The Greatest Generation Comes Home

99

TEXAS A&M UNIVERSITY MILITARY HISTORY SERIES

Joseph G. Dawson III, General Editor

Editorial Board:
Robert Doughty
Brian Linn
Craig Symonds
Robert Wooster

The Greatest

Generation

Comes Home

THE VETERAN

IN AMERICAN SOCIETY

Michael D. Gambone

Texas A&M University Press
College Station

Library of Congress Cataloging0in-Publication Data

Gambone, Michael D., 1963–
    The greatest generation comes home : the veteran in American society /
Michael D. Gambone.– 1st ed.
        p. cm. — (Texas A&M University military history series ; no. 99)
    Includes bibliographical references and index.
    ISBN 1-58544-455-3 (cloth : alk. paper)
    ISBN 1-58544-488-X (pbk. : alk. paper)
    1. World War, 1939–1945—Veterans—United States.   2. Veterans—United
States—Social conditions—20th century.   3. United
States—History—1945–1953.   4. United States—Social conditions—1945–
I. Title.   II. Texas A&M University military history series ; 99.
D810.V42U65 2005
973.918'086'97–dc22   2005002899

This work is dedicated to

Sergeant First Class C. J. MacAllister

Medical Platoon Sergeant

Headquarters

Headquarters Company

2nd Battalion

508th Infantry (ABN)

Thank God for sergeants

CONTENTS

ACKNOWLEDGMENTS

I lack adequate time and space to thank everyone involved in this project. Many people have lent key support as the work has evolved over the years. Some people, however, stand out for particular recognition. I would like to thank Joseph Hovish and Kevin Flanagan at the American Legion Library. I would also like to thank R. L. Baker and the staff of the U.S. Military History Institute. My appreciation extends to Mike Smith, Curt Hansen, and Jennifer Hecker at the Walter Reuther Library. Col. Gary Solis and Fred H. Allison at the Marine Corps Historical Center also deserve mention for their assistance as do Willis Shirk at the Pennsylvania State Archives, Josie Harvey at the American GI Forum National Veterans Outreach Program, and Mark Mederski, Executive Director of the Motorcycle Hall of Fame Museum.

Librarians throughout southeastern Pennsylvania deserve special recognition for their invaluable assistance as I trolled endlessly for secondary readings and primary sources. I am very grateful to Bill Yurvati and the staff of Kutztown University's Rohrbach Library for their rapid and professional support of my research. Additional kudos also go to the library personnel at the University of Pennsylvania, Albright College, and Franklin and Marshall College.

A great deal of research for this book was made possible by grants from Kutztown University. I would like to thank Sandra Hammann and the Research Committee for their generosity in funding my many sojourns to archives and collections scattered around the country.

My colleagues in the Department of History also lent critical support in the developmental stages of this project. Their ideas and comments gave clarity to my research and the early drafts of the manuscript. Thanks to John Delaney, Patricia Derr, Patricia Kelleher, and Louis Rodriquez.

My research assistant Vaneesa Cook was a rare find in the draft stages of the manuscript. Her insight and attention to detail undoubtedly saved many portions of the project as it unfolded over the past year.

I look forward to the day when she joins the discipline in her own right.

The most important influence on my work is my family. I am very fortunate to have a scholar as a spouse. My wife, Rachel, has been a sounding board for the many ideas explored in this book. Through her intellect and good graces, each part of the work was made better before words were ever typed on my computer. My young son, Michael, a growing boy of six, also lent his own contribution by being blissfully unaware of my work and always insisting that it was time for play. I can appreciate his perspective most of all.

The Greatest Generation Comes Home

INTRODUCTION

*People usually think that wars are a great cleansing; that, pu-
rified through sacrifice, they can start from scratch along their
ideal paths after it is all over. Because of their innate wishful-
ness, people inevitably forget that every event is interrelated
and one cannot go outside of history and "start over."*
— *American sailor writing home from the Pacific in 1945*

Veterans have always been with us. In the beginning, as tiny
settlements of colonists clung to the New England and Virginia
shorelines, they were often the only thing standing between survival
and death. At the start of the seventeenth century, veterans of past
wars constituted a body of experience in arms, and they used that
know-how to defend their communities and prosecute war against the
Native Americans. They imported a body of military knowledge from
Europe that accompanied their weapons and bulky armor. Although
the latter would be discarded as impractical, the tradition of military
service would increase in importance as America grew.[1]

Veterans participating in local militias remained the backbone of
colonial America as the frontier first clustered along the Atlantic seaboard and then began to move west. In the bloody clashes between
Virginians and the Powhatan in the 1620s and during the vicious fighting that erupted between the scattered settlements in New England
and an alliance of Native American tribes led by Metacomet (otherwise
known to the English as King Philip) in 1675, militias constituted the
single barrier to outright annihilation. As each generation fought, it
passed the benefits of experience to the next generation of citizen
soldiers.[2]

Not every lesson was learned, however. Colonial America's militias remained notoriously inconsistent in their training, equipment, and discipline. While a few attempted to keep a sharp edge through periodic drills, most militias began to decline as the frontier moved and the proximity to danger moved with it. Without the presence of an imminent threat, it became difficult at best to convince local militias to render mutual aid or deploy beyond their colonial borders.[3]

Yet, they remained at the core of American life in a manner that gradually became more political than military. For colonists who were growing increasingly restive under the mantle of British rule, the veteran employed in his local militia began to serve as a bulwark not against the Native American but against the threat of a standing professional army. As the years passed and the seventeenth century moved into history, it became a distinctly American article of faith that a well-equipped militia served as a check against the coercive power of the national state.[4]

Even as these political concepts evolved and spread, the veteran, periodically employed in his local armory, developed yet another facet of his status and service. In many respects, local militias were key social-gathering points in America, where like-minded men and their families could not only meet and reinforce their common agreement regarding military duty but also pursue a broader spectrum of activities that included fund-raising for charity, business partnerships, and personal friendships. Once the mundane task of drill was complete, it was normal for wives, children, and soldiers to gather to drink, gossip, and enjoy each other's company.[5]

Certain units also reflected the social status of their sponsoring communities. The well-bred elites of Philadelphia created the first and oldest cavalry troop in America. Other militias that were located in the rural western reaches of the colonies were composed primarily of farmers, tradespeople, and simpler folk. Consequently, veterans' status, like membership in a particular church congregation or private club, was an early means of establishing a bond within an American community and defining—or defending—one's place in the social hierarchy.[6]

Veterans' status rather quickly became an American litmus test for leadership. George Washington's experience at the conclusion of the Revolution illustrated what would become a very strong thread in American history. When the commander in chief of the Continental forces bade farewell to his officers on a cold December day in 1783, the moment was marked by Washington's quiet modesty and the deeply held devotion of his senior officers. The same could not be said of the crowds of boisterous New Yorkers who gathered along the old general's route to Whitehall Ferry and what he thought would be a restful retirement.[7] The outpouring of public adulation would be Washington's greatest burden and his greatest asset for the rest of his life. For years after the Revolution, one of his greatest difficulties was attempting to allay fears that he would use his old military network to transform the fledgling American republic into a dictatorship.[8] This never came to pass. However, Washington's credibility as the first president of the United States clearly benefited from the reputation for leadership he had accumulated during the war. The common features of his performance in combat—Washington's coolness under fire and almost foolhardy bravery—and, perhaps more important, his dogged determination to pursue victory despite defeat, definitely shaped a conventional wisdom that prepared a path to the presidency in 1789.

For many of Washington's presidential successors, war served as a crucible for political leadership. A belated victory over the British in 1815 thrust Andrew Jackson into national prominence. Many a lawmaker grumbled that Jackson's prowess in battle resonated dangerously with the growing number of Americans who were gaining the ability to vote. Henry Clay famously lamented during the election of 1824 that "I cannot believe that killing 2,500 Englishmen at New Orleans qualifies for the various, difficult and complicated duties of the Chief Magistracy."[9] To an older cadre of Americans who had been raised in a much more exclusive version of democracy, the glorification of military service represented all of the worst qualities of low politics and misguided public passions. Yet, as the century wore on, it became a key test of leadership and something that had to be treated carefully. Candidates with less than distinguished military records handled their veterans' status gingerly. Throughout his political career, Abraham Lincoln often joked about his lack of combat service during the Black Hawk War of 1832 but considered his election as a militia company commander to be one of the highlights of his life.[10]

Certain politicians have recognized the value that military service has provided at key moments in American history. In 1868, in the aftermath of the Civil War, it was no coincidence that U.S. Grant was first unofficially nominated for the presidency at the Soldiers and

Sailors Convention in Chicago. Nor was it an accident that former Union officers joined the national speech circuit for him, while enlisted veterans of the Grand Army of the Republic organized torchlight parades to campaign for their old leader.[11] Similarly, Theodore Roosevelt understood the value of military service as a means of appealing to the country, particularly at the end of the nineteenth century, when the horrors of the Civil War had passed into popular nostalgia. From the tailored Brooks Brothers uniforms he had made before departing for the Spanish-American War, to the still and motion-picture camera operators who accompanied his regiment to Cuba to capture his performance, Roosevelt's campaign for veteran's status was homage to the concept. It was also highly successful. Although Col. Teddy Roosevelt was relatively well known as a Progressive reformer before 1898, it was his famous reputed moment at San Juan Hill that made him and his Rough Riders national celebrities. On the campaign trail only a few weeks after the war, he was commonly seen addressing crowds flanked by old veterans of the regiment and in many cases introduced by his old bugler, Emil Cassi. Colonel Roosevelt, as he was now known, rode on public acclaim into the New York governor's mansion in 1899 and the Republican national convention to receive the vice presidential nomination a year later.[12]

As they created a place for themselves in American politics, veterans gradually established a dominant place in public policy. Very early on, it was commonplace for the colonies to establish benefits for old soldiers and their families. In 1636, the Plymouth Colony decided that any soldier who was disabled as a result of his service should be maintained by the colony for the rest of his life. In 1718, Rhode Island enacted a law that included medical care and an annual pension drawn from the colony's treasury.[13] Once a national government began to form, it too addressed the issues of benefits for veterans of the Continental Army, promising bounty lands to the west and pensions for Revolutionary War soldiers. Rudimentary programs for disabled veterans were also created by the federal government shortly after the war. In 1782, Congress agreed to provide a pension of five dollars a month to sick and wounded soldiers for the duration of their lives.[14]

In the years following the Revolution, the issue of veterans' benefits became the subject of moments of great generosity and debate over excessive cost. Programs often appeared in the flush of enthusiasm that followed the end of the conflict. Unfortunately, as the years passed and sobriety returned to Congress and the public alike, the financial realities of a cash-strapped republic soon set in. One senator's statement during the debate over an 1818 bill expanding veterans' pensions illustrated what would become the most common and formidable obstacle to veterans' benefits: "I consider this bill as a branch of a great system, calculated and intended to create a permanent change upon the Treasury, with a view to delay the payment of the public debt, and to postpone, indefinitely, the claims of the people for a reduction in taxes, when the debt shall finally be extinguished."[15]

Controversy and scandal clung to the administration of veterans' benefits throughout the eighteenth and nineteenth centuries. Poor record keeping at the state and federal levels left the veterans' pension system ripe for fraud and manipulation. When a pension act for Revolutionary War veterans was passed in 1832, for example, the War Department had complete records for militia service from only Virginia and New Hampshire. Protests regarding favoritism flared up almost as soon as the American Revolution ended. When Congress granted lifetime pensions for Washington's officers, an uproar ensued. The Massachusetts legislature denounced the decision in a public letter to federal lawmakers, claiming the policy was "inconsistent with the equality which ought to subsist among citizens of free and republican States." Problems evolved from that point onward. Almost as soon as benefits payments to veterans began, a small cottage industry sprang up to falsify service records or conjure up dependent family members to claim the pensions of deceased veterans. Over time, lawmakers invested more effort in defending veterans' programs from these assaults at the expense of new legislation.[16]

It was not until the Civil War that veterans' benefits programs took a major step forward. Contemplating hundreds of thousands of new additions to the ranks of American veterans, Congress began significant revisions of existing policy in the spring of 1862. One author has described the result as "epoch-making" law. It provided for extensive increases in pensions for disability and disease. The definition of family dependents also changed significantly. Widows and children under sixteen qualified for benefits after the death of the veteran head of the household. Mothers and orphan sisters, previously excluded by federal law, could also receive the pensions of their sons and brothers. All in all, the veterans' law of 1862 committed the federal government to an enormous and costly benefits program that would extend far past the lives of the original veteran beneficiaries. The rapidly rising cost of this program mirrored its commitments. Although Congress estimated that the 1862 law would cost the treasury $7 million per year, two years later the budget for pensioners had almost doubled, to $13.4 million. By 1874, it had increased to $30.5 million. By 1893, it had ballooned to a breathtaking $158.1 million.[17]

Substantial holes in the law remained despite the massive increases in expenditures for veterans. In the post–Civil War era, benefits did not include hospitalization or rehabilitation for former soldiers and sailors. Most veterans and their families were expected to rely upon their own devices for long-term recovery. When individual resources proved inadequate, private charity was often the only recourse. The years following the war saw the expansion of organizations such as the American Red Cross and the National Home for Disabled Volunteer Soldiers to meet the needs of this large body of sick and wounded veterans.[18]

The next major breakthrough in veterans' benefits did not appear until the First World War. The unprecedented scale of mobilization for the war, a process that saw four million Americans wear their country's uniform, and the staggering lethality of modern industrial combat produced the largest number of veterans in the nation's history—and the greatest need for care in three generations. By the time the guns fell silent in Europe, more than two hundred thousand Americans had been wounded in the war.[19]

New laws and programs soon emerged to meet a staggering demand. The War Risk Act of 1918 provided rehabilitation for the war injured. Approximately 675,000 veterans of the Great War would apply for benefits through this one law. Under the Rehabilitation Law of 1919, disabled veterans received tuition, books, and a subsistence allowance of between $90 and $145 per month. To meet the acute need for hospital care, the Wilson administration initially assigned responsibility for veterans to the Public Health Service in 1919.[20]

However, many unmet problems remained for the millions seeking work, homes, and a means to reassimilate after the war. Demobilization for the vast majority of veterans was abrupt, and little attention was paid to their transition back into civilian life. Discharged soldiers normally received a sixty-dollar separation payment and a railroad ticket home.[21] Beyond these most rudimentary steps, individual veterans were left alone to negotiate a postwar American climate that was characterized by a sharp economic recession that lasted until 1921, the Red Scare, the outbreak of the great influenza epidemic, and a general consensus to tuck the war as far away in the public memory as possible.

For its own part, the federal government attempted in 1921 to redress some of these difficulties by consolidating all of the old functions of the benefits system into the Veterans' Bureau. Unfortunately, corruption quickly overwhelmed the new agency. One of the most famous scandals of the decade enmeshed Col. Charles R. Forbes, a loyal campaign worker appointed by Warren Harding, as the first director of the bureau. Forbes was charged with fraud while arranging bids for the construction of veterans' hospitals. Criminal investigators discovered that he had accepted bribes for bids on contracts and a kickback of up to one-third of the profit made on the construction of each facility during his time in office. Forbes was eventually convicted and sentenced to two years in prison.[22]

Disgruntled over what appeared to be public apathy regarding their plight and doubting that policy makers could successfully create an agency to represent their interests, veterans began to organize for themselves. In 1919, the American Legion (AL) joined the Veterans of Foreign Wars (VFW) as the second major national institution designed to protect and promote the interests of former service members.[23] In many important respects, the legion and VFW represented the time-honored desire for veterans to simply congregate and enjoy the camaraderie that was rooted in common service. Meeting halls became cultural enclaves in which old soldiers could not only meet and exchange "war stories" but also, and perhaps more importantly, maintain an identity that represented one of the most profound and important aspects of their lives.[24] Locally, chapters of the VFW and American Legion became aggressive community activists, sponsoring charity fundraisers, youth sports, educational contests, and a host of other activities.

At the state and national levels, the two veterans' groups rather quickly became political forces to be reckoned with in the post–World War I era. With its headquarters in Indianapolis, the American Legion, for example, maintained constant contact with state and local chapters through telegrams, correspondence, and the American Legion Magazine. Overall, veterans represented a highly organized and integrated constituency that formed a powerful voting bloc at nearly every level of the political process. Attaining an endorsement from the Veterans of Foreign Wars and the American Legion became a rite of passage for aspiring American politicians. Drawing on war chests created by the membership dues of hundreds of thousands of veterans, both organizations were able to maintain lobbyists in state capitals and Washington.[25] There they maintained constant pressure for the expansion and refinement of existing veterans' programs. In many cases, they were hugely successful. It is somewhat ironic that, by 1932, the year of the disastrous Bonus March on Washington, 12.8 percent of the total federal budget was dedicated to veterans. A year after the march, the Veterans' Administration recorded 412,482 beneficiaries who were receiving compensation for non-service-connected disabilities.[26]

World War II changed everything. The conflict catapulted the United States to the permanent status of global superpower. In 1945, America could blacken the skies and cover the visible horizon of the sea with its fleets of planes and ships. Also in 1945, after the dramatic test at Trinity site, the United States could claim an atomic monopoly. Perhaps more important to the next generation was America's position as the sole, untouched industrial power in the world, a standing that would grant the country both an advantage in technology and production and access to global markets that it would maintain for the next thirty years. With this dominance came a new optimism and sometimes a new arrogance about what Henry Luce called "the American Century," a time when the fundamental blueprint of the world might be reshaped by American hands, where democracy, free markets, cultural mores, and security would find more American forms.[27]

At home, dramatic change was also afoot. When Franklin Delano Roosevelt died near the end of the war, many assumed that the New Deal might expire with him. Republicans in particular, hearkening back to the days of balanced budgets and a laissez-faire approach to regulation, hoped for a postwar era of government retrenchment. However, none of this came to pass. The grasp and reach of the federal government grew to gargantuan proportions during the war.[28] Contained in selective service, the federal income tax, the Office of Price Administration, or the alphabet soup of agencies that descended upon the country, the national government attained a permanent and fixed place in American conventional wisdom. As it did, so too did public expectations that the government would provide for not only security but also a host of other functions contributing to the public good. Nowhere is this better illustrated than in the Servicemen's Readjustment

Act of 1944 (popularly known as the GI Bill of Rights), arguably the greatest social-welfare program in U.S. history, and a host of programs in nearly every state mirrored or extended the benefits set down by the federal government.[29] For millions of Americans—veterans and their families—the GI Bill would solidify the link between public expectations and public policymaking.

Cracks in the American social status quo began to form as a result of the war. Pragmatism and the need for utility driven by national survival burst apart the taboos that encompassed life. Women, married or not, flocked to the workplace and demonstrated unrivaled competence. Their efforts, particularly in meeting the massive administrative needs of the modern War Department, proved crucial to victory. Minorities surged into factories and recruiting offices intent on demonstrating a patriotism on par with, if not greater than, the mainstream and with great hopes that the goals of the war would find their way home. Millions of GIs, contemplating their discharge from the service, saw in the future an opportunity for upward mobility for both themselves and their children. Their attitudes reflected a nation perched on the brink of enormous social change.

Despite the collective enormity of these events, historians today tend to gloss over the post–World War II period, particularly as it applies to veterans. In this instance, the problem might lie in the simple passage of time and our tendency to compress the past into manageable, but increasingly inaccurate, clichés that are useful for the sake of their brevity. Nearly every teacher has confronted the fundamental conflict between details and time remaining on the classroom clock. Serious scholars of modern American history have fewer excuses. Yet, the tendency in too many contemporary treatments of the postwar forties is to focus on victory in 1945; address the general political, economic, and social difficulties faced in the first Truman administration; and segue immediately to McCarthyism, the Cold War, the Baby Boom, and the fifties.[30]

Although valuable, all of this scholarship ignores a question that is fundamental to the forties and much of American history of subsequent decades: How did sixteen million veterans come home after World War II? From this basic staring point, questions multiply. Beyond the accommodations made by new law, how did society prepare for them? How would men who had been weaned on bloody combat fare as husbands and the fathers of an emerging and massive generation of children? How did the economy manage to incorporate them as productive wage earners without plunging the country into a postwar depression? How might American politics evolve to capture a formidable new constituency?

Second, but perhaps of even greater importance, how did these veterans change America? Their numbers alone tell a story that is hard to ignore. In 1945, approximately sixteen million Americans with a common experience of sacrifice, separation, and service came home to a country that was, in many ways, alien terrain after their years of military service. Did these former soldiers create what amounted to their own subculture within American society? If not, how did these veterans, both individually and collectively, reshape the nation to achieve what they perceived to be a better future? What imprint did they leave on the ballot box, the classroom, and popular culture?[31] This second area of study offers what might be one of the most rewarding and untouched segments of twentieth-century American history.

When looking at the veterans of World War II, scholars have tended to focus on key institutions or specific attributes of the veterans' experiences. The impact of the GI Bill on American higher education has garnered a great deal of attention.[32] Studies of the rise and decline of the veterans' health-care system, motivated to a degree by the Vietnam War experience, have also appeared in historical scholarship over the years.[33]

It is only in the very recent past that scholars have begun to examine the diverse components of the experiences of the World War II veterans. Social historians have broadened the field beyond examinations of law and bureaucracies to include the impact of race and ethnicity on military service and veterans' status. A significant body of work has appeared that addresses the histories of African American, Latino, and Nisei service personnel.[34] The past ten years have also seen significant growth in histories of women veterans.[35] Moreover, in the aftermath of Tom Brokaw's *Greatest Generation* series and with the enormous popularity of Steven Spielberg's movie *Saving Private Ryan*, both amateur and professional historians have received an enormous boost to expand oral-history collections drawn from World War II veterans.[36]

Despite this growing body of work, comprehensive histories of the World War II veteran are rare. The most recent example, *To Hear Only Thunder Again*, published by Mark D. Van Ells in 2001, is an important addition to what remains a fairly anemic historical field.[37] This is unfortunate, particularly since these veterans touched so many facets of American life—from their raucous demands for redeployment home that stampeded lawmakers who were eyeing the rapidly approaching 1946 congressional elections, to the revolution in medical care the Veterans' Administration established to treat hundreds of thousands of sick and disabled members of the armed forces, to the more subtle changes they invoked in college classrooms once the GI Bill began to pick up momentum. The broad array of places where veterans touched America after World War II deserve to be integrated into one complete story.

That is the contribution I would like to make with this book. As I have pursued this research over the years, it has led me to social, political, and economic subjects related to the veteran. It has also pushed me outside the traditional bounds of my own historical discipline to include the relevant aspects of medicine, psychology, psychiatry, and film. In the process, this search has led me to undiscovered areas that may add to the texture and depth of our understanding of the legacy these veterans bestowed upon a nation in the forties and fifties and beyond.

The structure of the book follows a fairly logical order. In chapter 1 I address the impact that military service had on the veterans' perceptions of home, from the time basic training rewrote the basic elements of social normalcy, to the image that civilian life retained while military personnel served around the world, to their first reactions upon returning to a much different country when the war finally ended. Chapter 2 focuses on the need to heal the many wounds inflicted by World War II. It covers the scandalous situation that greeted returning veterans in need of medical care in 1945 and the truly Herculean efforts by Omar Bradley to reverse this situation in the Veterans' Administration. Chapter 3 follows the veterans as they gradually found their way back into civilian life through work, education, and politics, leaving a significant imprint upon each as the decade progressed. Chapters 4 and 5 introduce distinct groups of veterans—women, African Americans, Latinos, and Japanese Americans—who not only shared some of the specific attributes and accomplishments of military service but also served under the burdens of discrimination distinct to midcentury American society.

Nevertheless, the wartime experience proved a catalyst for change and rising postwar expectations for veterans as much as for the majority population. Arguably, the war was also a catalyst for both modern-day feminism and the civil rights movement. Chapter 6 addresses the influence of World War II upon popular culture, specifically as it applies to the movies, one of the most popular contemporary-entertainment mediums in American history. With the arrival and substantial success of *The Best Years of Our Lives* in 1946, veterans appeared prominently in Hollywood drama, including the increasingly popular film noir crime films that appeared after the war. As veterans found their way onto the screen, their numbers in movie audiences also markedly altered the manner in which war was depicted on film. In a clear departure from wartime portrayals of conflict, war movies after 1945 placed a much higher premium on realism and the perspective of the common soldier. Chapter 7 brings the story full circle, to a time when thousands of comfortably demobilized veterans once again faced military service in Korea. Accompanying the national story that unfolded, the chapter also examines the service experience of the 28th Pennsylvania National Guard Division from its first mobilization, through training, and to its eventual deployment overseas. Chapter 8 addresses the long-term legacy that World War II veterans had for the baby-boom generation, which grew to adulthood during the Vietnam era.

Clearly, this is a story made complex by the massive size of the GI generation, the vastly different qualities that veterans introduced to American history, and the scope of the six decades that have followed World War II. The enormity of the task is daunting to say the least. However, I hope that this book will contribute in some way to an understanding of a pivotal moment in time and render appropriate justice to those who served in time of war and helped to build the subsequent peace.

CHAPTER 1   *Home*

Home is what they all dreamed about. It became their refuge after the first shock of induction into military service and the completely alien experience that enveloped them. Home was the yardstick they used to measure the rigors of military life. It came to them in the predawn hours of the basic-training depot, as nameless men shouted for them to awaken. It came to them as their "rack" replaced their beds, as "chow" replaced the morning congregation around the breakfast table, as every feature of their individual lives—birthdays, clothes, tastes, and preferences—vanished into a system designed to produce the "GI"—"government issue"—a term that wryly recognized the transformation of a civilian into a soldier and the disappearance of everything an individual had held dear in the past.

These new American GIs were taught the finer points of the military arts in their new home. Close-order drill, group punishments, and military routine became the new standards of the day. Marion Hargrove, in *See Here, Private Hargrove,* would comment during the war, "All your persecution is deliberate, calculated, systematic. It is the collegiate practice of hazing, applied to the grim and highly important task of transforming a civilian into a soldier, a boy into a man. It is the Hardening Process."[1]

The enforced unfairness of discipline and the callousness that was common to military life were designed to toughen millions of rank amateurs and prepare them for what was to come on battlefields in Europe and the Pacific. The hardening process was critical to their future survival. In order for it to be successful, it had to abolish everything the rookies had learned in a lifetime at home.[2] Recruits were taught the real depths of their physical endurance. Obstacle courses and calisthenics pushed them to limits they had barely explored in civilian life. Enduring bloody, blistered feet on a twenty-five-mile march eventually became an afterthought. More importantly, the hardening process taught the young GI the art of death, whether it came from a rifle, a bayonet, or bare hands. Values embedded over the course of a lifetime were forced aside. Trainees learned instead to aim at "center mass" and squeeze the trigger, using the infantry rifle as if it were a physical extension of themselves. Those who were best able to adapt to this new system were celebrated and promoted. Those who could not became the subject of ridicule and derision. James Baker's "Sad Sack" was not only an icon of the long-suffering common private but also an example of an abject failure at the soldier's craft.

In the absence of fathers and mothers, new figures emerged to govern the soldiers' new home. First among them was the sergeant. From the GIs' very first introduction to military culture, the sergeant was the core of their life. He was the first and best example of bearing and behavior. He became the taskmaster for the basic skills they learned in the first weeks of training and a teacher for most of their remaining years of service. The comparisons veterans later made between their sergeants and their parents do not come as a surprise. Marine T. Grady Gallant describes his drill instructor at Parris Island this way: "Corporal Blaskewitz did his best to prepare us for the difficult days ahead, and it was something like rearing children." Yet even at this point, most service members understood the differences that still separated their old homes from their new one. As they toughened themselves, they reflected upon the sacrifices they were being asked to make for the necessities of war. In an important sense, the home that the GIs knew and the one they occupied in uniform coexisted throughout the war. Gallant draws the distinction well when he sums up his drill instructor: "Blaskewitz was a good DI. Our mothers would not have liked him."[3]

Once their training was complete, deployment overseas reinforced the physical and mental distance from home. The prospect of the long journey to points unknown caused many to reflect upon the final, tangible separation from America. In 1943, Thomas R. St. George wrote about the gravity of this realization: "Back in the barracks something of significance had appeared on the bulletin board. 'Tomorrow's K.P.s' had been gleefully crossed out, and, added at the bottom of the roster, in scrawling print, was the information: 'NEW ADDRESS—C/O POSTMASTER, SAN FRANCISCO.' That did it. 'C/O Postmaster.' I was going overseas, away from home, to God knew where or what or for how long, maybe the rest of my life. And there was too much to do to give a particular damn about the significance of it all. Probably it was just as well."[4] That outlook would change once the thousands of troop transports bound for Europe and Asia left port. In the slow weeks that passed between their departure from the United States to assembly points in the war zone, service members had long stretches of time in which to contemplate life back in the States. Between scheduled meals, classes, and half-hearted attempts at training were long periods devoted to reading and rereading mail and speculating about the first battle to come. Time was not a friend to the homesick.

Combat left its own imprint on the GIs' vision of home. In the mud and snow of Western Europe, in the steaming jungles of Asia, on islands scattered across the Pacific, and in the vast fleets that populated oceans throughout the world, Americans were exposed to the unprecedented horrors of modern mass warfare. As they unfolded, the lengths and depths of human suffering placed civilian life in a completely new perspective. Home became a tiny anchor in a human disaster, a touchstone. Many combat veterans learned to treasure small keepsakes that linked them to the past and a safer, saner place. In "The Things Men Live By," which appeared in the Marine Corps *Headquarters Bulletin,* Sgt. Bem Price notes that "Pictures of folks back home were things that men clung to with desperation. They might lose everything but their rifles, ammunition and a raggedy pair of pants, but tucked in some torn pocket would be a snapshot of a girl, a mother or whole family. That picture might be wrinkled but more often it had been carefully preserved—perhaps between two flat bits of wood tied together with a string."[5]

Scattered throughout the war narratives are constant references to places back in the United States. Some GIs commented on how much the battlefield looked like home. Ernie Pyle remarked during the Okinawan invasion that "Southern boys said the reddish clay and the pine trees reminded them of Georgia. Westerners saw California in the green rolling hills, partly wooded, partly patchworked with little green fields. And the farmed plains looked like our Midwest."[6] One soldier, upon meeting a Russian when U.S. forces linked up with their Soviet counterparts on the Elbe river, compared him to a "Garfield High quarterback."[7]

Home ties would also unknowingly affect combat soldiers during the times when they made contact with the enemy. Despite their training and despite the substantial efforts to toughen and desensitize the GIs to the prospect of combat, a study by S. L. A. Marshall speculates that only 15 percent actually fired their weapons and directly participated in the act of combat.[8] This low percentage is a reflection of the psychological strain created on the modern battlefield. More importantly, it is also a commentary on the strong grip that civilian mores maintained on the soldiers who were faced with the prospect of bloodletting. After the war, the army and marines would devote considerable effort to addressing the problem of participation in combat.[9]

As the war progressed, the perception of home altered with it. The home front remained the carrot that motivated millions to continue the conflict to final victory. However, as the war dragged on and attrition and exhaustion began to decimate frontline units, this link assumed an almost desperate quality. In this context, home became an ideal, a sanctuary from the grinding horror that embodied the final bitter months of World War II. The prospect of clean sheets, a home-cooked meal, and peace took on connotations far out of proportion to reality. Moreover, new expectations accompanied these older standards. War Department surveys of personnel stationed in Europe in April and August, 1945, indicate that two-thirds or more of American soldiers believed that people back home had "a real sense of gratitude and appreciation for what the soldiers have done."[10] In other words, after the war, home would offer not only comfort but also acknowledgement for a job well done. The obvious problem with this assumption was the belief that veterans and civilian society would both possess a clear understanding of the veterans' experience and be able to have a meaningful dialogue based on this knowledge. Unfortunately, no such consensus existed in 1945 or in the years afterward.[11]

Very little of this disconnect was apparent at the end of the war, however. When news of peace finally arrived in August, 1945, it was the cause for joy around the world. A letter from a woman in Brooklyn to her husband in the Pacific recalls similar reactions across the country: "People outside were dancing in the streets with their nightgowns and pajamas on. Children from one year and up were running through the dark street banging pots and pans, blowing horns and ringing bells. There were some young boys on East 3rd Street that have a small band of music and they began to play in the middle of the street as everyone danced. People shouted from their windows and small bon-fires were started all along the street. Victory! Glorious Victory! How good it felt!"[12]

Troops stationed abroad celebrated with equal enthusiasm. Many of the luckiest indulged themselves in the vast captured caches of alcohol the Germans had left behind.[13] One servicewoman stationed in France witnessed a scene in which delirious Parisians disassembled a U.S. Army vehicle on the spot for souvenirs.[14]

Once the celebrations died down, joy was tempered by an increasing sense of impatience. The headline over war correspondent Andy Rooney's last column for *Stars and Stripes,* written on VE Day, speaks volumes about the troops' sentiments: "Good! When Do We Leave This Hole and Go Home?"[15] Even the general who had led these soldiers for four hard years, Dwight Eisenhower, openly contemplated the possibility of retirement now that the fighting was finally over.[16]

And so began the clamor for redeployment home. In barracks and tent cities scattered around the world, GIs waited for word from headquarters about plans that would set their homecoming in motion. As weeks turned into months, the wait itself became unbearable, made worse by the fact that some service members had not seen their families in years. A rotation policy instituted by the War Department in 1944 was quickly overwhelmed by personnel shortages.[17] For a lucky few who had enjoyed furloughs to the United States during the war, a brief, tantalizing glimpse of civilian life offered little respite before their return to combat. According to an army survey conducted in 1945, two out of three soldiers awaiting discharge thought that the military was mishandling the process.[18]

Few GIs understood or cared that the system that had been created to send them home was simply unprepared for the enormity of the task. Originally, returnees were to be governed by a point system that granted discharges from the military according to merit and need. Specific points were awarded for combat experience, marital status, overseas service, and a number of other categories. One point was granted for each month of military service, with an additional point for each month overseas. Five points were awarded for campaign stars or decorations, and five were awarded for each Purple Heart received for wounds. Veterans with children received twelve points for each child under eighteen (up to three). A total of eighty-five points could send a GI home in the fall of 1945.[19]

The problem was that no one had expected the war to end so early. In August, 1945, most of the strategic planners in the Pentagon were anticipating months, if not years, of additional fighting to subdue the Japanese home islands, but the atomic bomb short-circuited all of that. As the month wound to a close, the leadership that had guided the war effort confronted the gargantuan task of bringing back almost twelve million service members from nearly every continent. Where were the ships that would transport them? Where were the doctors to examine them? Where was the army of clerks needed to handle back pay, lost equipment, and a myriad of other details? In August, 1945, Washington had few answers and even less time to contemplate them.

At home, the public lobbied hard to speed up demobilization. Secretary of War Robert Patterson attempted to hold firm, citing the need to occupy recently captured territory and repatriate millions of former enemy combatants. But the people did not listen. Following VJ Day, a Gallup poll reported that 63 percent of Americans had decided that the Japanese were not incurably warlike. A year earlier, 62 percent of polled citizens had reached the exact opposite conclusion.[20] It seemed, at least in the public's mind, that the contingency for defense had disappeared. In the first weeks of peacetime, the Senate Military Affairs Committee was deluged with ten thousand letters a day demanding the return of husbands, fathers, and sons. Extensive hearings were held throughout the fall to examine the minutiae of the separation process in order to find methods to expedite it.[21]

American industry also lent its two cents to the debate. Railroad companies demanded the return of 75,000 workers they deemed essential to handle the anticipated postwar increase in traffic.[22] The coal states argued for the early release of miners, who would be necessary to produce an energy supply adequate for reconversion. Responding to pressure from this vote-laden area of the industrial Northeast, the Senate offered a friendly resolution for the immediate return of miners from military service. Bowing to this pressure, Patterson finally agreed and ordered the expedited discharge of 10,000 miners and furloughs for an additional 20,000 a few weeks after the Japanese officially surrendered in Tokyo harbor.[23]

Efforts to slow down demobilization and impose some type of rational order were met with angry protests, in some cases led by GIs still in uniform. In January, 1946, between 8,000 and 10,000 troops demonstrated in Manila. Sponsored by a committee of service members headed by UAW leader Emil Mazey, they protested a "hopelessly confused demobilization program" in full-page ads featured in fifteen major dailies around the United States. Other rallies sprang up spontaneously in Western Europe, India, China, and Korea. When Patterson toured bases on a swing through the Pacific, he was greeted by angry service personnel. On a visit to Guam, he was burned in effigy.[24]

In response to this pressure, the system gave way, and redeployments home to the United States accelerated rapidly. Separation centers mushroomed at places like Ft. Dix, New Jersey; Ft. McPherson, Georgia; Jefferson Barracks, Missouri; and dozens of other locations.[25] The total number of points required for discharge was reduced from 85 to 80 in September, 1945, to 60 in October, and finally to 50 by the end of December. The separation process itself was streamlined from an eighteen-day ordeal to an average of forty-four hours per serviceperson. Soldiers, sailors, and marines were mustered out at a rate of twenty-six thousand per day. In September, 1945, Patterson promised to reduce the wartime army from 8 million to 2 million within a year.[26]

The stream of veterans coming home became a deluge. Between May and October, 1945, the port of New York alone received 759,715 returnees.[27] In the months that followed, the mass redeployment of troops continued unabated despite the massive problems that began to crop up in regions as far apart as southern Korea and western Germany. American and Allied commanders struggled with the disposition of millions of displaced refugees and the absolute destruction of rail systems, bridges, hospitals, and sewage-treatment plants. More importantly, in these early days of the Cold War, it was an open question as to whether the American military still possessed the capability to carry out even the most fundamental military missions. Pres. Harry Truman commented in his memoirs that, "so far as I was concerned, the program we were following was no longer demobilization—it was disintegration of our armed forces."[28] Writing to the chair of a committee investigating national defense, Maj. Gen. W. S. Paul commented, "[F]or better or for worse, the Army has reached a stage where it is so stripped of experienced men that in the opinion of most military experts, it would take a year to reach the stage it had at the beginning of the war."[29] General Paul was largely correct in his assessment. By 1946, U.S. forces had evaporated from their overseas bases. Visitors to Western Europe were amazed to find thousands of pieces of American equipment and vehicles summarily abandoned and left to rust in the open air by units hell-bent on returning home.[30]

When they finally arrived home, veterans of the war were treated to a glorious sight. The great landmarks of either coast, San Francisco's Golden Gate Bridge or the Statue of Liberty in New York, greeted hundreds of thousands as their first real signs of America.

Army nurse Theresa Archard's description of her arrival is typical of many: "Land was in sight!—American land, too. The ambulatory patients were going wild. Men minus a leg hobbled around on crutches; others had decided limps. Some were extremely emaciated, but one and all had a glint in their eyes. This was something like it—good old American soil."[31]

Once home, the veterans were able to indulge in their first tastes of normalcy. Most of them initially sought out incredibly simple things often taken for granted by civilians on the home front. One returning GI spoke only of wanting to "climb in between a pair of clean sheets and sleep for a week." Upon arriving in Camp Kilmore, New Jersey, Nisei veteran Ark G. Chin, newly returned from France, enjoyed one of the largest steaks he had ever seen. Theresa Archard came back from Europe jaundiced and malnourished and was immediately admitted to a military hospital in Charleston, South Carolina. Her first request was for a highly prized glass of fresh milk. She received a whole quart to slowly savor.[32]

After these most basic needs were satisfied, the returning veterans began to take stock of how much the United States had changed during the war. Most had read accounts about the country in the newspapers that arrived from home. Millions of letters sent by family members during the course of the conflict had kept many service members apprised of events. However, neither of these prepared the veterans for what was the greatest domestic upheaval in U.S. history. The enormity of the war could in large part be measured by the tremendous movement of people after 1941. Nearly 16 million had left their homes to serve in uniform. An additional 15 million had crisscrossed America in search of job opportunities in the shipyards and war plants that mushroomed around the country.[33] Overall, approximately one-quarter of the nation had departed familiar territory when duty called or opportunity presented itself. Regional identity mattered considerably less in a postwar country that began to place a much greater emphasis on mobility. Some of the basic underpinnings of life—homes, towns, neighborhoods—that provided critical landmarks to the veteran were vanishing from the landscape.

Changes in the economic state of the union were equally profound. By 1945, faced with rationing and shortages as well as constant demands from industry for overtime, Americans were able to save up to 25 percent of their take-home pay. When Japan finally surrendered, bank accounts across the country bulged with an estimated $140 billion in personal savings.[34] Although some people worried that demobilization might cause the economy to lose the ground it had gained during the war, many Americans anticipated a postwar boom led by consumer demand that had been pent up since the Great Depression.

Not all of the economic news was good, however. In the months following the war, strikes paralyzed major sections of the country. Workers for Ford and General Motors walked off their jobs in September, 1945. More than 750,000 steelworkers and 400,000 coal miners soon followed suit, demanding substantial pay and increases in benefits.[35] They were joined by meat packers, communications workers, and tradespeople. During the winter of 1945–1946, as power brownouts and blackouts rolled across the country and concerns about the coal shortage grew, veterans found themselves trapped in bitter labor-management disputes, while strikes froze plans for new hiring. In 1946, one complained to a *Collier's* magazine reporter that "I was too young for a job when I enlisted but I wasn't too young to get into the war. I've been four years in the service, two at the front in Europe. I have no seniority, no references, nothing. The big corporations say, 'Have you got a union card?'"[36]

The postwar housing shortage made the prospect of normal life more complex for veterans. During the war, materials for home construction vanished from the market into military hands. Consequently, new housing starts dropped to slightly more than 200,000 units a year between 1942 and 1945. According to federal-government estimates after the war, there was an "urgent need" for more than 3 million low- and moderately priced housing units. Although the number of new homes constructed in 1946 tripled, the construction industry could not keep pace with demand.

Rents also skyrocketed as waiting lists lengthened. A one-room apartment without a bath could cost the prospective renter as much as $75 a month, an enormous sum in 1945. Families were often forced to share housing or rely on relatives. In 1946, 64 percent of married veterans and 80 percent of single veterans lived with family or friends.[37] As late as 1947, approximately four million veterans were reportedly still seeking housing. In September, the Congress on Industrial Organizations Committee on Housing reported that

30 percent of married veterans continued to live under what it called "shameful circumstances."[38]

Inflation added yet another layer of difficulty to life and readjustment in postwar America. Throughout World War II, the Office of Price Administration was relatively successful in keeping prices in check. During the conflict, they had increased by 28 percent overall. Once mandated controls were removed, however, prices, like pent-up consumer demand, exploded. Between June and December, 1946, alone, wholesale prices in the country rose by 24 percent, while food prices leaped upward by 40 percent in the same period.[39] The simplest, most basic market-basket goods—meat, butter, eggs—began to disappear from grocers' shelves. The home-cooked meal that many a GI had dreamed about while in uniform continued to be a fantasy as shortages in 1946 began to rival the rationing of only a year earlier.

As veterans struggled with the simplest functions of life in postwar America, more profound challenges awaited millions of them when they came home. New families welcomed them, populated by the leading edge of what would become known as the baby boom. For children, the returning father was a revelation. In some cases, he was a person who had been built up to heroic proportions during the war. To see veterans bandaged and carrying physical wounds or hear them crying out from lingering nightmares created confusion in the children's minds. In others cases, the veteran father, who had been absent when the child was born, was a complete stranger to his toddler. His arrival was often a painful anticlimax between two people who had never met. Some youngsters asked whether their father's return was permanent, and they wondered whether another crisis might call him away.[40]

New fathers sometimes found themselves at sea when contending with the unaccustomed responsibilities of parenthood. In some respects, their time spent in uniform certainly prepared them for meeting the needs of an infant. The proverbial 2 A.M. feeding, after years of living according to the tempo of a military schedule, was a much less daunting task to a veteran. However, a child was neither a recruit nor an enlisted soldier. An infant was an unpredictable bundle of new joys and frustrations who had priorities quite apart from those of the new father. In their own unique way, the children of these veterans led their fathers down the path of readjustment by redefining the idea of duty to a greater cause and obligation to the betterment of the next generation. In pursuing the American dream for these children, the

CHAPTER 1

veteran was given a new, noble purpose in the postwar years.

Relationships between husbands and wives suffered similar strains in the process of readjustment as well. A boom in marriage paralleled the war. Many of these unions reflected the tumult of the time, when traditional courtship was abandoned by the near prospect of death, the absence of parental authority, and the desire to live for the moment. The boom was also promoted by the changing sexual mores of the time. Between 1939 and 1945, American society saw a 42 percent increase in illegitimate births. Consequently, many marriages that had begun on uncertain ground failed after the war. Divorce rates rose significantly, from 16 percent in 1942 to 27 percent two years later. More than three million marriages failed during this period. By 1945, the United States had, at 31 percent, one of the highest recorded divorce rates in the world.[41]

Young couples faced the formidable task of building lives together at a time when upheaval was more the rule than the exception. Many of these changes were fundamental. The war drastically altered the role of a wife in America. A woman's say in daily household decisions increased significantly when her husband relocated to a military assignment and the burden of childrearing and employment fell on her shoulders. As a result of the war, millions of women entered the workforce for the first time. Unprecedented numbers of them were married women who did so out of patriotism and basic necessity. Peacetime brought only a partial return to the past. Although millions of women departed work willingly or were forced out of their positions, a higher percentage worked than in the prewar years. By 1947, they constituted 28 percent of the total workforce, and their numbers were growing.[42] Again, many of these women were married, this time supporting not only their growing broods of children but also their veteran husbands, who had decided to defer work for the educational benefits the GI Bill offered. The postwar years would see an important redefinition of the American family and the roles performed by men and women in the modern household.

Facing this array of economic and social challenges, veterans found their sense of anticipation tempered by a sense of ambivalence. Many of them contemplated the meaning of their new status in postwar America. Army surveys conducted at the conclusion of the war noted that a large majority of veterans considered themselves "technically and morally superior to the men who had not done so much in the war as they had." In August, 1945, although a large number (71 percent) thought that people at home were doing all they could to help win the war, a somewhat smaller number (61 percent) thought that the home front was appropriately grateful for their military service.[43] Was this America prepared to acknowledge them and the sacrifices they had made? Upon their return, many veterans were disturbed by evidence that the cooperation of the war years had completely given way to a breakneck competition for the bounties of peacetime. Seemingly endless labor strife, the bitter partisan bickering between the new president and Congress, the rush to buy as many long-deferred luxuries as possible all seemed to indicate a decline in the great republic they had fought to preserve.[44]

Peacetime social conflict created a disturbing segue for veterans who had seen some of the very worst examples of humanity in a world made desperate by war. Soldiers in the Italian campaign recalled mobs scrambling to glean scraps of food from American garbage dumps. Veterans of the dash through France and the Netherlands remembered vengeful crowds inflicting terrible punishment on collaborators. Immediately after the war, John Dos Passos wrote that "Frankfurt resembles a city as much as a pile of bones and a smashed skull resemble a prize Hereford steer, but white enameled street cars packed with people jingle purposefully as they run along the cleared asphalt streets. People in city clothes with city faces and briefcases under their arms trot busily about among the high rubbish piles, dart into punched-out doorways under tottering walls. They behave horribly like ants when you have kicked over an anthill."[45]

Veterans of the Pacific war carried with them the spectacle of civilians on Saipan and Okinawa committing suicide rather than surrender to advancing American units. More ominous were the examples of suffering—created by design—that American forces uncovered in the death camps in Germany and the Japanese prisoner-of-war compounds in Asia. Was "normalcy" possible in such a world? Could safe routines be re-created in the wake of such horrors? For many veterans, a profound inner struggle developed over the sense of alienation they felt about a society widely separated from even the most basic standards of human behavior.

Other veterans worried about the damage to their own humanity. In June, 1945, one marine wrote this to his family: "I can't expect you to understand me at times but try to realize that under a normal cycle my trend of thought would be considerably different. I feel very lonesome and my mood keyed to a pitch that to hold what I am thinking about within me would only burn like a fire longed to be cooled. I have changed, Mom and Dad, so please be patient with me when I am home."[46]

Many were unsure of the effects of the war on themselves and whether they would be able to fit into civil society again. After years of service with their units, some service members had become accustomed to the same faces and personalities in a manner that made the military a surrogate family. Common experiences and common suffering created a bond that was incomprehensible to a civilian. The loss of this bond gave veterans pause to consider what had happened to them. When units began to fold their flags and break up at the conclusion of the war, this realization hit especially hard. In July, 1945, one soldier reflected in his diary: "They're all gone. All of them. Just a few of us left who feel like the last leaves on the trees. . . . We've been together two & a half years—cussed, bitched, griped, been scared to death together, got drunk, chased women, razzed the hell out of each other, borrowed & loaned, helped each other & been helped. I love every damn one of them, but saying goodby [sic] to some was about the hardest thing I ever had to do in my life."[47]

Could they make the transition from a life based upon contingency to one based upon normalcy? Throughout their military experiences, their actions had been devoted to simple survival. The yardstick they used to measure behavior was straightforward: It reduced everything to commonsense responses to basic physical needs—sleep, food, and the threat of imminent danger. Justifying or explaining these decisions after the fact became a problem. William Manchester, a marine in the Pacific, put it in this context: "We were all animals, really, torn between fear—I was mostly frightened—and a murderous rage at events. One strange feeling, which I remember clearly, was a powerful link with the slain, particularly those who had fallen within the past hour or two. There was so much death around that life seemed almost indecent. Some men's uniforms were soaked with gobs of blood. The ground was sodden with it. I killed, too."[48]

After having taken this step between duty and moral consciousness, could the veteran return completely to the "normal" bounds of law and morality?[49] The degree of concern among veterans was not small. An army survey recorded that 48 percent of returning GIs worried whether they would be able to settle down and return to civilian life. Many had no idea what the future held. One soldier awaiting his return while on occupation duty in Germany reflected years later: "We seldom talked about our futures. Few of us had clear goals, other than getting on with our lives. Returning to the civilian jobs we left was guaranteed, though I did not much relish being a file clerk for an insurance company the rest of my life."[50]

"What to do next?" That was the question uniting GIs and the public alike. Back in the United States, as millions of returning veterans began filtering home, a cottage industry arose to answer the question as it lingered in the minds of families and spouses: Was the returning soldier a threat or an asset to society?[51] Contemporary publications were stuffed full of advice to calm anxieties or inflame them. American publishing houses churned out dozens of how-to guides on topics related to marriage, work, sex, and the resocialization of veterans. Most were written in simple lay terms or were filled with anecdotal examples of the difficulties veterans initially faced upon their return.[52] Readers were urged to keep an eye out for "danger signals"—frustrations, anger, or anxiety about "vocational insecurity"—as returnees struggled to find a place in the job market. In most cases these guides emphasized tolerance during the transition to civilian life and patient efforts to inspire veterans.[53] In terms that required whole families and communities to act in concert, a common theme they expressed was the need to collectively come to grips with reintegration. Contemporary experts noted that the veterans' familiarity with groups in the service demanded that civilian society cooperate in dealing with their rehabilitation.[54] This appeal resonated with an American public that was already used to mobilization on the home front. After 1945, the public campaign to serve the veterans became in many respects an extension of the war effort.

In the early months of peacetime, however, the pessimists' voices were the loudest. One author made the point that veterans had fashioned a fantasy regarding their awaiting homes, one that would be impossible to rediscover. He predicted widespread disillusionment once this reality began to dawn on millions of returned service personnel.[55] Many American educators also chimed in with their own misgivings.

The American Association of University Women editorialized that the tidal wave of veterans entering colleges might come at the expense of more qualified female applicants.[56] At the University of Chicago, Robert M. Hutchins stated that the number of competent instructors necessary to teach the new influx of veteran students simply did not exist. Others argued that the fundamental idea behind the new Servicemen's Readjustment Act (the so-called GI Bill) for university-level training was a fallacy of the first order. James Conant, president of Harvard University, declared the GI Bill a mistake because it did not "distinguish between those who can profit most by advanced education and those who cannot." He worried that the academic integrity of American colleges would be bankrupted by veterans. How could people who had been subjected to military regimentation devote themselves to intellectual exploration? Universities would become what one writer in *American Scholar* magazine described as "merely a housing for the mass production of degrees."[57]

Willard Waller, a professor at Barnard College, Columbia University, made perhaps the direst prediction for the future of both the veterans and the country. In his widely read 1944 book, *The Veteran Comes Back*, Waller foretells a repetition of the years immediately following the First World War, when millions found themselves bewildered, without future prospects, and severely alienated from civilian society. He darkly intones that "Every veteran is at least mildly shell-shocked." As these millions began to grapple with new peacetime conditions, Waller states, they would form a separate subculture within America, one that possessed its own language, humor, and ethical standards. The result would be two Americas: one with combat-honed skills that had become obsolete and one that warily eyed a new, potentially dangerous social minority.[58] Under these circumstances, assimilation would be impossible. As another author, Dixon Wecter, puts it, "A civilian can be licked into shape as a soldier by the manual of arms and a drillmaster, but no manual has ever been written for changing him back into a civilian."[59]

Additional anxiety centered around the belief that reincorporating veterans into normal life would break the back of the postwar economy. Many Americans were concerned that full employment would vanish in the wake of the millions of returning soldiers. Another economic collapse on par with that of 1929, something that John Kenneth Galbraith later described as a "Depression psychosis," became almost an article of faith among Americans in 1945.[60] Hard facts reinforced this anxiety. Faced with the cancellation of billions of dollars in War Department orders, American industry responded by drastically reducing production. Mass layoffs followed. In the first ten days of peace, 1.8 million Americans lost their jobs, and 620,000 filed for unemployment insurance. In September, 1945, Boeing and Ford alone fired 71,000 workers. By February, 1946, American economic productivity had fallen 31 percent below its peak the previous June.[61] As a hedge against the future, people throughout the country began to migrate to lower-paying jobs not related to war production.[62]

The prospect of a new economic decline awaiting Waller's millions of antisocial veterans combined to produce a bleak scenario more reminiscent of Germany in the twenties than America in the forties. Many social scientists expressed concern that the conditions prevalent in 1946 were a perfect catalyst for the Fascist and Communist movements that had appeared in Europe after the First World War.[63] At the very least, the ground seemed fertile for a future climate of radicalism.

More optimistic appraisals of the postwar era served as a counterpoint to Waller's vision, and much of this goodwill and hope came from the GIs themselves. As a group, they registered enormous relief that the war was over. Decades after the conflict, one veteran noted in a survey that he had "No reaction—just contented to be with my family and friends and try to forget the past service years. Glad that there were no scars or missing limbs." Most considered the transition from war to peace to be a relatively simple process and were straightforward about their expectations. A veteran of the 1st Armored Division expressed the feelings of many contemporaries when he said, "All I expected was to find work and live a normal life."[64] Contemporary surveys of returning soldiers indicate an overwhelming desire to leave military service behind. In August, 1945, 81 percent of soldiers who were asked asserted that they had already done their share and should be discharged as soon as possible. After examining data collected from surveys in 1945, the War Department noted that the collective needs of the army were quickly being displaced by the desires of individual soldiers for their civilian futures.[65] Ironically, the best evidence against the alarmists' predictions of an America plagued by disgruntled veterans was coming from the soldiers themselves.

Recognizing the value of this desire for normalcy, lawmakers worked hard to capture and transform the veterans' expectations into law.

What motivated some was an interesting combination of altruism and true respect for the accomplishments of American men and women in uniform. By 1946, almost half of Congress had served in uniform at one point in their lives, some as far back as the Spanish-American War. They had lived the story that was unfolding before them and recognized an opportunity to right past mistakes. For others, political pragmatists who may or may not have served, the prospect of a campaign in the upcoming 1946 midterm congressional elections, without any action for millions of likely voters, beggared common sense. Regardless of motive, the list of laws dedicated to veterans began to grow.

The original GI Bill showed the way. Franklin Roosevelt signed Public Law 346, the Servicemen's Readjustment Act, on June 22, 1944. Its purpose was to create concrete means to ease the veterans' transition back to civilian life. The original law consisted of three major components: education and vocational training; unemployment compensation; and loan guarantees for homes, farms, and businesses. All of these provisions were largely untried and unprecedented in the history of veterans' programs.[66] A veteran with only ninety days of service and with any discharge other than dishonorable could qualify for benefits. Many returning veterans joined the so-called 52-20 Club, which provided them with payment of a "readjustment allowance" of twenty dollars a week for up to fifty-two weeks.[67]

Fiscal conservatives like House Veterans' Committee chair John E. Rankin of Mississippi cried foul, citing the potential cost of such broad proposals, but they found themselves drowned out by overwhelming public support. The American Legion and the Veterans of Foreign Wars both endorsed the law.[68] Although organized labor grumbled about later provisions for the hiring and rehiring of veterans, they too eventually jumped on the growing public bandwagon. Proponents of the GI Bill tried to soothe fears by stressing the fact that it was not intended as a substitute for employment or permanent training and that benefit payments to veterans were limited.

Yet, additions to the original GI Bill continued without interruption. Additional legislation addressed preference for veterans in civil-service jobs, the sale of surplus property, hospitalization, domiciliary care, disability, and survivor and burial benefits.[69] Washington bureaucracies that were dedicated to the veterans began to hemorrhage. Separate offices for new programs were created by the Selective Service System, the Department of Labor, the U.S. Employment Service, the Veterans'

Security Agency, the War Manpower Commission, and the Veterans' Administration. A reemployment committeeperson served on each of the 6,500 local draft boards in the United States. Selective Service created nearly 10,000 Veterans' Information Centers around the country. Not to be outdone, the U.S. Employment Service established 1,500 offices nationwide for veterans.[70]

State and local governments followed suit and passed their own laws dedicated to veterans' benefits. Many jurisdictions created their own civil-service preference for veterans as well as aid programs for spouses and dependents. Florida provided state unemployment compensation to veterans. Louisiana offered them homestead land. California actually established a welfare board to assist veterans in prosecuting claims against the federal government.[71] A few Southern states removed the poll-tax requirement for veterans, a decision that would later have an important impact on the civil rights movement of the forties.

Collectively, veterans began to confront a well-meaning morass of red tape, conflicting advice, and interagency turf wars. Confusion became the rule rather than the exception as every tier of American government struggled to keep pace with new legislation. In relatively short order, an additional cottage industry sprang up in postwar America, one dedicated to helping individual returnees to navigate their way through a bewildering, often redundant, array of institutions and programs.[72]

Leaders who could cut through this red tape were a premium commodity after the war. More than a few were taken directly from the ranks of the military. Marine Maj. Gen. Graves B. Erskine was reassigned from combat command in the Pacific to take charge of the Department of Labor's Retraining and Reemployment Administration (RRA). Displaying a warrior's tact, Erskine rode roughshod over the entrenched civil servants he now led. When confronted with standard bureaucratic operating procedures, he responded "I haven't got time to monkey with that kind of business. And the President has put me in here to do the job, and I am going to do it and nobody is going to get in my way."[73] In a December, 1945, conference with representatives of forty separate agencies, one of Erskine's first acts was to lay out clear lines of responsibility within the RRA. More importantly, like many military leaders pressed into civilian service after World War II, Erskine delegated control of his agency to local field offices. He based this decision on the logic that officials closer to the problems would be better able to craft solutions for them. This type of flexibility would be a hallmark of the early postwar period.[74]

The Veterans' Administration experienced an even more profound change. Less than two weeks after the surrender of Nazi Germany, Dwight D. Eisenhower summoned Gen. Omar N. Bradley to his headquarters. The purpose of the meeting was to inform Bradley of his appointment to head the Veterans' Administration. Bradley had been a key subordinate to Eisenhower throughout the war and had served him in campaigns stretching back to North Africa and Sicily. When he received the news about his VA assignment, Bradley was nearing the apex of his military career. In 1945, he commanded the 12th Army Group. Bradley could count George S. Patton as a subordinate and British field marshall Bernard Law Montgomery as a peer. In the near term, he had expected to parlay his position into the prestigious appointment as chief of staff of the army. News of the unexpected civilian assignment, according to Bradley, "devastated" him. However, his sense of duty and his understanding that the VA position would be temporary overcame this initial reluctance. The general returned to the United States in June, 1945, and on June 7, President Harry Truman announced Bradley's appointment as the new leader of the Veterans' Administration.[75]

Beyond his implacable sense of duty, Bradley also possessed other features that made him ideally suited for the Veterans' Administration job. He had an innate sense of coolness and fairness that complemented an aptitude for attacking large problems. According to historian Forest C. Pogue, "Bradley was [George C.] Marshall's model of a field commander. Calm, utterly without flamboyance, patient, capable of hard decisions without screaming and cursing, cooperative, successful in molding winning armies, Bradley would have been Marshall's choice for Chairman of the Joint Chiefs of Staff had he not already been in the job."[76]

In other words, Bradley was not a Patton or a Curtis "Bombs Away" LeMay. He had all the qualities of a successful civilian administrator who was plunked down in middle of the internecine warfare of Washington, D.C. His fame was an additional asset. When Bradley returned to the United States in the summer of 1945, he was nearly as famous as Eisenhower. Parades greeted him everywhere. One of the most popular writers of the time, Ernie Pyle, wrote of him in this way: "If I could pick any two men in the world for my father, except my own dad, I would pick Gen. Omar Bradley or Gen. Ike Eisenhower. If I had a son, I would like him to go to Bradley or Ike for advice."[77]

Upon taking charge of the Veterans' Administration, Bradley needed every ounce of this personal discipline and public acclaim. What he found at the VA was the largest independent federal agency in America. In 1945, it contained more than 65,000 employees scattered throughout the forty-eight states. Its previous head was its founder, retired army Brig. Gen. Frank T. Hines, who had served the agency as administrator for twenty-two years. A Hoover appointee, Bradley described Hines as "a colorless but scrupulously honest, conservative and conscientious administrator."[78] Unfortunately for the bureaucracy, Hines was more suited to the limited role that his organization had played during peacetime than the enormous demands awaiting the VA in the postwar period. During his tenure, Hines had centralized decision making within the confines of the national headquarters. Judgments regarding benefits, health care, insurance, and a host of other matters rarely escaped his personal attention. As Bradley later recounted, "When we came in we found it impossible to pile the huge load of World War II on a chassis built for World War I."[79]

Hines's antiquated system buckled and broke under the strain of nearly sixteen million new veterans. Once the war ended, claims for health, education, and insurance benefits flooded the national office. As early as June, 1945, the VA had received 66,000 disability claims from World War II veterans. It was the very tip of the proverbial iceberg. Within a matter of months, the VA was handling between 75,000 and a quarter of a million pieces of mail each day.[80] During these hectic months, public criticism grew. One journalist has described the administration as a "vast dehumanized bureaucracy, enmeshed in mountains of red tape, ingrown with entrenched mediocrity, undemocratically operated under autocratic control centered in Washington, prescribing medieval medicine to its sick and disabled wards, highly susceptible to political pressures, rigidly resistant to proposed reforms."[81]

Bradley acted quickly to address the many problems plaguing the Veterans' Administration. Like Erskine, he immediately began to decentralize the basic functions of the organization. Operational control of daily affairs was delegated to thirteen branch offices headed by deputy administrators. While Bradley chipped away at the larger problems of budgets, staffing, and facility construction, these people were granted the latitude to shape policy to their own particular region.

Such responsibility did not come without accountability, however. As Bradley commented a year after assuming his job at the VA, "I believe that any man, when given a job, must also be given the freedom to do that job. I do not believe in doing it for him. I do not believe in telling him precisely how it shall be done. I prefer to hold him responsible instead for his performance."[82]

Risks also accompanied this liberal policy. Veterans' Administration officials in the South commonly segregated black veterans according to local and state practice. As the months of peace accumulated, a rising chorus of complaints from African American veterans regarding health care, job placement, and the deliberately lax processing of benefits claims soon pushed the problem into the national debate.[83]

Despite a number of lingering problems, the VA began to change for the better during Bradley's first year. The number of people employed by the VA swelled from 70,000 in 1945 to 173,000 by 1946. The total number of field offices they served surged from 160 to 753. The total volume of veterans seen by administration staff more than tripled—from 400,000 to 1.5 million.[84] The quality of work also improved. As administrator, Bradley was able to dragoon a large number of staff officers from the 12th Army Group and incorporate them into many parts of the Veterans' Administration. One key addition to the VA's Department of Medicine and Surgery was Paul Hawley, former surgeon general for the European theater of operations.[85] Although often blunt in their assessment of civilian government and at odds with long-standing procedures, these newly minted civil servants stiffened the ranks of the administration and added a sense of urgency to its work. Perhaps more importantly, they provided Bradley with a degree of loyalty in an institution in which he enjoyed no seniority or status. The veterans of the 12th Army Group would prove crucial to his success at the Veterans' Administration.

Bradley's approach to public relations also reveals a shrewdness that belied his modest image. Almost from the very start of his time at the VA, Bradley was constantly cultivating major American media outlets. One of his first acts was to compile a staff of three hundred who were assigned the specific task of promoting the VA to the American people.[86] He was a frequent visitor to the major networks and appeared almost monthly as a guest on radio talk shows. The general made himself constantly available to print journalists around the country.[87] When *The Best Years of Our Lives,* a 1946 movie about veterans in transition after the war, began to accumulate public and critical acclaim, Bradley told the *New York Times* that it would be required viewing for all VA personnel.[88]

Bradley's battle for the hearts and minds of the American people was important. In his quick and decisive handling of veterans' problems, he offered an important degree of comfort to former GIs and the American public. This was no small feat in 1945. Roosevelt was gone. Few people were confident that the foundering Truman administration was up to the task of overcoming the massive problems that confronted the country with the rapid onset of peace. In a tumultuous time, Bradley became a touchstone of calm.

In the closing months of 1945, America was an unsettled country. Not many citizens could say with any conviction what the future might bring. Abroad, tensions with the Soviet Union were on the rise. Starvation and desperation threatened Europe. Hovering over it all was the atomic bomb, the wonder weapon that had ended the war but was now a new, ominous presence in postwar American culture.[89] At home, the signs were equally discouraging. The strikes, the shortages, and the bitter, renewed partisan bickering between Democrats and Republicans reflected a vanishing unity that, while not perfect by any means during the war, had at least held the country together in a common effort. In 1945, the consensus at home had apparently disappeared. The open question was, what would take its place?

The role that the veterans might play in this future was equally murky. Would they follow Willard Waller's path and become a challenge to social stability? Was America in the forties destined to repeat the history of the Weimar Republic twenty years earlier? Or would problems emerge in smaller, but still significant, ways? Could families and marriages survive the strain of reunion? Could educators adapt to the large numbers of veterans clamoring for entrance into universities and develop new teaching methods to accommodate them?

The times required a reconstruction of Americans' priorities. In a sense, this was a cause for cautious optimism. If there was one thing Americans had demonstrated during World War II, it was their ability to adapt to changing circumstances. Much the same challenge now confronted the country. Both veterans and civilians alike were faced with a new mission to recraft civil society in a manner that would account for change but still try to maintain a degree of continuity. Although home would be rebuilt, it would still be recognizable.

The first and most obvious task ahead was to handle the most immediate damage the war had caused. In 1945, Americans soon focused on the needs of the war wounded—the service members who had suffered in mind and body because of the conflict. To this objective, the country would devote enormous, uncapped energy to alleviate their suffering and honor the veterans' ultimate commitment to their country. Healing the wounds of these thousands would become the first rallying point for the country and the first real effort to remake the American homeland for its returning GIs.

Healing the Wounds

Shock is what they felt first. Disbelief that it could happen. Sometimes the wound felt like nothing at all, a tug on the uniform as
fighting raged around them, a minor item in a maelstrom. Sometimes
it came all at once, after the explosion and concussion, in a cloudburst
of steel fragments. Either way, the body failed as shock set in and the
central nervous system collapsed. The GI lost control of himself at
that moment. His future passed to others' hands: his own buddies,
who would carry him to safety, and the medic who might eventually
appear to treat him. What he could do was observe and remember:
the copper scent of his own blood, the acrid odor of sulfa powder, his
own feces.

In time, once the panic subsided, realization dawned as to the extent
of the wounds. For the first time in many a young life, a hard bound-
ary appeared, the product of ruptured blood vessels, fractures that
never quite healed, or the loss of an ability so long taken for granted.
Time became a precious commodity. Patience became a virtue at a
time of life when few young men practiced it. Recovery was possible.
But before life could begin again, a time of healing was necessary.

World War II produced the largest number of American wounded
casualties of any conflict in U.S. history. For Americans, the Second
World War narrowly followed only the Civil War in terms of its total
cost. In approximately four years of fighting, 291,557 Americans died
in combat, and 113,842 perished from wounds, disease, and accidents.
A total of 671,846 Americans were wounded during the war.[1]

Advances in conventional military technology produced these casualties in unprecedented numbers. Modern science had, for example,
significantly improved the yield, range, and accuracy of existing weapons. The centuries-old art of artillery benefited from refinements in
the types of alloys used for gun barrels, the growing catalog of shells
fired, and the use of radio communication to coordinate bombard-
ments over vast areas. Old tools like these were joined by ever-improv-

ing generations of deadly military devices, from antipersonnel mines to strategic bombers. Combined, they made combat in the Second World War the most lethal in recorded history.

The closing months of the war riveted public attention on the issue of casualties. While the war wound down in Western Europe, the battles for Iwo Jima and Okinawa raged on land and sea. After only two days of fighting for Iwo Jima, 3,650 Marines were dead, more than the total casualties of Tarawa, and nearly as many as all of the marine casualties after five months of fighting on Guadalcanal.[2] One military history describes the carnage during the three-month battle for Okinawa as the "Asian Götterdämmerung." Under the punishing attacks of Japanese kamikazes, the U.S. 5th Fleet suffered 10,000 killed, wounded, and missing. During the ground campaign, the U.S. 10th Army endured an additional 40,000 casualties.[3]

More bloodshed appeared likely in the future. As the summer of 1945 drew to a close, American planners began final preparations for the invasion of the Japanese home islands. Although hotly debated within the confines of the Pentagon, casualty estimates for this final stage of the war ran as high as 500,000.[4]

Paradoxically, unlike in previous conflicts, more Americans also survived their wounds during World War II. The use of blood plasma close to the front line and the availability of rapid evacuation by ground and air transportation dramatically improved the survival rates of the wounded. Breakthroughs in modern medicine, such as the availability of sulfa drugs and penicillin, saved many paralyzed soldiers from infections of the bladder and kidneys that would have killed them in the First World War.[5] Improved surgical techniques allowed soldiers with traumatic amputations to survive at a higher rate.[6] Contemporary treatments for fractures reduced the incidence of permanent disability from 46 percent during World War I to 10 percent by 1945.[7]

The same trends were also apparent with respect to the mental injuries of combatants during the Second World War. "For the duration" was the most common yardstick used to describe the term of service in the war. In comparison to combat in the First World War and the Spanish-American War, World War II saw sustained fighting for longer periods than at any time since the Civil War. Some of the older units, such as the 1st Marine Division or the 82nd Airborne Division, deployed overseas for the entire war and stayed in combat for years, with minor respites for retraining and refitting. By 1945, the strain on the survivors of these campaigns had begun to tell.[8]

During World War II, it was a generally accepted medical fact that a soldier could endure approximately two hundred days of combat before the first signs of mental breakdown began to appear.[9] This number alone, however, only scratched the surface of the true nature of the stress that combatants experienced between 1939 and 1945. The World War II–era soldier fought regardless of climate, terrain, or weather in campaigns that lasted for months.[10] The short, sharp battles of the past were gone. Moreover, unlike previous wars, the Second World War placed an inordinate amount of strain upon an increasingly isolated soldier. Because of the destructive power of weapons fielded, units were required to disperse in order to improve their survivability. According to one military historian, Civil War units had concentrated 5,359 men per square mile. In the First World War, the number shrank to 558 men per square mile. During the Second World War, it was reduced again to 50 men per square mile.[11]

The obvious result of this trend was that the soldier or marine on the ground rarely saw the enemy. "Where are the targets?" asked S. L. A. Marshall. "How does one engage an enemy who does not seem to be present?"[12] Isolation compounded the feeling of powerlessness and tension in individual combatants. So too did the increasing sophistication of the World War II–era soldier with regard to mental disease. Prior to the war, the general public was beginning to understand that mental illness could appear in "ordinary people" without invoking images of insanity or permanent disability.[13] Consequently, soldiers in the Second World War were more prone to reveal their psychological problems and had a higher expectation that these injuries would be treated with a greater degree of urgency than in the past.[14]

The American military medical system struggled to keep pace with mental-health diagnosis and treatment throughout the war. The shortage of personnel who were qualified to conduct induction screening was so severe that the army conducted a four-week crash course in military psychiatry for physicians in an attempt to weed out potential problems from the draftee population. One recent study of the issue describes the number of qualified mental-health professionals as "hopelessly inadequate" to meet wartime needs. Shortages continued on into the postwar period. In 1946, the American Psychiatric Association had 3,655 members, of whom only 900 were treating military patients.[15] At the same time, demands on the mental-health system grew. The number of neuropsychiatric patients in the United States nearly doubled between 1944 and 1945, increasing from 39 percent to 62.54 percent of the total military patient load by the end of the war.[16]

Overall, the postwar medical challenge that veterans presented was unparalleled in its complexity and scale. In 1945, more than 1,000 army veterans were permanently blinded and required attention. Another 40,000 were listed as "hard of hearing cases." Nearly 2,000 veterans suffered from severe spinal-cord injuries.[17] The total number of medical cases in need of immediate care was staggering. Among the three-quarters of a million troops who came home through the port of New York were more than 51,543 wounded who required transport to medical facilities around the country for further treatment.[18] Tens of thousands more arrived at ports on both coasts with similar needs.

And so the flow of casualties grew. As it did, the situation presented the American public with an interesting dilemma. The month of August, 1945, marked the first real taste of peace in nearly four years. Few citizens wanted the celebrations that started during that late summer to end. Unfortunately for them, the flood of casualties coming home caught the country on the brink of this transition. It was a moment pregnant with possibilities. Americans had a choice to make: either indulge themselves after a hard-won conflict or turn to duty once again.

By the millions, people embraced the latter option. As they had during the buildup for the war itself, the American public attacked the challenge of caring for wounded veterans with remarkable vigor. As the war wound down, hundreds of publications appeared that provided guidance to anxious people who wanted to help ease the wounded veterans back into normal life. The advice addressed issues as diverse as the medical benefits contained in the new GI Bill and the difficulties that families experienced in coping with the signs of posttraumatic stress that began to appear among the returning soldiers.[19] Popular publications like *Collier's*, the *Saturday Evening Post,* and *Life* offered millions of Americans suggestions on the dos and don'ts of everyday encounters with veterans.[20] Self-help was a dominant theme in books and articles as early as 1944. Thousands of people joined local chapters of the American Red Cross and the American Legion Auxiliary, inspired in part by the work of authors such as Helen Keller, who celebrated the "heroic and often triumphant efforts of the wounded to surmount obstacles."[21] Oscar winner Harold Russell, the handicapped army veteran featured in *The Best Years of Our Lives,* became a national celebrity and the focus of a national outpouring of support.[22]

What also motivated Americans was the plight of the wounded veterans. In 1945, the American public seethed as the treatment problems that former GIs encountered exploded into a national scandal. A series of investigative reports by Albert Deutsch revealed horrific problems within the hospital system run by the Veterans' Administration. Deutsch uncovered evidence of exorbitant fees charged by some VA hospitals to cash the federal-assistance checks the veterans received, of four hundred patients at the Castle Point, New York, Tuberculosis Hospital who signed a complaint about the inedible food the facility served, and of a mental patient at the Lyons, New York, VA facility who was given shock treatments—over his repeated objections—as a demonstration to medical students.[23] The *New Republic* and *Reader's Digest* reported instances of VA hospitals plagued by unsanitary conditions and medical treatment that was "often perfunctory and incompetent," allegations supported by the *Journal of the American Medical Association.*[24] In June, 1945, the *New York Times* reported the court-martial of fifteen soldiers accused of abusing VA patients.[25] That same month, both the Veterans of Foreign Wars (VFW) and the American Legion (AL) lodged complaints about overcrowded facilities, where mental patients were housed with general hospital populations, and about medical staffs who were overwhelmed by their workloads.[26] As the reports accumulated, the unfolding scandal rocked the country.[27]

Before long, this rising tide of public discontent reached the offices of those who were charged with overseeing veterans' affairs. The House Committee on World War Veterans' Legislation, chaired by Rep. John E. Rankin of Mississippi, began to draw fire for its slow response to the widespread criticism. According to one journalist's account, the committee had "followed a policy for several weeks of using the most adroit policy maneuvers to avoid involving itself in any form of investigation of procedures built on legislation which it sponsored in the first place." According to another account, Rankin had publicly chastised Rep. Philip J. Philbin for presenting hundreds of letters of complaint during the hearings that were held in May, 1945. In response to the Deutsch exposé, Rankin investigated the reporter rather than the stories themselves and held him in contempt for refusing to reveal his sources.[28]

In fact, a very strong bureaucratic undertow was working against veterans' care that went far beyond the Rankin committee. Throughout the war, the Veterans' Administration had struggled against a priority system that gave the military branches first choice for personnel, supplies, and facilities. Those already assigned to the VA, for example, did not receive draft deferments during the war. Many also volunteered to serve. In the year following Pearl Harbor, more than seven thousand VA employees enlisted. One thousand of these enlistees were virtually irreplaceable nurses.[29] Many who remained after conscription were tempted by higher-paying jobs in the war industries. In 1942 alone, the VA Supply Service experienced an 85 percent turnover rate.[30] Throughout the war, administrators struggled with staff shortages. Lacking adequate secretarial support, VA officials used obsolescent Dictaphones to record routine letters, shipped the recording cylinders from Washington to New York to be transcribed onto paper, and then waited until they were sent back to the capital for signature and distribution.[31]

The lack of doctors to treat veterans was particularly acute. Even though 3,000 physicians flocked to recruiting stations after Pearl Harbor, the Pentagon reported a shortage of 13,000 medical-corps officers in the first six months of the war and scoured medical schools to fill open slots.[32] By the spring of 1943, the War Department was prepared to take into military service physicians who were color-blind, deaf in one ear, or missing limbs.[33] Consequently, in 1943, it came as little surprise when Assistant Secretary of War John J. McCloy wrote that he would "have no difficulty in refusing any augmentation of Veterans' Administration doctors at the expense of the Army." Moreover, he doubted that the army could provide help, given that its own patient load "is only commencing."[34] At his headquarters in Washington, VA administrator Frank T. Hines noted with some frustration the "necessarily sustained serious inroads by the needs of the armed services" on the number of physicians available for veterans' care. Specific shortages existed in general medicine, surgical specialties, and neuropsychiatry.[35]

As the war progressed, so did the burden placed on military medicine and the Veterans' Administration. The total number of patients who returned to the United States increased from 71,823 in 1943 to 172,968 in 1944 to 385,972 in 1945.[36] While this outpouring created logistical nightmares for medical facilities all over the country, it proved especially difficult for the VA's doctors. At a time when the number and type of injuries were increasing beyond the capabilities of even the most experienced physicians, Veterans' Administration staffs suffered under treatment regimens prescribed by the cumbersome *Rules and Procedures* manual. Hines's tendency to micromanage doctors—he required the approval of all new medical techniques by the Washington headquarters—was an additional and unnecessary obstacle to patient care.[37]

The return to peace made all these conditions worse. When the War Department began to rapidly demobilize in 1945, medical units were not always exempted from the process. Doctors, nurses, and orderlies followed the soldiers home. Consequently, the number of hospital beds in Europe shrank from a peak of more than 250,000 on VE Day to 19,955 by January, 1946.[38] As the medical capabilities evaporated, the demands on them grew geometrically. The number of medical admissions more than doubled, from 243,994 to 532,881, in the two years after the war. The number of patients hospitalized in VA and non-VA facilities increased by 21 percent between 1946 and 1947. Tuberculosis (47 percent), neuropsychiatric (35 percent), and general surgical (27 percent) categories recorded the largest gains. Hospital admissions grew by 63 percent during the same period.[39] Problems became so widespread that, in November, 1945, a formal Senate resolution accused the army surgeon general of incompetence.[40]

With the need for combat readiness relaxed, veterans and service members alike began to opt for elective medical care. The backaches, tooth problems, and other ailments they had deferred "for the duration" now began to claim the time and attention of doctors and nurses both overseas and in the United States.[41] Added to this task were the millions of exit physicals required by processing centers all over the country. And this was just the beginning. The new GI Bill of Rights mandated medical care for both service- and non-service-related injuries as well as therapy and rehabilitation. These provisions promised to create enormous burdens in the very near future.[42]

Further complicating the situation were the medical demands placed upon the American military by occupation duty in Europe and Asia. Allied armies moving into Italy, Germany, and Japan were forced to contend with devastated nations. American soldiers presided over a complete breakdown of the infrastructure and basic services in Germany. Millions of displaced persons (DPs) from a host of nations roamed the countryside. The American forces alone were respon-

CHAPTER 2

sible for four million prisoners of war (POWs). Contagious diseases became a chronic problem in both DP camps and POW compounds. Overtaxed medical units struggled with widespread malnutrition and a typhoid epidemic during the fall of 1946. In Japan, the same massive physical destruction prevailed. Items as simple as fresh drinking water were at a premium. Upon arriving in Tokyo, the American occupation forces were informed by Japanese officials of a spreading cholera epidemic.[43]

At war's end, the need for reform was obvious to everyone. Changes in policy, particularly with respect to medical care, dominated the landscape. In an interview conducted by the *New York Times*, the first priority cited by new VA Administrator Omar N. Bradley was meeting the needs of disabled veterans.[44] Improving veterans' medical care presented a formidable challenge for Eisenhower's old subordinate. In 1945, the Veterans' Administration maintained ninety-seven hospitals in forty-five states and the District of Columbia. More than 71,000 patients resided in these facilities, a population that included 45,000 veterans from the First World War, 2,800 from the Spanish-American War, and 8 from the Civil War.[45]

Undaunted, Bradley attacked the problems confronting his agency with the same determination that had characterized his command of the 12th Army Group in Europe. One of his first actions was to address the problem of transportation for the war wounded. During the chaotic weeks that had followed the Japanese surrender, the Veterans' Administration had been embarrassed by reports of long delays for medical patients awaiting railroad berths. Patients in need of convalescent care and treatment were forced to wait for days—sometimes weeks—for priority on the nation's overstressed rail system. In relatively short order, Bradley won an agreement from the War Department reassigning additional passenger cars for his veterans.[46]

Next Bradley addressed larger problems. One of the most prominent was the old VA practice of hiring medical staff through the U.S. Civil Service. By Bradley's own account, the doctors in this system were "the dregs of the medical profession," a body of physicians more notable for their seniority and political connections than their quality.[47] This assessment was reinforced by a September, 1945, report issued by longtime presidential advisor Bernard Baruch that highlighted the need to separate medical services from other nonmedical responsibilities within the Veterans' Administration. Baruch's report recommended salary increases, hiring and promotion policies based upon professional ability, and an emphasis on postgraduate training for both doctors and nursing staffs.[48]

Bradley implemented all of these proposals and added a few new twists of his own. One of his earliest and most important appointments was Paul R. Hawley to oversee medical care within the VA. Hawley, the son of a doctor and trained at the College of Medicine of the University of Cincinnati, was a regular army officer who had served as Eisenhower's chief surgeon for the entire European theater. In Bradley's words, Hawley "was an outspoken iconoclast with a great distaste for red tape—an able and forceful administrator."[49] Hawley combined his boss's hard-nosed professionalism with an unimpeachable zeal to improve the professional quality of the VA doctors.

Hawley's first mission was to bolster the anemic ranks of the VA physicians. In 1945, 1,700 of the Veterans' Administration's 2,300 doctors were on loan from the army and navy. Most were scheduled for demobilization, a prospect that would leave him far short of the projected 3,600 doctors he needed to meet the immediate medical needs of veterans. Even more alarming was his own prediction that the total number of physicians necessary to treat the rapidly growing veteran population would have to double by 1946.[50]

Hawley planned to attack this problem from a number of directions. First, he recommended the creation of a separate VA medical staff that would resemble the existing military medical corps or the U.S. Public Health Service and pry away control over hiring from the hands of the U.S. Civil Service. Both Bradley and Hawley considered the Civil Service to be a significant obstacle to meaningful reform. For example, all personnel decisions were subject to byzantine civil-service regulations, particularly those that granted first hires to people with the most seniority. In testimony before the House Committee on World War Veterans' Legislation, Hawley noted that the first doctor on the list presented to him by the Civil Service was 87 years old. The second was 76 years old. Overall, more than half of the doctors awaiting assignment were over the age of 60.[51]

Ideally, what he wanted was a younger breed of physician, one who had not only benefited from modern training but was also from a generation that was more willing and able to vigorously pursue patient treatment. Second, Hawley wanted to establish affiliate memberships between the Veterans' Administration and medical teaching institutions around the country. The use of civilian affiliation was common practice for military general hospitals in both world wars, one that did wonders for physicians' exposure to contemporary medical training and the newest techniques. It seemed to be common sense to continue this relationship into peacetime.[52] Collectively, Hawley wanted to introduce the VA to the cutting edge of modern medicine. To accomplish this and to build ties with the American Medical Association and other professional societies, he enlisted the help of Paul B. Magnuson, head of the Department of Bone and Joint Surgery at Northwestern University. Magnuson placed the VA reforms in simple terms: "You can't hire good doctors to go anywhere, for any amount of money, unless you give them the chance to do what they really want to do—make progress in medicine by teaching, doing research, and keeping in close touch with the best men in the profession."[53]

Congress and President Truman agreed. On January 3, 1946, Public Law 293 reorganized the VA's Department of Medicine and Surgery. The act provided for a 25 percent bonus for medical specialists and finalized support for residency training programs. All of the personnel decisions were to be controlled by Hawley, who was acting as chief medical director. After the bill was signed, the VA announced an immediate need for 1,125 physicians, 1,200 nurses, and 100 dentists.[54] The drive to establish affiliations with teaching institutions followed soon afterward. Before the annual convention of the American Medical Association, Hawley assured doctors that they would keep a "free rein" on medical decisions, "unhampered by Washington." By the summer of 1946, the Veterans' Administration was able to establish a physician's residency program that included 63 of the 77 medical schools in the country. Young, well-trained doctors applied in droves to a system that offered modern training as well as the prospect of service. By August, the VA fielded four applications for every position available in the Department of Medicine and Surgery.[55]

The Veterans' Administration scored equally substantial victories in the field of nursing care. From his new position in the Department of Medicine and Surgery, Hawley promised "a nursing service second to none." He increased the base salary for nurses, then at $1,800–2,000 per year, to $2,644–3,397 per year. The VA also separated nursing salaries from position assignments and made compensation a function of experience, education, and competence.[56] Hawley's most important decision was his appointment of Dorothy Wheeler as the new director of VA nursing. Wheeler, at age thirty-four, rejuvenated the inspection system used throughout the administration and aggressively pursued improvements in patient treatment. Her goal was to have a nurse-patient ratio of 5:1, half the army's wartime standard. Wheeler argued for—and achieved—specialized training in fields such as neuropsychiatry and surgery, making the point that nurses needed to keep pace with the improving standards for doctors.[57]

Veterans' mental health care made impressive gains under Hawley's guidance. During World War II, it was normal to classify psychological problems as "combat exhaustion" and attribute illness to physical fatigue or a condition that predated military service. The most common solution was to treat the soldiers as close to the front line as possible and return them to combat. Evacuation to the United States for further treatment was always a last resort.[58] Military medicine devoted precious little attention to the idea that mental disability might continue after a serviceperson left the military.[59] Once the war was over, however, it was up to the Veterans' Administration to address the long-term mental-health treatment of thousands of former service members.

VA doctors tackled the problem with the same vigor they applied to physical injuries. At the Menninger Clinic in Topeka, Kansas, doctors Karl Menninger and William Menninger constructed a therapy regime built around a well-planned, thirteen-hour day of activity fitted to the individual patient's needs. They encouraged self-governing wards that elected their own ward officers and committees and created a degree of patient control over the day-to-day routine. The use of mutual aid through group therapy, originally an expedient to deal with the large influx of patients, became a treatment staple that encouraged discharged veterans to discuss their problems among peers. According to journalist Albert Deutsch, once one of the loudest critics of the Veterans' Administration, the Menningers had sparked a "revolution" in the VA hospitals.[60]

The Veterans' Administration also embarked upon an ambitious medical-construction program after the war. The administration estimated that as many as 300,000 new beds would be needed to accommodate the new patients.[61] When Bradley took charge in August, 1945, more than 70 new VA hospitals were already in the planning stages. Interestingly, his greatest difficulty was not the number of facilities proposed, but their location. Veterans' Administration hospitals traditionally were notorious sources of congressional pork. Buildings located in a remote district of a favored legislative son—and far away from counterpart civilian institutions—were commonplace. With the reform of the VA's hiring practices already in his pocket, Bradley neither challenged this congressional prerogative nor substantively guided the $95 million dollars appropriated for hospital construction during the fiscal year of 1945.[62] However, he was able to acquire 37 surplus military hospitals as well as facilities transferred from other civilian agencies that were more accessible for veterans. In this manner, Bradley added 39,622 new beds to the VA inventory in 1946.[63]

As building plans moved forward, Bradley and Hawley focused on reconstructing VA facilities from within, expanding the number of hospitals treating amputations, spinal-cord injuries, and thoracic surgery to sixteen nationwide. The VA created partnerships with specialized-training institutions such as the Mayo Clinic, ones that allowed their doctors to explore the cutting edge of patient treatment.[64] Veterans' Administration hospitals improved their physical-therapy departments by incorporating the latest breakthroughs in lighter, more flexible metals and plastics for prosthetic devices.[65] Although sometimes a patient's progress could be measured only in the days of excruciating effort expended to move a thumb or shrug both shoulders, thousands of veterans benefited from improvements in therapist training.[66]

The Veterans' Administration also placed increasing emphasis on job placement once medical treatment was complete. Occupational-therapy programs retrained medically disabled veterans in woodworking, weaving, and other crafts.[67] In cooperation with the VA, the major trade unions opened their doors to these people. Bradley pressed for and received early cooperation from private businesses in hiring and training disabled veterans. International Harvester, Ford, Bulova, and Westinghouse all established hiring programs that produced excellent results.[68]

By many measures, the medical revolution that followed World War II was a dramatic success story for American veterans. Millions of lives were immediately affected in the years after the war. A generation would benefit from the medical standards set in 1945. Future generations of veterans, particularly those of the Vietnam War, would shape their expectations according to precedents that were established in the forties.

Central to this success was Omar N. Bradley. In his memoirs, Bradley attributed his progress in running the VA to a friendly press, which usually spoke of him in the glowing terms that were commonly used to describe a war hero. One journalist summed up the thrust of dozens of articles when he described Bradley as "a man who had a knack for getting at the heart of a situation."[69] Conventional American wisdom saw the general as a figure born of the war against fascism, tempered by success on the battlefields of Europe, and burnished by total victory in 1945. More importantly, Bradley's prestige resonated not only with the general public but also with the many veterans who populated the media after 1945. Former marine Sam Stavisky of the *Washington Post* would prove to be an asset to the VA long after Bradley's departure in 1947.[70]

However, there is more to the story than Bradley's formidable strength of character. As a politician, Bradley was shrewd enough to understand the important leverage that the public's confidence gave him at a key moment in history. This public faith in him gave Bradley an enormous bargaining chip that broke the legislative and special-interest logjams that repeatedly threatened his efforts to reform the Veterans' Administration. When confronted by civil-service lobbying against proposed changes to the Department of Medicine and Surgery, Bradley offered to resign, a move that sent opponents backpedaling furiously in an effort to avoid the inevitable national outcry such a move might produce.[71]

In a larger sense, Bradley's rise also reflected the growing importance of military service in American politics. Only five years earlier, it would have been almost unthinkable for the Roosevelt administration to openly appoint military officers to what were traditionally civilian administrative domains. By 1945, it was commonplace to see uniformed military personnel overseeing the operations of civilian agencies. Bradley was charged with the Veterans' Administration.[72] Other soldiers followed him. Their staffs went with them, displacing long-standing civilian officeholders by the dozen. Paul Hawley was not alone when he wrested control of medical decisions from the Civil Service Commission. When Bradley transplanted his 12th Army Group staff to the VA, he did so for practical reasons. This group of men was a skilled, disciplined contingent of soldiers who were prepared to unleash their talents on an important new mission.

The postwar political atmosphere not only tolerated but also demanded such moves. As more than sixteen million veterans returned to civilian life, they redrew the fundamental expectations of the American electorate. Veterans' medical care became a critical issue for perhaps the most potent political constituency in the twentieth century. The stories of scandal that bombarded the Veterans' Administration in the summer of 1945 resonated with this population. Far from posing a liability, military service became the new currency of American politics. Service created a sense of legitimacy and reinforced the confidence that public policy would benefit from the same talents that had won the war. Not since the Civil War had time in uniform become such a critical test for public office at the local, state, and federal levels. Military leaders like Bradley built a path that would eventually lead to Dwight D. Eisenhower's presidency barely a decade later.

World War II also initiated profound changes in the method of American governance that aided the change and growth of the Veterans' Administration. The war years were a fluid time, when expediency superseded established protocol in importance. Ever the great improviser, Roosevelt created an alphabet soup of agencies that were designed to mobilize the nation and that dwarfed the New Deal. After 1941, the Office of Price Administration, the Office of War Information, the War Manpower Commission, and dozens of other new bureaus appeared on the American landscape. Each was intended as a short-term solution to an immediate wartime need. The president favored this approach because it allowed him to often bypass stubborn legislators and older federal departments that were primarily interested in protecting their bureaucratic turf.[73] What Roosevelt did not anticipate was the climate that he would cultivate within Washington, D.C., one that embraced new ideas and demonstrated an unprecedented flexibility for a short time after his death. In the summer of 1945, American lawmakers were prepared to tolerate change to a degree unheard of only a few years earlier. When Omar Bradley approached Congress asking for sweeping reforms of veterans' medical treatment, he did so in an environment that was remarkably different from the prewar norm.[74]

An even more profound development in American governance occurred in its scale. The Second World War saw an explosive growth in what the national government both consumed and produced. Millions of citizens were introduced to federal income taxes for the first time. In 1943, employers deducted $686 million from American workers' paychecks. Only two years later, more than $10 billion was withheld from paychecks around the country.[75] This vast increase helped make

Washington the largest procurer of goods and services in the nation's history. In the first six months of 1942, the federal government ordered $100 billion for war production, more than the American economy had ever produced in a single year.

This flow of revenue also allowed the number of federal employees to skyrocket. Between 1940 and 1945, the number of civilian workers in the federal government nearly quadrupled, from slightly more than 1 million to 3.8 million.[76] If the New Deal introduced Americans to institutionalized big government, the war increased its size to gargantuan proportions. No longer did lawmakers look aghast at the prospect of multibillion-dollar programs controlled by tens of thousands of federal employees. In the climate of 1945, these had become almost routine.

The Veterans' Administration followed suit. In 1945, the VA was the largest independent agency in the federal government. That year, $177.6 million was allocated for veterans' affairs. By 1947, the VA's budget had surpassed the half-billion-dollar mark. "Readjustment benefits" increased more than sevenfold, from $295 million to $2.1 billion. Funding for "hospital and domiciliary facilities" increased from $17.9 million to an impressive $242.8 million.[77] The total number of VA employees increased substantially on Bradley's watch, from nearly 65,000 in 1945 to 200,000 by 1947. Throughout the two years following the war, the question most often asked was not "why" funding for veterans should increase, but by how much.

The final, decisive component of the veterans' postwar medical "revolution" was not the VA but the American public. During the war, the public had endured the hardships of rationing, housing shortages, new taxes, and the unprecedented growth of federal authority in their everyday lives. They had tolerated the conscription of millions of their sons, husbands, and fathers. When these men came home, the American people became the most important first step that linked the veteran and his medical rehabilitation. Bradley made this connection as early as December, 1945: "While we can assist with benefits and offer guidance, it is the community that must do the grass-roots work. For it is in his daily association with his neighbors that the veteran rubs shoulders with so many troublesome problems Washington cannot hope to solve."[78]

People volunteered for this mission by the millions. Again, the war opened the door for volunteer service. Between 1941 and 1945,

Americans of all ages served as air-raid wardens, canteen workers, or child-care aides. As one periodical observed in 1946, the conflict had "smoked most men and women out of inactivity and aloofness."[79]

After the war, volunteer groups, once dedicated to easing the hardships of the GIs, turned their attention toward rehabilitating them. In practical terms, local community groups became the first step in a system of referrals that led veterans to medical treatment. At the foundation of the growing federal bureaucracy dedicated to veterans' problems were families, churches, and charities spread across towns and cities throughout America. Some of this cooperation came as a result of federal outreach programs. The Retraining and Reemployment Administration of the Department of Labor offered step-by-step guidelines for community organization. Its goal was "to bring together, in one place, complete and accurate information, obtain the services of agencies and experts, and give individual assistance in solving personal problems."[80]

The VA Volunteer Service (VAVS) fostered community cooperation in reassimilation. By the end of the forties, 72,700 volunteers in thirty-eight states contributed an average of 344,700 hours each month to the cause. Many psychiatric patients without families, who would have otherwise been hospitalized, were taken in by private homes as part of a foster-care program.[81] The VA Auxiliary sponsored a nationwide, three-week training program for hospital aides to relieve the burdens faced by the veterans' hospital system nationwide.[82] The Veterans' Administration also encouraged local participation in this process through the "hometown" program that allowed veterans to see their local doctors, dentists, and pharmacists (once approved) for treatment at government expense. By 1950, more than 100,000 physicians were participating in the project.[83]

Privately run national organizations also took the initiative at the grassroots level. The American Legion expanded the work of its Child Welfare Division to aid war widows and the surviving children of veterans. By 1946, the AL National Rehabilitation Program had 650 full-time staff and 18,000 volunteer auxiliaries across the country.[84] The American Red Cross became one of the most important venues for veterans who were seeking mental-health counseling. Home service workers became a primary bridge between returning disabled veterans and their homes.[85] Similarly, the YMCA created its own counseling service to address the needs of veterans. In the months following the war, the list of philanthropic groups grew to include the Military Order of the Purple Heart; the Fleet Reserve Association; Catholic War Veterans, Inc.; the Navy Mutual Aid Association; and a host of other organizations.[86]

Local agencies contributed a final layer of volunteers. The Junior League and Mental Hygiene Society of Los Angeles, for example, established a community clinic for "disturbed" veterans soon after the war.[87] In September, 1945, the Detroit Council of Veterans' Affairs Information Center fielded more than four thousand calls, most of them addressing employment (19 percent), education benefits (16 percent), and insurance (9 percent).[88]

Community organizations became the mortar that held the national veterans' medical network together. Although at times they battled over jurisdiction and sometimes presented the new returnee with a dizzying array of choices, the private sector was decisive in overcoming any initial reluctance to seek treatment. Because these organizations were often composed of friends, families, and neighbors, they were much more effective in translating the monolithic federal bureaucracies into a human face. Equally important was the ability of these local groups to monitor the progress the veterans made and to modify their care as each person required it. In the end, the peacetime home front became a crucial contributor to the veterans' healing process.

U nfortunately, the momentum behind this medical crusade did not last. As the decade progressed, the laserlike focus on veterans' medical issues diminished and eventually receded into the background. What had for a time been the focal point of intense public scrutiny eventually became an afterthought.

A number of factors explain this development. The most obvious was Omar Bradley's return to active duty military in December, 1947. At that time, the general received what he had craved at the end of the war: the post of army chief of staff. His departure represented a victory of sorts for the U.S. Civil Service and the prewar status quo. When Bradley left, he took with him significant political capital as well as his personal access to President Truman. Subordinates like Magnuson and Hawley lost their best patron in Washington circles. So too did the innovators that the VA had supported up to that time.

The arrival of Carl R. Gray as the new administrator of the Veterans' Administration was small consolation to these people. Gray, a former vice president of the Northwestern Railroad Company, embodied the VA's loss of prestige and dynamism after Bradley's departure. A man with notoriously poor eyesight, he could barely read the documents that passed through his office each day. When conducting inspection tours of VA hospitals, Gray would briskly walk through each room, unable to clearly see their occupants or equipment. According to Paul Magnuson, who was unrestrained in his criticism, "Carl Gray has been described as affable. His geniality was of the heavy-handed kind; and he had quite a reputation in some places as a raconteur, specializing in railroad stories. I found out early in the game that he was a compulsive talker. He could not listen. This was particularly true if anybody had anything sensible to tell him."[89]

Gray restored the centralized VA bureaucracy that had flourished before 1945 under Frank T. Hines. Control of medical affairs was rerouted directly to his office, a decision that placed him in constant conflict with Magnuson, who, in 1948, threatened to resign and was finally fired in 1951. The priority for hospital construction and facilities purchases again passed to the congressional pork barrel. Gray himself was forced out as VA administrator after a Senate investigation chaired by Hubert Humphrey revealed a familiar story of politicization and bureaucratic incompetence.[90]

In truth, the blame for the decline of the Veterans' Administration does not rest on any one person's shoulders. Bradley's arrival as the head of a traditionally civilian agency highlighted broad hostility between new military personnel and the old guard of civilian administrators. When Gen. Graves B. Erskine of the U.S. Marines took over the Retraining and Reemployment Administration, he railed against General Hines, who "had used the Administration as a sort of haven for his old broken down drunks, to push them over the edge so they could retire."[91] Statements like these were an expression of sometimes well-deserved contempt. In the crisis months that followed the war, they were tolerable reflections of conventional wisdom. However, there were limits to how much abuse the long-suffering civilian rank and file were willing to accept. After a point, the obvious lack of tact displayed by the new regime of military administrators added to a growing reservoir of resentment that fueled a backlash against reform. Ironically, from this perspective, Carl R. Gray was a breath of fresh air that followed years of often clumsy, confrontational policymaking.

In a larger sense, America itself was changing as the VA struggled to heal the country's veterans. The political climate following the war represented a backlash of its own kind. In 1945 and 1946, the early stumbles of the Truman administration became fertile soil for the Republican Party. Whether the problem applied to rising prices, the coal shortage, the imminent breakdown of the national railroad system, or Truman's highly public battles with labor leaders such as the United Mine Workers' president, John L. Lewis, the time seemed ripe for change.[92] Consequently, the Republican message in the fall "beefsteak election" of 1946 was simple: "Had enough? Vote Republican."[93] And vote they did. When Americans went to the polls that November, they dealt the worst blow to Roosevelt's party in a generation. Democrats lost control of both houses of the federal legislature that year. When the Eightieth Congress convened, Republicans outnumbered Democrats by 246 to 188 in the House of Representatives and 45 to 41 in the Senate.[94]

The new leadership represented a marked change from what the country had enjoyed throughout Roosevelt's four terms. Joseph Martin of Massachusetts took the place of Sam Rayburn as Speaker of the House of Representatives. In the Senate, Robert A. Taft of Ohio and Arthur Vandenberg of Michigan directed the agenda. As a group, the Republican majority in the Eightieth Congress represented an approach to public affairs that hearkened back to the days of Calvin Coolidge. Most of them were hostile to the principle of federal government embodied by the New Deal and the rapid growth of programs they had witnessed in the thirties and early forties. Perhaps more importantly, congressional Republicans were interested in taking down presidential authority a few pegs. From their standpoint, FDR had enjoyed too much power as a result of the New Deal and the war. The significant Republican gains in the 1946 election seemed to signify that the time had arrived for restoring the primacy of Congress in national leadership.[95] Robert A. Taft spoke for many of his compatriots as the new Congress prepared to convene in 1947: "The main issue of the election was the restoration of freedom and the elimination or reduction of constantly increasing interference with family life and with business by autocratic government bureaus and autocratic labor leaders."[96]

In many of the legislative battles that unfolded over the next two years, the Eightieth Congress stayed true to its intentions. It attempted with some success to peel away the many layers of federal administrative agencies that had been added during the Depression and the war. It rejected federal funding for public housing, the creation of a national health-care system, and civil rights reform. Overall, federal spending shrank, shaped by a new emphasis on balanced budgets and fiscal conservatism. The numbers tell the story. Total federal outlays declined from $38.9 billion in 1947 to $32.9 the following year.[97]

Bitter partisanship also defined the politics of the postwar era. Lawmaking degenerated into a running political gun battle between Congress and Truman, a relationship that would only worsen as the presidential election of 1948 approached and the Cold War with the Soviet Union grew in intensity. Aggressive, irresponsible politicians, people whom Secretary of State Dean Acheson would contemptuously refer to as "the primitives," men like Joseph P. McCarthy and Richard M. Nixon, would capture the dialogue of these years and transform it with vicious attacks that ignored the line between substance and pure fantasy, scarring a generation of Americans. So too would the president, who developed confrontational politics into an art form as he gave his legislature hell during his 1948 campaign stops around the country.[98]

Eventually this fight spilled over into veterans' affairs. The Veterans' Administration was a tempting target for fiscal conservatives. It managed a popular array of programs that enjoyed considerable public support, particularly among politically powerful and conservative groups like the American Legion. However, the VA was also expensive and had a demonstrated capacity to expand far beyond its originally intended mandate. Data on veterans' massive college enrollment for the 1946–1947 academic year, for example, came as a surprise to many and indicated the gigantic impact the GI Bill was having on higher education. The confusion and inefficiency that characterized certain portions of the VA medical plan suggested the vulnerability of a public program to abuse. Overall, veterans' benefits represented the worst aspects of New Deal–era programs and their costly, inefficient, and intrusive nature. The problem for Republicans lay in crafting a strategy to pare back veterans' benefits without provoking a public backlash.

The response of the Republican-controlled Congress to this dilemma is a case study in political backsliding. As the forties moved forward, the Republicans avoided direct public attacks on specific veterans' programs. In the meantime, during the drawn-out process of crafting appropriations legislation, they cut these same programs' budgets. In this way, lawmakers could support the principle of veterans' assistance while hewing closely to the Republican Party's principle of fiscal responsibility.

In 1946, even before the new Republican cohort reached Capitol Hill, Omar Bradley found an increasingly hostile audience for his budget requests. When he testified before the House Veterans' Affairs Committee in June, Bradley reported that the VA could not keep pace with the burgeoning numbers of veterans entering the system. New claims for readjustment allowances under Title V of the GI Bill alone had reached one hundred thousand per week that month. Paying for these increases, after what many legislators considered lavish expenditures on veterans' benefits, was becoming a hard case to make. Bradley drew immediate fire when he appeared before the House Appropriations Committee to request supplemental funding for the fiscal year, noting that the VA would run out of money on June 30, 1947, if additional revenues were not forthcoming.[99]

Ironically, the additional cost was a reflection of progress. By 1946, salaries for medical specialists, advanced training, and the cost of new drugs and treatment regimes were all indicators of the quantum leap in medical care available to veterans. Bradley was blunt about the trade-off: "Progressive hospital treatment at the hands of competent doctors and nurses is neither cheap nor inexpensive."[100] The larger staffs required to process and answer the medical claims that poured into VA offices across the country also required more robust budgets. As veterans began to understand that the benefits package offered by the VA was reliable and accessible, both their confidence and the number of their medical claims grew. And so the cycle repeated itself.

What undercut Bradley's argument was the VA's ongoing problem of not spending money already allocated for medical care. In 1943 and 1944, funding for 74 new VA hospitals had been approved by Congress. Three years later, 68 construction sites had been chosen, and planning was under way for 59 hospitals. However, contracts had been awarded for only 8 facilities, and construction on only 3 had actually begun. Cost overruns also plagued the administration. Prices for basic building materials, reflecting competition with the booming postwar housing market and equally heavy demands for commercial construction, rapidly outpaced the original estimates. The skilled labor necessary for each project, from the contractors necessary to pour concrete foundations to the electricians and plumbers who outfitted the finished structure, was at a premium as Levittowns mushroomed around America. The cost of a VA psychiatric hospital in Peekskill, New York, for example, nearly tripled, from $8 million to $22 million in only two years.[101] Facilities like this became more the rule than the exception.

The unpredictability of VA spending was fresh meat for the budget hawks in Washington. As essential as some of the veterans' programs were, and it was hard to argue that medical rehabilitation was not, the fact that money remained unspent for years made it hard to justify more. The open-ended problem of higher costs, while not always the product of the VA's incompetence or inaction, lent exactly that air to the political atmosphere. Even when Bradley was able to win a few tactical victories in his budget battles, he drew fire for supporting partisan interests. The general eventually received two supplemental-funding amendments to his budget in 1946 but prompted criticism that he had allowed the American Medical Association to set prices for outpatient services.[102] Bradley's efforts to reach out to veterans' organizations also backfired. The VA officially recognized twenty-four separate veterans' groups and maintained office space for 3,600 of their representatives. While this allowed federal policy to rapidly reach the local, VFW, or American Legion–post level, it almost immediately created charges of favoritism.[103]

A severe budget clampdown followed shortly after Bradley's appeals to Congress. By February, 1947, the Veterans' Administration was forced to order a hiring freeze and curtail all but essential travel. The VA headquarters in Washington began to review all medical examinations and assess their cost before it authorized treatment through VA and affiliated hospitals.

Many doctors saw this type of health-care management as a fundamental betrayal of the promises made in 1945. A letter sent to Bradley by Karl A. Menninger of the Menninger Clinic expressed the feelings of many: "I came into this thing because I saw the possibility of developing a great thing for the veterans and for the Nation, under your leadership and that of General Hawley. But I, and many others like me, will drop it like a hotcake if penny wise, pound foolish politics are forced upon me."[104]

Faced with shrinking budgets and increasing micromanagement, doctors began to resign from the Veterans' Administration. The virtues of private practice beckoned. Many health-care providers followed America to the suburbs and the booming market in obstetrics and family practice. Shortages of trained doctors and specialists soon became widespread in the VA system. By 1950, more than four thousand authorized beds, the equivalent of sixteen average-sized hospitals, could not be used because the staffs needed to maintain them were unavailable.[105]

By the end of the forties, the debate over veterans' medical care had been transformed. The time when legislators once enthusiastically embraced the public's demands for more extensive and better quality care seemed very far away. Discussion of quality and quantity vanished. Retrenchment became the keynote of the day. The bureaucratic tide began to shift as agency after agency supported cutbacks in veterans' medical programs. In some cases, the military led the way. A 1949 study by the Armed Forces Medical Advisory Committee for the secretary of defense recommended that army and navy hospitals reduce or eliminate the care of veterans. That March, the Senate Committee on Labor and Public Welfare endorsed a sixteen-thousand-bed cutback in new construction of VA hospitals. The Bureau of Budget approved the elimination of more than eleven thousand VA positions during fiscal year 1950. In April, 1949, the House Appropriations Committee recommended reducing the VA's operating budget by $28 million. Private-interest groups also chimed in. The American Hospital Association, long an opponent of the Veterans' Administration, lobbied to have veterans with non-service-connected medical problems dropped from VA hospitals.[106]

On the brink of the Korean War, the Veterans' Administration began to shrink. Between 1949 and 1950, more than seven thousand staff personnel were fired. Cutbacks eliminated thirteen branch offices and office space totaling 1.3 million square feet.[107] VA officials were able to stave off the economic measures that directly threatened veterans' hospitalization benefits, however, and some new hospital construction continued. Nevertheless, these measures merely protected the status quo. The days of fiscal largess and unquestioning support of the VA's medical program were over by the spring of 1950.

The Republican Party's political philosophy and new budgetary priorities explain only part of the overall decline in veterans' medical care by 1950. In some respects, the VA was a victim of its own success. The treatment programs rapidly brought to bear on the hundreds of thousands of wounded in 1945 worked when applied during Bradley's short tenure. The medical breakthroughs that Hawley and his cadre of doctors introduced were a success.[108] Much of the physical damage caused by the war was repaired. Tissue damage healed to the extent that it could in the months and years following the war. The physical therapy that was made available worked within the same limits. It addressed the patients' immediate needs, offered a proscribed treatment regimen, and ceased after a period of time. What could not be healed by medicine was subsidized through veterans' disability payments and the continued hard work by the veterans to adapt to their circumstances. In the process, thousands moved off of patient rolls. Still, as the number of hospitalized veterans shrank, some never left their beds. This was particularly the case for hundreds of veterans with severe physical injuries. It was also true for those who were still plagued by psychological disorders. The VA's annual report for 1950 noted that its mental-health facilities had more than a 95 percent occupancy rate. While a relatively small group, the needs of the mentally disabled veterans prompted much of the VA's hospital construction that persisted into the fifties.[109]

As the forties ended, the American business sector, once an enthusiastic supporter of the disabled veteran, appeared to be moving toward other vistas. The accommodation agreements that Bradley won early in his administration began to dissipate soon afterward. According to one article published at the end of 1946, only about 10 percent of blind veterans had found work, a number slightly less than comparable civilian cases.[110] The following year, the American Legion reported that more than 170,000 permanently disabled veterans remained unemployed. Many firms expressed a reluctance to hire these people because of insurance costs. By 1947, many state legislatures had bowed to this pressure and began to require veterans to sign "second-injury" agreements that absolved employers from coverage of any physical ailments on the job that might be related to a worker's military service.[111]

The American public also seemed increasingly anxious to finally enjoy the benefits of peacetime. The various grassroots campaigns to work with injured veterans faded as their overall need diminished and attention began to focus on the postwar economic boom. The energy put into the various local and municipal campaigns had been impressive, even more so given the public's impatience with mobilization that was apparent at the end of the war. But the need for mobilization seemed over. Priorities now shifted toward affluence, normalcy, and the baby boom. In those years, stability was what the country craved. Safety for new children. Security in the job market. Sacrifice remained but stood closer to home as people crafted their own versions of the American dream.

Life moved on. For most people, the tempo of daily routines began to reflect individual preferences and ambitions. While much of the wartime consensus regarding patriotism and military service persisted into the early days of the Cold War, conformity was tempered by the desire to progress and leave the war, the Great Depression, and almost a generation of deferred gratification behind. Americans wanted to enjoy life again. As the postwar boom developed, the means to do this arrived for most people and offered them an opportunity to explore new worlds of travel, entertainment, and leisure.[112] In this emerging climate, it would be left to the veterans themselves to take the final steps toward fitting in with general society.

Fitting In

Eventually the celebrations died down. The tears dried. The "welcome home" banners were removed from front porches. Uniforms found their way to a footlocker in the attic. A decent interval of rest followed the days and weeks of excitement. Veterans caught up on lost sleep. They regained lost weight. The tempo of life settled to a comfortable civilian routine.

As time passed, the awkward moments grew. Gentle questions about future plans evolved into more pointed reminders that one could not drift through the rest of life. Comfort was not an end unto itself. Parents and spouses reminded the returnees that the tempo of postwar life was increasing by leaps and bounds. There were opportunities to be had if one could rediscover focus and discipline.

For the veteran, too, the welcome home became cloying after a time. It was wonderful to be the center of attention, but reverting to old roles was sometimes difficult. Boyhood did not seem to fit any better than the old civilian clothes they had left behind in the dresser. Many a wartime marriage, forged in the first blush of romance, now took on a harder reality as responsibility for a home and children moved to center stage. It was time to move on, time to map out a future, and time to take charge of a life just beginning.

How would the GI, now returned home, begin the final transition back into civilian life? This was not a small concern. As Omar Bradley himself put it in January, 1946, "Until these veterans find employment, rebuild their lives, and resume their responsibilities as civilians, the war is not ended and we cannot escape or evade our duties to them."[1] James B. Conant at Harvard University portrayed the issue in even more dramatic terms: "The demobilization of our armed forces is a God-given moment for reintroducing the American concept of a fluid society. If it is handled properly, we can insure a healthy body politic for at least a generation. Handle it improperly and we may well sow the seed of civil war within a decade."[2]

Veterans' actual expectations about the final process of reassimilation were markedly simpler. For the young returnee in his late teens,
school seemed an obvious choice, whether this meant finishing secondary education or moving on to college. A 1951 study of college-bound
veterans indicates that a large number had already planned to enroll
before military service interrupted their education. In these cases,
the education benefits provided by the GI Bill augmented an already
existing goal.[3] Most of the men and women who left the service in
their twenties saw the next steps in terms of marriage, families, home,
and work. In surveys conducted during the war and in the years after
it, the common aspirations they expressed for these things remained
remarkably consistent.

Perhaps the most important tool assisting the process of reassimilation was the GI Bill. In the short term, this one act of Congress
provided for some of the basic elements—medical treatment and
insurance—necessary to reestablish a foundation for a normal life.
Other provisions for business loans, home-loan guarantees, and aid to
agriculture addressed the longer-term needs that would occupy their
later lives once they had established a career and a family. Of these
long-term programs, the greatest was the part of the bill that dealt with
veterans' education. In this one area, lawmakers vested their faith in
the American educational system's ability to bridge the gap between
military and civilian life.

In 1945, Americans appeared to agree that education offered a solution to the multitude of difficulties associated with returning veterans.
By resocializing them, schools would stave off the behavioral problems
they suffered. Following this conventional wisdom, classrooms would
serve as a new template for the veterans in organizing their thoughts,
exploring their intellectual curiosity, and doing both in a civil environment. Schools would also make up for the country's intellectual
capacity, which had been sacrificed for wartime military service. According to one estimate published in the *History of Education Quarterly*,
more than 1.5 million student years of college training had been lost
to the war.[4]

The transition from military service to civilian school, while not
seamless, was aided by the basic nature of the modern military. Most
of the veterans of the Second World War were not combat soldiers or
sailors. It was a basic fact that the twentieth-century military, dependent
as it was on the complex organization and maintenance of materials

necessary to wage war, relied heavily on its logistical "tail" to conduct combat. As it turned out, the ratio of service to combat personnel was roughly 3:1 throughout the war. Every rifleman was backed up by a medic, an administrative clerk, and a truck driver. Every pilot relied on a mechanic, a fuel handler, and an armorer.[5]

All of these skills were the product of extensive training. Throughout the war, the military branches invested enormous energy into a massive military-school program that provided the intellectual means to support the war. Large parts of this program by their very nature were technically more complex than the military could provide for and required assistance from the civilian sector. American colleges were enlisted to fill the gap. From the Army Specialized Training Program (ASTP) to the U.S. Navy V-12 program to the Army Air Corps College Training Program, thousands of military personnel entered campuses around the country. At its peak in 1943, the army had 141,953 personnel enrolled in institutions of higher learning. In addition to the growing military representation in college classrooms, thousands of civilian employees of the War Department also went to school. Through the Engineering, Science, and Management War Training Program managed by the U.S. Office of Education, nearly 900,000 Americans completed course work in areas related to national defense. By 1943, more than 21 percent of these students were women.[6]

The impact of these programs was enormous. For service members, they offered the first real taste of life and thought in the ivy tower. In many cases, the curriculum for military training courses read like that of a standard liberal-arts core in any university. The ASTP "basic phase" of training, for example, required courses in math, physics, chemistry, English, history, and geography. Significantly, military students were also exposed for the first time to the more intensive demands of college-level study, even more so when training was compressed and sped up to accommodate the war effort. Many were pleasantly surprised to find that they could not only cope with the rigors of academic life but also excel in this new environment. This was not a small thing. Prior to the war, higher education was a rare milestone in American life. In 1930, a total of only about one million Americans attended college—2 percent of the total population. In 1940, colleges and universities produced 160,000 degrees. As late as 1945, approximately 40 out of 100 young people graduated from high school. Of this number, only 16 went to college.[7] What the war successfully accomplished, even before the GI Bill became law, was to bridge the gap between the general public and the university.

The wartime partnership with the federal government also fundamentally changed American universities. Gone were the days when campuses moved at a leisurely pace determined primarily by academic priorities. The Manhattan Project, conducted in research laboratories in schools across the nation, became a signpost of the near future when Cold War priorities transformed private research institutions. Contract deadlines now drove the train. Contemplation of academic principles still mattered, as long as they were harnessed to national security and driven by the Defense Department.

Gone also from the American university was the cachet of exclusiveness that surrounded college life. The demands for research both during and after the war opened up federal coffers for equipment, staffs, and building space that were unheard of before 1941. But these new perks came at a cost. Federal dollars created federal leverage over security requirements, hiring decisions, and the basic trajectory of the university system. Physicists, mathematicians, linguists, and historians—all the products of traditional liberal arts and sciences—became the Cold Warriors of the period. The interweaving of federal priorities with those of the existing higher-education system forever pierced the membrane that had surrounded American campuses and paved the way for millions of GIs who would enroll in the forties.[8]

Most of those in the academic community believed that great changes were unlikely in the first school year following the war. Informed sources speculated that as few as 1 percent of veterans might take advantage of the college training the GI Bill offered. In early 1946, the *South Atlantic Quarterly* estimated that the figure might go as high as 10 percent (1.6 million) of all veterans.[9] Statistics initially seemed to bear these predictions out. In the bill's first year of operation, a mere 83,016 veterans applied for educational benefits.[10]

To the shock of many, these figures were only the tip of the iceberg. By June, 1946, the Veterans' Administration reported that 3.3 million veterans had applied for educational benefits.[11] A year later, 6.6 million veterans had applied to the VA for assistance in school and job training. This number included more than 315,000 disabled veterans who had applied for vocational rehabilitation under Public Law 16.[12]

The draw to schools is easy to understand. According to the provisions established by the GI Bill, a veteran could receive payment for up to thirty-six months of instruction. An additional $500 was also provided for books and other school fees. Single veterans initially received a $50 stipend each month for room and board. Those who were married received $75, although later amendments to the GI Bill raised both amounts. Taken as a whole, the education benefit was an incredible boon to a generation of former soldiers. While the living stipend barely covered basic needs, particularly for veterans with children, and never kept pace with inflation, the total amount offered toward an education was unprecedented. The fact that the educational benefit itself was measured in months and not dollars was significant. It gave the veteran a choice of the gamut of American colleges and universities. Most chose relatively inexpensive state-run schools. However, many could—and did—choose from among the private, ivy-league institutions because the GI Bill included their costs as well.[13]

Once they arrived, what did the veterans expect from college? One service member who had been stationed in the Western Pacific wrote to the dean of Columbia College and expressed the sentiments of millions: "I am a civilian at heart and don't want any special treatment." An infantryman in Germany, responding to a survey sent by Columbia to 1,200 former undergraduates serving in uniform, was optimistic about the prospects for veterans, noting that "servicemen will adjust themselves to civilian life much quicker than if they should continue to stay in separate groups."[14]

One clear trend that emerged after the war was the impact that military service had made on the choice of academic majors. A survey of 51,100 officers and enlisted men in the Army Air Corps revealed that 63 percent had altered their educational plans because of their military experience. The three top areas of study that those surveyed wanted to pursue were engineering (26 percent), business (24 percent), and science (16 percent).[15] Many of them wanted to build upon the technical or managerial skills they had acquired in the military school system and honed in their years of service. Numerous veterans were equally confident that, since they had survived the rigors of military campaigns, they would flourish in the civilian marketplace. One veteran from Pennsylvania remarked, "I was a salesman, but I thought I'd like some kind of engineering. The Army made me a refrigeration mechanic and now I think I'd like that; so it's college and a good course in engineering for me."[16]

As the number of applicants grew, higher education began to prepare for a new and distinct type of student. Many admissions departments, for example, allowed veterans who had not completed high school to take equivalency exams on campus before the start of the regular semester. Large numbers of schools granted exceptions to their transfer policies to accept old military training as academic credit. As early as 1944, the California State Federation of Junior Colleges recommended allowing six credits for military service regardless of training. That same year, the University of Wisconsin announced that it would accept credits earned through military correspondence courses. Many schools also augmented their basic administrative structure to better fit the veteran student population. The University of Illinois created a Special Division of War Veterans that was designed to create programs of study to make up shortfalls in course work and advise veterans on specific courses to improve their postgraduate job prospects.[17] All of this work was done with an eye toward the significant numbers of incoming, nontraditional students. In April, 1946, when the Veterans' Administration reported that colleges and universities had provided 162,485 openings for veterans in the upcoming school year, there was a sense that the situation was well in hand.[18]

Much of this confidence was badly misplaced, however. In the fall of 1946, 2 million applications deluged America's colleges and universities, a number that included 970,000 veterans. The problem for higher education was that institutions could accommodate only 1.6 million students. There were shortages everywhere—of classroom space, labs, dining halls, on-campus housing units (only about 300,000 were available), and qualified faculty (between 7,000 and 10,000) to teach the hordes who began appearing on class rosters.[19] In one year, many institutions doubled in size. Between 1945 and 1946, the University of Wisconsin grew from 9,000 to 18,000 students. Rutgers University expanded from 7,000 students to 16,000 by 1948.[20] In an effort to place veterans, the VA was forced to scour institutions to find remaining available spaces in programs. An administration study of 123 schools in May, 1946, revealed that the largest remaining number of openings were in liberal arts (13,554), engineering (2,612), and education (2,146). Some of the veterans found themselves in programs simply because they contained room. Overnight, former GIs with plans to enter the business world became English majors or students of modern history, careers that many of them kept for the remainder of their lives.[21]

The absence of accommodations both on campus and off was a particular challenge to new arrivals, one that reminded many not ironically of military life. Lacking adequate housing, more than a few schools resorted to Quonset huts and barracks buildings they bought at cost from federal-surplus stockpiles. Tent cities sprang up on campuses across the country. The familiar smell of damp canvas was often the first sensation that greeted many veterans in their early days of study. Otherwise, gymnasiums, study lounges, and mobile homes housed veterans and their families. At Rensselaer Polytech Institute in upstate New York, four Landing Ships (Tank) (LSTs) were moored in the Hudson River to accommodate the student overload.[22] In most cases, the facilities available in these places were primitive at best. Running water was a rare luxury. Private baths even more so. It was often the case that temporary housing areas, "Vetsvilles" as they became known locally, started their own general stores, Laundromats, and other businesses when the walking distance downtown made the alternative more practical.

As time passed, the problem of numbers simply grew worse. When the 1947 school year started, there were 1.1 million veterans enrolled in college courses—49 percent of all students.[23] In many schools, the proportion was even greater. New York University was an extreme example of the trend. In the summer of 1945, 89 percent of the student body was composed of veterans.[24]

Straining under the increasing enrollment, many schools were forced to make substantial modifications to their programs of study. The traditional school day began at an earlier time in the morning and often carried on late into the night, sometimes until 11:00 P.M. Class size grew, significantly in some cases. After the war, Brown University constructed a building that housed nine hundred students in a single classroom. The rapid increase in student-teacher ratios became a common feature in education all over the country and reflected a marked decline in the personal attention an earlier generation of scholars once enjoyed.[25] The frustration of competing for the finite time of an overburdened professor became an increasingly shared rite of passage for the American undergraduate.

Veterans also presented a unique challenge to many faculty in the way they ran their classrooms. Generally, they were better traveled than the traditional student, having seen parts of the world most Americans might have had difficulty finding on a map in 1940. As a group, they were also older than the normal undergraduate. Six out of ten of those who had served were between 18 and 24 years of age. When the war ended, most of them were not teenagers, either mentally or chronologically. Their work ethic also pleasantly surprised many faculty. One professor at the University of Illinois was highly impressed by "the dynamic working standards and the mental vigor which they bring to campus." Reflecting on "the adolescent mummery of the social fraternities, the synthetic sentimentalism of commercialized quasi-professional intercollegiate sports, and the anti-intellectualism of so much that in the prewar days passed for 'college spirit,'" Peter H. Odegard, president of Reed College in Portland, Oregon, commented, "The GI students, in a word, have not confused the side shows with the main performance."[26]

Still, many of the gaps in veterans' formal education that were created by the war were not filled by specialized military instruction or later "challenge exams" in college. Some faculty and administrators openly worried that the veterans had attained what one writer describes as "growth in a vacuum." Too many of these new students, this school of thought argued, had gone off to war for four years and benefited from physical maturity and "moral adulthood" but may also have languished mentally for lack of stimulation.[27] What was the value of teaching someone who was more mature and more assertive about a narrow range of topics in which they lacked adequate comprehension? Anecdotal knowledge was important but limited in its value.

The mission for faculty and administrators was to find a curriculum that would interest the veterans without alienating them. Their basic task was to create courses that would strike a balance between overly specific instruction and broad, muddled learning.[28] Many faculty discovered, some to their dismay, that the veteran students did not want to waste their time on rote memorization and an overemphasis on doctrinal uniformity. Instead, veterans stressed instruction that focused on the present day. The University of Iowa saw, for example, increased enrollments in courses such as "Politics in the Far East," "Background of the News," and "Man in Society." Even when they did not directly address current topics, many existing courses took on a more contemporary emphasis.[29] One academic periodical advised professors that this situation "may mean for some preparing new lectures, revising those old prewar notes with the dog-eared edges, and modernizing examinations and methods of testing." The expectations

CHAPTER 3

of these new students might also mean a change in teaching style. Faculty members needed to engage their audience. The older, time-tested method of lecturing might no longer suffice to capture much more inquisitive and assertive students. The summer, 1947, issue of the *American Scholar* states that professors were "no longer able to lecture dogmatically without proving points and drawing clear distinctions between opinion and fact."[30]

Faculty also had to worry about a new set of taboos that veterans might bring to their classrooms. Deference to past rank or accomplishment was frowned upon by many former service members. So too was recognition of a particular branch of the military or any portion of a lecture that might stray into specific military affairs.[31] What most veterans wanted was a businesslike approach to learning, one that stressed utility over what they considered to be the less important garnishes of academic language and abstract theory.

For their own part, veterans seemed to worry very little about the taboos that preceded them into the classroom. They were far from reticent about criticizing faculty. According to one 1947 survey, "The most frequent complaint made by students that I have talked with from various universities is that their instruction is not only incompetent, but also antiquated and unrealistic." Many complained about the obvious generation gap between them and the existing faculty at a large number of universities. A review of 71 faculty at one school revealed that 26 had been students prior to the First World War and that only 6 had received their advanced degrees after 1936.[32] Generally, this was not the fault of the institutions cited since many of them had to place new hires on hold as the war drained away talented young graduate students and faculty. It was only after the war that the search for new instructors could begin to catch up. In the meantime, until many of the veterans themselves could complete doctoral training, the faculty shortages and the generation gap persisted. The situation lasted for the remainder of the decade.

As they reshaped the classrooms, the veterans also redrew the boundaries of college social life in the forties. Most of these undergraduates had little interest in the traditional hijinks that had characterized the prewar campus: wearing beanies, patiently being victims of pranks, or deferring in general to members of the junior and senior classes. A 1947 article in *School and Society* remarks, "The average veteran thinks it is idiotic to wear freshman 'beanies,' to carry freshman 'bibles,' to have to stay off certain benches and areas which have been reserved, and, in general, to have to kowtow to upperclassmen, some of whom did not serve in the Armed Forces and many of whom are several years his junior."[33] Compared to the experiences accumulated during the war and the responsibilities of family, the demands of undergraduate culture seemed trivial at best and were easily trumped by the common-sense requirements of home and study.

As a group, veterans defied the early, pessimistic predictions that they would diminish American universities. Much to the chagrin of their professors and many of their classmates, they became pacesetters in many courses. An evaluation of winter-quarter grades at Ohio State University reveals that veteran students outperformed nonveterans in the colleges of agriculture, arts, commerce, and education. At Oklahoma Mechanical and Technical College, a similar study of seven academic divisions shows veterans were superior in all areas except engineering. Even when veterans' scores equaled or were slightly lower than those of traditional undergraduates, the more sophisticated studies of the time noted that their failure rates and dropout rates were also lower.[34]

Overall, the veterans' significant participation in college study also allowed for an important improvement in the intellectual capacity of the country. A cursory examination of census data reveals an across-the-board increase in the number of professional workers who entered the labor force between 1945 and 1950. During this five-year span, the number of Americans who were employed as engineers grew from 297,000 to 543,000; the number of accountants and auditors from 238,000 to 390,000; and the number of draftspersons from 82,000 to 127,000.[35] The millions who used the GI Bill to acquire professional training became a critical part of America's postindustrial economy. The transition from blue-collar to white-collar work, well on its way by 1950, was significantly affected by the generation of veterans who graduated from college after the Second World War.

On the negative side of the ledger, the transformation of college prompted by the veterans planted the seeds for later trouble at many institutions. The incessant demands for practicality and the emphasis on vocational learning was a boon to junior colleges, but it diminished the focus on the traditional humanities and liberal arts at the four-year universities. The contemplation of abstract ideas too often became an afterthought in the headlong rush to finish a degree.[36]

CHAPTER 3

More importantly, the rapid growth of universities' systems throughout the country came at the expense of personal contact between faculty and students. Although an intangible quality, the growing separation that appeared between the large undergraduate populations and their schools foreshadowed the frustration with and criticism of the anonymity and corporate culture that would come to define higher education in the sixties.[37]

O ne of the most basic ways for a veteran to readjust to America was to find work. To the GIs who had returned from the war, a job was more than a simple paycheck. It was a concrete way for them to be a productive part of society again.[38] Whether they were the breadwinner for a family or individuals striking out on a career, work allowed them to contribute to and participate in a productive, measurable occupation. Work offered the chance to wipe away the ambiguity that clouded the social place a veteran occupied as someone who was no longer a member of the military but also not quite a full-fledged civilian. It created a new yardstick that could be used to measure the man or woman, one not based on the past but on future value.[39]

And the jobs were there. Although the need for workers shrank immediately after August, 1945, as war plants closed their doors, the overall demand for labor throughout the country remained high. Part of this need came from existing sectors of the economy that had benefited from wartime mobilization. An additional part was driven by companies that had been absent from the economy before 1940 and were later created by the war. In the Sunbelt region of the western United States, particularly in Texas and Oklahoma, the oil industry flourished, initially fed by the War Department and later expanded by the booming auto industry. Federal subsidies for the chemical industry to create synthetic materials for the military rapidly translated into a whole line of civilian products, from dinnerware to clothing and portable radios. In California, the most rapidly growing state in the union, more than $17 billion in War Department contracts created virtually overnight new companies devoted to shipbuilding, aircraft manufacturing, chemical production, and dozens of other enterprises. In this hothouse environment were thousands of new opportunities. In older industrial states such as Illinois and Pennsylvania, the war built upon existing manufacturing and industry. At the peak of the conflict, manufacturing employment in Illinois rose 45 percent from its prewar levels. Companies that were devoted to the production of machinery, iron, and steel maintained a workforce that was more than 50 percent larger than it had been in 1939. Although it experienced some layoffs in 1945, Pennsylvania retained half a million additional manufacturing jobs after the war. Corporate projections for the products of heavy industry, particularly steel that would be used for home and commercial construction and the millions of new cars that Detroit would soon produce, made the prospects for employment good. Overall, the demand for skilled labor remained high and consistent throughout the forties in industries that could still offer significant salaries and benefits. A great deal of blue-collar work in the old smokestack industries of the Northeast and the booming manufacturing areas of the Southwest offered millions of Americans their first steps toward the middle class.[40]

As they pursued this part of the American dream, most veterans did not go to college. Instead, they chose to learn a trade or complete their secondary education, achievements that would allow them access to the flourishing manufacturing and industrial economy. After the war, 3.5 million veterans used their educational benefits to acquire a specific skill or to obtain a high-school equivalency certificate. This latter step was a major accomplishment for them. Of the male enlisted personnel serving in the Second World War, 29.4 percent had not finished grade school. Within this same group, 57.2 percent had between one and four years of high school.[41] Literacy translated into an escape from menial work, a critical step for those interested in abandoning the physical and economic limits of backbreaking labor. A high-school diploma signified a higher order of capability, something demanded by a modern workplace increasingly driven by the expansion of technology.

The technical training that followed functional literacy further improved a veteran's potential employment. The average annual wage of someone employed in communications and public utilities in 1950 ($3,346) was more than double that of an agricultural worker ($1,282), significantly higher than that of someone employed in the service sector ($2,183), and comparable with manufacturing ($3,302) and construction ($3,333).[42] With the educational benefits for training available through the GI Bill, the potential for better pay and upward mobility was well within the veterans' grasp. According to estimates generated by the War Manpower Commission in 1945, some 300,000 positions opened for veterans who were interested in apprenticeship programs.[43] In fact, this substantial number barely scratched the surface of the opportunities available in the late forties. The demand for work in the building trades increased in the first five years after the war. One hundred and eleven thousand electricians joined the workforce during this period, more than a 30 percent increase over the number employed in 1945. Comparable opportunities appeared for plumbers and pipe fitters (93,000) and carpenters (240,000). The same could be said of the jobs created by the booming service industry. In the first five years after the war, 245,000 auto mechanics joined the workforce to maintain the millions of new vehicles Americans purchased. The total number of aircraft mechanics nearly tripled, from 28,000 to 75,000, in part to keep pace with the expanding airline industry.[44]

Unfortunately, the process of completing job training was often cumbersome and unnecessarily confusing. It was common practice for individual states to delegate the maintenance of training programs to their own separate departments of education or labor or even to special committees designated by the legislature. Many schools did not wait for guidance, not a small fact given that more than 5,600 institutions were founded after the original GI Bill to provide noncollege education for veterans. Between official state-run programs, officially sanctioned private efforts, and the more dubious fly-by-night enterprises interested in snatching a federally subsidized dollar from the veteran's hand, consistency was a rare quality. It was sometimes difficult to find certified technical schools that adhered to specific industry standards for student certification. Regular guidelines for faculty credentials, salaries for instructors, and equipment were even more inexact.[45] As the number of complaints from employers and prospective students grew, the Retraining and Reemployment Administration (RRA) created a federal oversight committee to develop criteria and standards for training. By the summer of 1946, combining the efforts of the Departments of War, Agriculture, Commerce, and the Navy, as well as the Federal Security Agency, labor unions, and veterans' groups, the RRA was able to establish basic standards regarding curriculum and certification.[46]

As the story of veterans' training programs unfolded, American labor unions watched with increasing anticipation, clearly interested in incorporating the boom in new skills into their own membership rolls. Hundreds of thousands of workers newly trained in industrial and manufacturing fields represented an enormous potential windfall. The question facing organized labor in America was how best to appeal to this new and growing constituency.

In some respects, the link between veterans and organized labor was already well established by the war. Unions stood at the forefront of the mobilization effort that won the war. In the vast production plants that rose to churn out hundreds of thousands of aircraft, tanks, trucks, and ships worked millions of union workers. Baldwin "Butch" Hawes's 1942 ballad, "UAW-CIO," reflects a justifiable pride in the contribution that organized labor made to the war against Fascism:

I was there when the Union came to town,
I was there when old Henry Ford went down,
I was standing at Gate Four
When I heard the people roar:
"Ain't nobody keeps us Autoworkers down!"

It's that UAW-CIO
Makes the Army roll and go,
Turning out the jeeps and tanks
And airplanes every day.
It's that UAW-CIO
Makes the Army roll and go,
Puts wheels on the USA.

There'll be a union label in Berlin
When the union boys in uniform march in,
And rolling in the ranks
There'll be UAW tanks.

Roll Hitler out and roll the Union in![47]

Besides their contribution to production, union workers also served by the millions in uniform. One and a half million members of the Congress of Industrial Organizations (CIO) alone had enlisted or been drafted; they represented one-quarter of its total and nearly one out of ten veterans overall.[48] Thousands more from the United Auto Workers

(UAW) and the other national unions followed their coworkers into the conflict. To a large extent, the very act of service aided organized labor in dispelling a degree of the animosity that had been created not only by the strike activity of the late thirties but also, more importantly, by the strikes that had peppered the war years. Overt acts of patriotic sacrifice, reinforced by millions of union members, became a basis for common ground between veterans and the public.[49]

It was also a simple fact that unions needed veterans. The auto industry, for one, anticipated an enormous pent-up demand for its product after VJ Day. Keeping pace with it would require hundreds of thousands of new workers. As Ruth Milkman has pointed out, Detroit's preference for white males between the ages of 20 and 25 placed it squarely in the veteran population just then returning from the war. It was no coincidence that these people were heavily recruited by the likes of General Motors, Ford, and Chrysler. Between December, 1945, and July, 1946, veterans composed approximately 47 percent of all workers hired by the auto industry. Overall, the number of veterans employed in manufacturing grew from 1.2 million to 2.6 million during this period, accounting for one out of every five workers in thirty-five industries.[50]

The potential influence the veteran constituency might exercise within the rank-and-file membership of organized labor was considerable, a fact not lost on union leaders. In a 1944 letter to Victor Reuther, head of the UAW-CIO's War Activities Division, one official acknowledged the potential impact that veterans might have after the war: "The emotional ties of men who have gone through battle toward their comrades in arms will be much stronger than their attitudes and feelings toward their unions."[51] Unions subsequently pursued two separate, but complementary, objectives regarding veterans: first cultivating them as new members and then addressing the concerns of the existing population of veterans within organized labor.

This process had actually begun even before the war ended. As early as 1944, the UAW and CIO took note of the fact that, of the total number of Americans going into the military, one in five had never held a job.[52] To appeal to this significant group as well as the remainder of the more experienced workforce, unions jumped on the postwar veteran bandwagon, portraying themselves not only as defenders of labor rights but also as promoters of veterans' privileges. In October, 1944, when Joseph G. Velosky, director of the UAW's Veterans'

Department, offered advice to union locals preparing for the return of veterans, he recommended that they focus on pay rates, rising inflation, media reports of corporate profits, and the need for worker parity.[53] By including basic market-basket issues, the UAW attempted to build a bridge to the recent returnees by illuminating the commonsense concerns that awaited them.[54] From there, the UAW-CIO campaign extended to include more specific concessions to the veterans. Most CIO unions, for example, required employers to pay veterans cash bonuses that were the equivalent of earned vacation time once they returned to work. Most also included active-duty service as time toward civilian seniority. For new members, the UAW-CIO waived initiation fees with proof of military service.[55]

One major clash developed over the issue of seniority. In principle, the unions wanted to maintain a system that protected years of employment with a degree of security. As one CIO publication put it, "Seniority is a simple method, originated by labor unions and enforced with court sanction, to protect every worker's right to his job in proportion to his length in service. 'First hired, last fired' would be a pretty accurate definition."[56] Unfortunately, for this reason, large segments of organized labor found themselves in early opposition to the original GI Bill and subsequent legislation that guaranteed a veteran's right to reemployment. While acknowledging the need to recognize service, the veterans-preference system directly challenged many of the collective-bargaining agreements then in place in many industries. Unions contended that veterans could be used as a means to dilute their membership in the workplace with nonunion workers or, in cases where union veterans returned to their jobs, displace other union members with greater work seniority by granting the serviceperson "super seniority" status.

It did not help the unions' cause that many powerful veterans' organizations, the American Legion (AL) foremost among them, had long criticized union labor practices and were perfectly willing to wield the patriotic club when doing so. One AL official openly mocked the unions' sincerity in their treatment of veterans, noting that "some of the very elements in labor who have most actively discriminated against veterans have been giving the loudest lip service to veterans through self-styled veterans' committees or representatives."[57] Moreover, to veterans' groups, the wartime strikes led by unions such as John L. Lewis's United Mine Workers smacked of treason. When the American Legion's national employment director likened union seniority practices to an "iron seniority curtain," his reference to the emerging Cold War was as pointed as his questioning of organized labor's loyalty to the country.[58]

In the end, the Supreme Court decided the question of super seniority. As part of the 1946 *Fishgold v. Sullivan Drydock and Repair Corp.* decision, the Court held that veterans were not protected from layoffs made in accordance with seniority systems established by union agreements in effect at the time of their induction into the military.[59] Policies granting veterans' preference in hiring continued but were contained within labor contracts already in force.

In the postwar period, unions won significant victories in the war of economic affluence. Improvements in the overall aptitude of the American workforce bolstered their numbers. This was particularly the case in the trade unions. By the end of the Korean War, total union membership surpassed the 17-million mark and would continue to grow.[60] In terms of the union workers' quality of life, the late forties and early fifties saw an unprecedented improvement in pay and benefits. By the fifties, bargaining had expanded to include health insurance, disability coverage, and pensions.[61] By this point it was clear that many blue-collar workers possessed the means to enter America's expanding middle class.

However, as the forties marched on, unions lost the war for the patriotic high ground. The odor of radicalism clung to the labor movement despite its best efforts to recast itself. Fairly or not, many Americans could recall with disdain the thousands of strikes they endured during the war despite a no-strike pledge from the unions. John L. Lewis was a hero to many a miner during the 1946 coal strike when he declared, "I have pleaded your case not in the quavering tones of a mendicant asking alms, but in the thundering voice of the captain of a mighty host, demanding the rights to which free men are entitled." This militancy offered little solace to the average person who suffered through rolling blackouts (short-term power outages) and fuel shortages that winter. When the Truman administration took John L. Lewis to court for violating the Smith-Connally Act, which prohibited strikes against government-held facilities, he won not only a legal fight but also a battle for public opinion that had begun to turn against organized labor. The passage of the Taft-Hartley Act in 1947 and later congressional investigations of unions for socialist and communist members reflected not only the conservative bent of the Eightieth Congress and the Cold War paranoia of the times but also a growing public consensus to check union power even as its membership continued to grow.[62]

As public support for organized labor eroded, so too did its overt connection with the veterans. Once their uniforms were packed away, service members who had returned from the war took up the old causes of wages, benefits, and recruitment. Postwar priorities for many were captured by their particular vocations or family needs or personal ambitions for the future. Although the military bond remained, it faded in importance in the workplace.

As they pursued the paths of education and work to fit back into America, many veterans also considered politics as an additional way to assimilate. For many, the desire for public service began with their enlistments in the military. Common sense dictated that service could continue in civilian life, with all of the lessons of war contained in it. In 1946, one veteran wrote about the war's impact on his ideals: "Our travels have taught us much . . . people, action, thoughts, scenery, idealism, and conflict have created a ponderous juggernaut which strangely has not destroyed us. Rather, it has reformed, reshaped, in substance as well as in spirit, our peculiar scholastic idealism. It made us realistic idealists."[63] The desire to pursue duty tempered by this realism continued after the war. Marine S.Sgt. Frank V. Gardner wrote the following while on Okinawa: "I prayed to God for peace and resolve to make my life worthwhile. I told God that if I survived . . . I would return home and devote myself to the service of my country in peacetime."[64]

Early in the postwar era, the efforts to translate military service into public service were relatively simple. Today it is striking to see what sorts of tributes World War II veterans preferred after the war. Rather than large monuments, postwar dedications were largely limited to public auditoriums, hospitals, stadiums, and civic centers. Utility was the keynote of the day.[65]

The desire for service was not passive, however. Veterans sought out leadership roles in all aspects of their postwar years. On college campuses, they became a force in student government. They populated union offices.[66] They interjected themselves in state and local politics.

In some instances, direct action was a reflection of their impatience. Veterans besieged the New York State Senate Chamber in October, 1946, to demand redress for the housing shortage. Veterans in Missouri converged on the state capital to successfully lobby lawmakers for a bonus bill.[67]

In a short time, veterans became leaders embedded in activities at the state and local levels of society. They became unstoppable philanthropists, raising money for all manner of causes. In the first year after the war, New York City chapters of the American Legion, in cooperation with the March of Dimes, created two $25,000 fellowships for the study of rheumatic heart disease. Through the AL's efforts, a donation of $50,000 went to the American Council on Rheumatic Fever. Sometimes the dollar figures were smaller, but they were no less meaningful. The National Eight and Forty, a group affiliated with the American Legion Auxiliary, donated $2,000 to the National Jewish Hospital of Denver, Colorado, an amount that no doubt touched the lives of scores of people.[68] The Helen Fairchild American Legion Post, located in Philadelphia and composed of female veterans of both world wars, sponsored nursing students and supported sports, social events, and professional development.[69] By 1947, through the auspices of the American Legion, more than five million boys played Junior League baseball, which was coached and organized by veterans in neighborhoods and small towns around the country. On these teams, boys learned the fundamentals of hitting, catching, and base running. Perhaps more importantly, they learned the value of cooperation through teamwork and basic acts of personal dignity through good sportsmanship. At the end of each season, these skills were put to a final test when the league sponsored tournaments that culminated in a nationwide world series. Participation in this entire process became both a national fixture and a rite of passage for a generation of American fathers and sons.[70]

At other times, service translated into projects that were more complex than fund-raising. Individual veterans' groups sometimes lent their support to community-development projects and braved obstacle courses of a different sort created by zoning boards and local committee members. The American Legion Community Development Corporation, for example, forged a unique relationship with local, state, and federal authorities to solve the problem of the postwar housing shortage. In Greendale, Wisconsin, a Milwaukee suburb, the

AL created a joint public-private enterprise that built one thousand middle-income rental homes for veteran and nonveteran families.[71]

In all of these enterprises, veterans provided an important degree of substance to the postwar American culture. Contemporaries then and historians today have often portrayed the times as shallow, materialistic, and self-indulgent. Writers in the fifties, such as Vance Packard, commented on the seemingly endless search for status and self-assertion among the newly affluent.[72] Suburbs became a particular lightning rod for this commentary. For many historians, the proliferation of new housing developments represented the "crabgrass frontier," a landscape as devoid of inventiveness and public spirit as it was of architectural style.[73] Clearly, as the evidence attests, neither the suburbs in particular nor American society in general languished in a cycle of complacency or self-satisfied stagnation. After 1945, the veterans who spread throughout America took upon themselves the task of managing the social responsibilities of postwar reconstruction and the baby boom. By the millions, in many small ways they served as the backbone of an effort to improve the future and pass along a healthier, more affluent, and happier version of the American Dream.

As they proliferated at the grassroots level, veterans also became a fixture in national politics. Polling, still in its infancy after World War II but a growing force in American politics, reflected their emerging importance. In the years immediately following the war, the Gallup Poll began to elicit veterans' concerns as a category separate from those of the remainder of the population. Their opinions on atomic-bomb tests, foreign policy, the continuation of the peacetime draft, and other issues were recorded.[74]

The Eightieth Congress, elected in 1946, reflected the dominance of the veteran in American politics. More than half of those who took office in the national legislature at that moment had served the country in uniform. Their service represented what was almost a textbook on military conflicts in the nineteenth and twentieth centuries. Rep. Joseph J. Mansfield, a Democrat from Columbus, Texas, had raised two companies of National Guard troops in 1886, the year Geronimo surrendered to the U.S. Army. Edward V. Robertson, who would represent Wyoming as a senator in 1947, fought with the Third Battalion of the Welsh Regiment in the Boer War from 1899 to 1902. Six members of the Eightieth Congress had put on a uniform in the war against Spain in 1898. The largest group of lawmakers, 164 in all, had served in the Great War. The entire Iowa delegation to the House of Representatives fought in the war against Kaiser Wilhelm II. Ninety had served in the Second World War. Fifteen saw service in both world wars. Remarkably, one of them, Sen. Edward Martin (R-PA), had served in three wars, enlisting as a private in 1898 and holding all ranks until reaching major general in 1942, while earning two Purple Hearts and two Distinguished Service Crosses.[75]

The types of military service performed by veterans in Congress were as varied as the wars themselves. Many legislators enlisted in World War II as privates or apprentice sailors in the fervid days following Pearl Harbor and worked their way up the ranks. In 1942, Sen. John Sherman (D-KY) enlisted as an army private at the age of forty-one and went on to serve with Patton's Third Army in France. More than a few compiled distinguished-combat records marked by acts of valor. Democrat Olin Earl Teague of College Station, Texas, ended the war with three Silver Stars, the Bronze Star, the Combat Infantryman's Badge, and three Purple Hearts after serving with the 79th Division.[76]

What motivated these individuals varied from person to person. Some had watched the events unfolding in Asia and Europe with dismay and prepared for a conflict that seemed inevitable. Some were enraged by the Japanese attack in Hawaii and rushed to enlist along with tens of thousands of other Americans. However, many public figures were captured by their own heated rhetoric when the United States debated intervention in the final year of the nation's official neutrality. A young Lyndon Johnson, on the campaign trail for a Senate seat in 1941, had promised his constituents in Texas that he "would be in the front line, in the trenches, in the mud and blood with your boys, helping to do the fighting."[77]

Astute politicians like Johnson—and he was not alone—realized at this early stage that they needed to create a link with a public that had millions of its fathers and sons overseas. Military service became a means of forging a common bond with an electorate heavily invested in the war even before it ended. To have served with distinction or to have been recognized for an act of valor was to gain even more traction with this public.

After the war, service became an important—and expected—electoral litmus test. As a young navy officer returned from duty in the Pacific, Richard M. Nixon was prevailed upon to run against Jerry Voorhees for his congressional seat in California. Recalling his political coming-out speech in November, 1945, Nixon noted in his memoirs that, because he did not yet own a civilian suit, he was forced to wear his navy dress-blue uniform.[78] Yet, on the campaign trail the following year, Nixon became a fixture in the same uniform, greeting workers exiting factory gates by saying, "I am Lieutenant Commander Richard M. Nixon." Similarly, during his own run for office, Joseph P. McCarthy campaigned on the slogan "Wisconsin Needs a Tail Gunner in the Senate."[79] Upon winning his seat in Congress in 1946, John F. Kennedy reflected upon the war and reconfirmed his own link with military service: "Most of the courage shown in the war came from men's understanding of their interdependence with each other. Men were saving other men's lives at the risk of their own simply because they realized that perhaps the next day their lives would be saved in turn."[80]

At times during the 1946 campaign and in the years afterward, many politicians simply chose to lie about their wartime records. McCarthy fabricated his record as a marine in the Pacific. But perhaps the most celebrated embellishment of military service came from Lyndon Johnson. For most of his short tenure in a navy uniform, the future Senate majority leader and president toured stateside bases and shipyards. Johnson, however, chafed at the routine nature of the assignments and agonized over the slowly building chorus of criticism back in Texas that he was not joining in the "mud and blood" as had other boys from his home state. Finally, after repeated attempts to secure an assignment near the war zone, he was allowed an opportunity to visit the South Pacific. There Johnson served as an observer on one bombing mission and, for this effort, was awarded the Silver Star by Gen. Douglas MacArthur. For the rest of his life, Johnson would make a point of fingering the medal he wore on the lapel of his suit whenever speaking to the public. His constant allusions to the one air mission and his role in it, complete with color slides that he would trundle out on occasion, became something of an inside joke in Washington circles after the war.[81]

For all their importance in the electoral politics of the postwar period, veterans did very little to change American politics and policymaking in the forties. The old soldiers and sailors serving in the Eightieth Congress tended toward the political ideology of their parties and the interests of their constituents. Their joint service did not represent the creation of a "third way" in American politics that challenged the status quo. They did not save the nation from the bitter partisan debate that engulfed Washington during Joseph McCarthy's brief ascent to national notoriety. In fact, many veterans from the newcomer congressional class of 1946, most notably John F. Kennedy and Richard Nixon, made their reputations as ardent Cold Warriors regardless of party affiliation. Nor did they as a group affect domestic policymaking to any significant degree. The veteran contingent did not rescue the Veterans' Administration from the budget axe in the late forties.

The same story is true with respect to national-security policy. Despite the fact that literally hundreds of lawmakers possessed military experience, America's readiness languished in the years prior to the Korean War. Although Congress extended conscription into peacetime for the first time in U.S. history, it rejected Harry Truman's calls for universal military training. Military budgets, which had been cut as a result of demobilization, continued their precipitous decline. Stocks of spare parts dwindled. Ammunition for training vanished. Aside from some improvements made to the newly created U.S. Air Force, by the end of the decade the armed forces were moving backward.[82] One of the consummate ironies of history is that it was this body of American legislators who left the military in such a state of disrepair. Then, in June of 1950, North Korean forces crossed the 38th parallel.

Many veterans made a conscious decision not to fit in after the war. They maintained the clannishness that sometimes characterizes the combat soldier. They built boundaries around the type of service they had performed and its proximity to danger. Their loyalty was defined and reinforced by a common understanding of hardship that never left them. In 1945, one officer explained this attitude: "It accounts for the various demonstrations of sacrifice of one's self for the group, as epitomized by the submarine commander who gave the command to 'Take her down' though it meant his death. Such attitudes are more closely related to spirituality than to stoicism."[83]

His explanation illustrates the indifference demonstrated by combat veterans toward replacements during the war. Scorn was often heaped upon the soldier who was new to the unit. The proverbial "green apples" could never penetrate the layers that encompassed the "old-

timers" because they lacked a basic starting point: the shared experience of past training and fighting. They were viewed as a liability, in
many cases legitimately, because the qualities they lacked could result
in the deaths of their fellow soldiers. Contempt was, in this case, an
act of self-preservation.[84]

After the war, separation from civil society became an act of self-preservation of a different kind. Distance was an important way to gather
breathing space in what was a new and strangely alien culture. How
could a civilian comprehend the changes the war had produced? Upon
returning home to the United States in the summer of 1945, George
S. Patton noted in his diary that "None of them [civilians] realizes that
one cannot fight for two and a half years and be the same."[85]

It was better to seek out the company of those who understood, these
disaffected veterans believed. A 1948 article appearing in the *Saturday
Evening Post* notes that veterans who still remained in VA hospitals
were gravitating toward others with similar wounds, rehabilitation,
and recovery patterns. Quite a few of them claimed that they had no
intention of leaving their wards, having found peers and a new surrogate home.[86] To them, the outside world began beyond the bounds of
this very small circle of experiences. In 1946, a nurse, commenting on
her patients, perhaps unwittingly revealed the barriers these soldiers
erected against perceived outsiders: "But they are the same likable
kids I've found before—a trifle more reserved and harder to know,
all conforming externally to the accepted GI pattern, and all using it
to conceal highly individualized thoughts and emotions."[87]

Many of them dealt with their sense of anxiety by physically escap-
ing from their old patterns of life. Millions took to the road, taking
advantage of the readjustment benefits offered by the GI Bill to travel,
explore, and see America. Many veterans would happily claim membership in the 52-20 Club and subsist on the twenty dollars it provided
them each week for gas, meals, and a cheap place to sleep. Using this
allowance, tens of thousands crisscrossed the country, seeing firsthand
the changes the war had created, deciding what appealed to them and
what did not. Darrell Berrigan, writing for the *New Republic* in 1947,
compared this new breed of travelers with the men who had drifted
around America in the thirties: "It is not a breakdown of morals that
makes them more dangerous. They are just better trained and much
more conscious of themselves as citizens who have a right to jobs."[88]
However, even while striking this cautionary note, Berrigan admitted

that it was hope that motivated these latter-day "hoboes" to strike out and search for a means to improve their lives. The fact that this was eminently possible in 1947 makes this story dramatically different from the one shaped by the Great Depression years.

Sometimes, as veterans sought sanctuary from the war, they severed it completely from their new civilian life. For tens of thousands, silence separated the war years from their families and loved ones. In many cases, their reticence was a reflection of a generation raised with the ethic of personal modesty. Embellishing a tale or simply including a personal reference was simply not done.[89] For others, it was the result of a deliberate effort to spare the listener from the horror of the event. Perhaps more importantly, silence was a shield that protected them from recounting their participation in the horror. One of the more striking parts of James Bradley's book *Flags of Our Fathers* is his statement that his father, for most of his life, never mentioned the war or his experiences on Iwo Jima and for years refused to be interviewed about what he had witnessed during the battle. Even more remarkable is the fact that the Bradley family learned of his Navy Cross for valor only after his death.[90]

At other points in the postwar story, veterans decided to vicariously relive the parts of the war that they wanted to remember. Many would openly admit that World War II was, in many ways, the most exciting, challenging event of their young lives. As young men at the peak of physical fitness, they had embraced risks and survived, pursuing a way of life that made their new civilian routines pale by comparison. How could a veteran re-create the adrenaline rush of exiting the door of an aircraft in the midst of a mass parachute drop or the thrill of successfully landing a fighter on the pitching deck of an aircraft carrier?

For these veterans, in their actions and in their silence, service represented a social enclave. How much and how far they maintained the barrier varied from person to person. Aging veterans might display their branch emblem on a tie clip or lapel button. Old tattoos acquired during the war remained on display no matter what the social situation. Barracks language might occasionally slip into polite conversation. The old saying "Once a marine, always a marine" became a common refrain in social and business circles alike, whether this distinction referred to one's haircut, bearing, or work ethic.

On a much deeper level, the veteran subculture distinctly separated former service members from the civilian mainstream. Local VFW and

Foreign Legion halls acted as touchstones for many veterans. Annual reunions became opportunities not only to catch up on families and work but also to recount common war experiences that remained as vivid in the decades following World War II as the day they happened. Many of the memoirs and interviews published after the war contain references to a stream of letters, personal conversations, and late-night phone calls attempting to express feelings of personal loyalty, terror, and achievement, whose real meaning was restricted to what historian Stephen Ambrose refers to as a "band of brothers."[91] At any level and in any expressed form, service became a badge and a permanent distinction that many veterans carried with them for the rest of their lives.[92]

A fter World War II, there was no one way that American veterans chose to fit back into the mainstream. The methods they adopted—school, work, or service—represented the social diversity of a country that went into uniform after 1940 and was prepared, once peace broke out, to again pursue normal individual preferences and ambitions. There is little question, however, that the opportunities available after 1945 differed drastically from those present before the war. This was particularly the case with respect to education and work. While the educational opportunities offered by the GI Bill no doubt assisted tens of thousands of veterans to complete school plans they had already made before their service, the broad array of academic and vocational choices that federal funding made possible ultimately affected millions in shaping their postwar career plans.

The same can be said of job opportunities that appeared once the country overcame demobilization problems and embraced the postwar civilian boom. The period after 1945 offered the skilled worker unprecedented economic rewards. In the older areas of the Smokestack Belt, the demand for labor grew. Iron, coal, and steel remained basic necessities for both American consumers and a world recovering from the war. Outpacing the enclaves in the Northeast and the upper Midwest was the Sunbelt, where whole new additions to the manufacturing and service sectors were creating work for millions. Armed with training initiated by federal law and supported by thousands of schools, veterans leaped aboard this bandwagon and never looked back. Pursuit of the upper mobility offered by education and expanding job opportunities became both a means toward assimilation and an end unto itself.

As they took to the task of fitting in, veterans fundamentally altered many of the institutions they entered. In this instance, the common experiences of service and not individual preference came to fore. American higher education changed the courses it offered, its teaching methods, and the basic nature of campus life to suit the millions of former service personnel who overwhelmed U.S. colleges and universities in the forties. In other cases, American institutions in the postwar era shifted to address the perceived needs and wants of veterans but did so in more superficial ways that did not accurately understand or represent them. Unions successfully defended their own institutional interests against encroachment by the veterans while acknowledging their service. Patriotism and military service were keynotes in the political rhetoric of the late forties, but these did not shield the country or individual Americans from the budgetary politics, mudslinging, and rampant anti-Communist paranoia of the time. They did not embolden America's most famous veteran, Dwight D. Eisenhower, to defend George C. Marshall's record from McCarthy's attacks during the 1952 presidential campaign, a decision the former general regretted for the rest of his life.[93]

Some veterans never completely made the transition back into civilian life. For many, the gap between wartime experience and normalcy went unclosed for years. In the meantime, they found the company of other veterans, the distractions of civilian freedom, or their own silence to offer sanctuary within and from wartime memories.

Americans witnessed unprecedented destruction during the war. A U.S. soldier surveys a German town in 1945.

*...rmy nurses in France,
...944. Of all the women
...ho joined the Army Nurs-
...g Corps, 98 percent re-
...uested overseas service.*

*Reminders of home
were a fixture in bar-
racks around the
world.*

Mail call. Sometime[s] letters were few and far between, but they were always coveted.

Signposts such as this one appeared in every war zone. The bottom placard reflects the conventional wisdom about the war's duration and uncertainty about the postwar period.

The stress of modern war. A marine in the Pacific, 1944. Psychoneurotic cases made up an increasing proportion of American casualties in the last year of fighting.

African American marines who were wounded during the battle for Saipan, 1944. Black veterans could claim many hard-won contributions that shaped their peacetime expectations.

VJ Day, 1945. Celebrations sometimes lasting for days swept through the country with the news that the war was over.

As the public began to clamor for demobilization, troopships bound for the United States began appearing at ports on both coasts. Veterans of the China-Burma-India theater arrive in New York in September, 1945.

The walking wounded aboard a transport within sight of land. For many men, this was their first glimpse of home in years.

Families' reunions were a common sight in 1945. After the war, many children met their fathers for the first time.

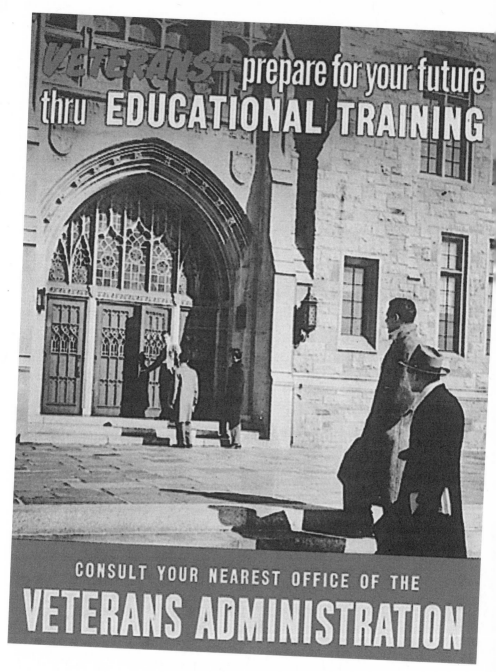

College became a viable option for GIs because of the Servicemen's Readjust-ment Act of 1944. Few experts accurately estimated the number of veterans who would take advantage of this benefit.

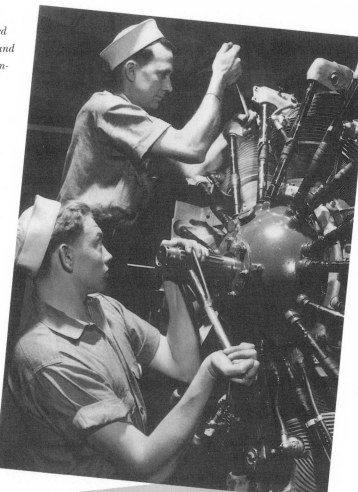

Millions of veterans turned to the postwar workplace and applied their military training to the civilian sector.

Job-placement services were available to veterans, who lined up to interview with the U.S. Civil Service, 1945.

CHAPTER 4   *GI Jane Comes Home*

*I am uncomfortable in a group now because I'm easily bored
with discussions of babies, food prices and home-making problems. People seem to be living behind walls, with no interest
in national or international events . . . and they look at you
strangely if you discuss any current problem other than what
they are going to have for breakfast the next morning.*
                                    —Female veteran surveyed
                        for a master's thesis on readjustment, 1947

It was their war, too. In 1940, women had watched as hundreds of
thousands of their fathers, husbands, sons, and brothers entered
military service, called to duty by peacetime conscription. After Pearl
Harbor, they sat on the sidelines again as millions more marched off
to war. At best, women could follow their progress through letters
hastily written in training camps or dispatched overseas via V-mail.
Otherwise, in the early days of the war, their role was limited to scrap
drives, civil-defense drills, volunteer work, and the growing number of
jobs appearing in the defense industry. In a larger sense, a new national
consensus appeared that made women responsible for preserving the
home front that the soldier was fighting to protect.[1]

It was not enough. Patriotism was not the province of one gender any
more than military service to the country. In a very real way, World War
II was a battle for American women to achieve direct participation in
the conflict. After the war was finished, the postwar period developed
into a story of women veterans gaining the acknowledgment that was
also their just due.

To accomplish both entry into the war and recognition afterward,
American women had to overcome a complex series of social and

legal obstacles to service. One of the first and most easily negotiated barriers addressed a woman's capacity for patriotism and duty. In this one respect, the heavy weight of the historical record and the contemporary conventional wisdom illustrated that the love of America could not be confined to men. Common sense dictated that women could participate in productive ways. Few could argue against the overall benefit of unleashing millions of motivated citizens against the common enemy. Moreover, as the discussion of women's military service moved forward, federal agencies concerned with civilian policy were already making deliberate efforts to integrate females into the war effort. The Department of Labor, faced with massive labor shortages as conscription drained millions from manufacturing and industry, initiated a deliberate campaign to encourage women to move from the home into the factory, all the while stressing their historical contributions to the preservation and progress of the nation. The subsequent demonstrations of women's adaptability and utility to the war industry alleviated a great many concerns regarding their transition into uniform.[2]

A more difficult debate centered on the exact nature of their military service once women joined the war effort. Initially, both the public and American lawmakers treated the idea as a concession to expedience. In this light, it was assumed that once the war was won, "normalcy" would again dictate the status quo, just as it had in past conflicts.

However, this expectation undercut the legitimacy of women's service at its starting point. By definition, participation in the military required an enormous sacrifice of personal freedom to the priorities of the particular branch of service and the nation as a whole. Women in uniform accepted the regimentation of their lives from first call in the barracks, through each day of training, to taps. Defining these women as "auxiliaries" and consigning their work to the periphery of the war itself, almost as an afterthought, is an insult to their sacrifices and the meaning of American citizenship.

Contemporary perceptions regarding the temporary nature of military service also prolonged and encouraged the social stigma attached to a woman's involvement in the military. In 1946, a writer noted that families who might give their sons and husbands to the war found it "disgraceful that a daughter should be held in the Service or even evince a desire to enlist."[3] A wartime questionnaire reported that 41 percent of those women who volunteered did so despite resistance from relatives. Many Americans treated the desire for military service as the product of a character flaw. An army nurse reflected on this attitude decades after the war: "They'd call us queer. You were in there because you wanted to be around nothing but women or because you wanted to chase men or you had some moral problems." Insults, deliberate slander campaigns, and rumors dogged women in uniform for the duration of the war.[4]

Staking out a place within the military proved to be a difficult task from the start. Organizationally, women were segregated into separate branches of the traditional military services. The Women's Army Auxiliary Corps (WAAC), created in 1941, was not intended to be equal, but rather an adjunct of the active-duty army. Its status did not change until the creation of the Women's Army Corps (WAC) two years later.[5] In the meantime, citizens were treated to a potpourri of organizations—WACs, WAVES (Women Accepted for Volunteer Emergency Service), WASPs (Women's Air Force Service Pilots), and SPARs (Coast Guard Women Reserves; the acronym comes from the Coast Guard's motto, "Semper Paratus," which means "always ready")—dedicated to organizing women's service in the military. Most were brand-new constructions that had barely caught on with the general public by the time the war ended.[6] Moreover, once women began to move into command assignments, it was difficult for the formerly all-male members of the services to comprehend or acknowledge their authority or contributions as true peers. These same difficulties appeared in the assignment of women to occupational specialties. At the start of the war, it was often the case that women were relegated to the most rudimentary duties. Trained nurses found themselves acting as hospital orderlies responsible for basic housekeeping functions.[7] It took years before the War Department resolved these issues and many others.

Overall, the number of women who served was significant. Approximately 350,000 entered active duty in all of the major branches of the U.S. military, more than ten times the number who put on the uniform during World War I. All of them were volunteers. Selective-service law, written in 1940 and amended afterward, never applied to female citizens.

As the number of women in uniform grew, so did the range of their duties. At the start of the war, women were allowed to serve in four occupational specialties. By its conclusion, the War Department had expanded this meager list to include 239 separate job titles. By 1945, women worked as engine mechanics, photographers, pharmacists, and parachute riggers. Despite significant congressional resistance, women were also authorized to perform these tasks overseas in combat theaters as well as in the United States.[8]

The War Department also briefly experimented with the idea of using women in combat. Between December, 1942, and April, 1943, as part of a project approved by George C. Marshall, army chief of staff, women were included in composite antiaircraft and searchlight units in the Washington military district and allowed to work alongside their male counterparts for extended periods. The experiment was a success and an endorsement of the women's ability to meet the physical and mental standards of combat duties. However, the greatest obstacle to utilizing women in a new combat role was not their ability but rather the army's more pressing need for qualified women in logistical positions, where they served as the underpinning for U.S. forces deployed overseas. Military logic was that women's capacity for administration would free up tens, if not hundreds, of thousands of male service members for more hazardous duty. With this in mind, the Pentagon quietly retired the concept of a direct combat role for women.[9]

Among the women who served in World War II, a number of basic characteristics stand out. Most of those who were surveyed reported their family background as "average." As many as one-third had fathers who were managers or professionals. Servicewomen were generally better educated than their contemporaries of both genders, progressing farther at both the secondary and college levels. This was particularly true for female officers.[10] In some cases, their motivation for service reflected many of the beliefs common at the time. A Marine Corps survey of female recruits reported that 35 percent had enlisted because their families already had men in the service. In the same group, 15 percent said that they had joined for the adventure.[11] Many were attracted to the military culture and believed that they would thrive in an environment that demanded discipline and decisiveness. Many were indeed born soldiers. Recounting her earliest days in the service, WAAC officer Charlotte Morehouse wrote the following: "Of course for a week I have eaten, dreamed, slept and breathed nothing but

Auxiliary, in fact never suspected myself of so much military furor. This thing gets in your blood, it is a chase, a fascinating contrast, and the farther you go, the more it takes hold on you."[12]

Some volunteers' motivation was a combination of conventional patriotic belief and a sensibility unique to women. Among the female marines who were asked, 6 percent responded that they had joined because they were from families with no men to send.[13] The desire to match the patriotism of male family members was a strong undercurrent appearing in surveys and individual memoirs. In an interview forty years after the war, a former WAC recounted her own story: "Well, I am an Army daughter, and that was the reason. I received father's first V-Letter when he was somewhere in North Africa. I went to the recruiting office the same day and enlisted."[14]

Many of the young women who volunteered were simply bored and saw the risks of service as preferable to the security of the home front. For a demographic made up of relatively well-educated women in their twenties, the prospect of scrap drives, salvage efforts, and volunteer causes through the Red Cross or the American Women's Voluntary Service was fairly thin gruel.[15] Instead, they sought a means of satisfying their inborn curiosity about the world and their personal limits. Perhaps more importantly, many also sensed that the war had created a break with the existing social status quo in America. The seismic shifts that mobilization mandated were reinventing social conventions on what sometimes seemed like a daily basis. Women understood that this atmosphere placed within their hands a chance to shape the future. As one young woman who worked in the Chicago steel industry simply put it, "I was behind the same machine for three years. I want my country to give me the same opportunities it gives the boys. I want to learn something in the Army."[16]

Once in uniform, most women wanted to make a direct and practical contribution. It was this motivation that prompted many to request overseas duty to be as close to the war as possible. One female veteran commented at the conclusion of the war that "It would be difficult to live with oneself and not do it."[17] Of all of the women who joined the Army Nursing Corps, 98 percent requested overseas service.[18] However, it was not until late in the conflict that the War Department, facing severe personnel shortages throughout the world, grudgingly began to loosen restrictions on women who were requesting overseas service.

Lacking a chance to deploy to Europe or the Pacific, women proved

CHAPTER 4

their utility at home. Nursing, a vocation that contained one of the largest reservoirs of professional female talent early in the war, both satisfied the individual desire to make a practical contribution to the war effort and became an ongoing demonstration to the nation of the truly critical role that women were playing.[19] As the military expanded its list of vocations open to women, evidence of this contribution spread accordingly, much as it did in industry and manufacturing at the time.

At the conclusion of the war, women discovered that they had earned a newfound degree of respect for what they had accomplished. Placing themselves at the core of the conflict, sometimes in its ugliest and most depraved parts, these women had separated themselves from their civilian female contemporaries. A nurse stationed in Western Europe or the Pacific who managed a ward full of mentally and physically wounded men did so by combining important measures of professional aptitude, compassion, and bearing, qualities that did not compare with the shift worker or fund-raiser back in America, however well intentioned or motivated.[20]

It was not just their jobs that began to make women veterans distinct. More important than the daily grind was their overall exposure to the war itself. In this, women, as much as male service members, became submerged in the exhaustion and horror that defined the nature of the conflict. Susie McPherson, a Red Cross worker in Italy, describes the war in terms that illustrate her own changing world view: "The thing about life in the war zone which is almost impossible to communicate is not the spectacular aspect—that is really the least of it—but it is the everydayness, the imperceptibly accumulating fatigue and boredom and everlasting homesickness. What you eat, the sameness of it; what identical filthy stone villages you drive through, most of them partially or wholly smashed. The background you don't notice anymore, but it is there."[21] What James Jones would describe thirty years after World War II as "the evolution of a soldier" was a process that began to affect women as well.[22] Whether women were directly involved in combat became less important than their overall immersion in the unequal measures of suffering and triumph that shaped life during wartime.

When peace arrived, women veterans treated it in much the same way as men did, with a shared excitement and an important degree of anxiety. It was thrilling to contemplate a release from the service and return home after several years of separation. Conversely, after the celebrations had died down, many wondered what the war had changed in them. Women veterans, like their male counterparts, began to consider whether it would be possible to jettison an experience that had become integral to their lives. Elizabeth R. Pollock, an early member of the WAAC, wrote the following more than a year before VJ Day: "It seems hard to believe that we were ever so carefree. But that is only a small part of it. Something is happening to all of us who *are* in this thing (and we are in it, even if we never get close enough to hear the sound of any gun besides the reveille cannon) and I wonder if we're going to find ourselves misfits when we go back to the life we had before."[23] The same sort of restlessness that inhabited the thoughts of men contemplating demobilization also resided in the ranks of uniformed women. Unsure about their prospects in the postwar period, these female soldiers were nevertheless impatient to test the waters of rediscovered freedom.

As they mulled over these issues, women tackled the short-term problems confronting them as demobilization proceeded in the fall of 1945. Many fumed at what were obvious biases in the blueprint the Pentagon created to send the troops home. The point system, controversial enough throughout the military, was especially so for women. As noncombatants, they had virtually no chance to accumulate points given for heroism and wounds. Moreover, when the War Department initially granted points for married veterans, it did so at the exclusion of women, a blind spot in policy that took months to rectify.[24]

Compounding the difficulties the women veterans faced was the War Department's reluctance to send them home because of the essential service they provided in processing the paperwork of millions of returning GIs. In late 1945, commanders in Europe actually requested fifty thousand additional WACs to handle the anticipated administrative demand of demobilization. As men boarded boats bound for American ports, the call went out for more women to leave the United States for points abroad.[25]

They completed these missions generally without complaint. Although many women privately grumbled about official policy and a small number translated these concerns into letters to their congressional representatives, women did not participate in any great numbers in the widespread soldiers' protests that broke out in January, 1946. Instead, they met the practical needs that were a dominant part of postwar demobilization and eased the transition of millions of men back into civilian life. More than fifty-two thousand military nurses provided convalescent care in six hundred army hospitals overseas and in eighty U.S. facilities.[26] Their labor was critical to building the foundation for wounded former combatants who were anxiously eying new civilian lives under drastically different circumstances.

B ack in the United States, life for American women on the home front was also undergoing profound changes. The war had created the thin tip of the wedge that many expected would pry open additional opportunities and a change in status once the guns fell silent. The rapid proliferation of women in civilian and military vocations as well as their arrival in positions of leadership was a contingency produced by conflict. However, the general understanding in the country that much of this change was temporary did not belie women's expectations for an American future that was substantially different from the prewar norm.[27] This was the case with respect to married women who were responsible for supporting their growing families while their veteran husbands were enrolled in GI Bill educational programs. It was also the case for a younger generation of women who had reached adulthood during the war. In her landmark study of the Roosevelt years, historian Doris Kearns Goodwin cites a 1946 *Senior Scholastic* survey that reports that 88 percent of thirty-three thousand female students who were polled aspired to a career other than homemaking.[28] In an important sense, the late forties marked a significant generational change in social expectations for women.[29]

Women veterans stood at the forefront of this shift in American society. Service presented them with an undeniable opportunity to transcend the social status quo that previous generations of American women could not have comprehended. The many surveys of female service members convey their desire to move past the conventional roles that awaited them once out of uniform. A Veterans' Administration study of eighteen hundred former enlisted WAACs and WAVES in February, 1946, points out some interesting trends. According to the VA, women were taking jobs more slowly than their male counterparts. Fewer female veterans had dependents, and most of those who did were married women returning home to families. Nevertheless, three to four months after discharge, more than half of the group surveyed were employed, and 6 percent were attending school. Only 22 percent returned to prewar employment, half the rate for males. Four in five believed that they had acquired skills in the military that would be valuable in the civilian job market. Education also figured substantially in their postwar plans. Besides those women who were attending courses, an additional 11 percent had applied to schools, and 13 percent had definite plans to attend at some point in the future.[30]

Obstructing these ambitions were the problems women veterans faced in the transition from military to civilian life. Like many men leaving the service, women experienced what was often euphemistically described as "personal problems," difficulties that ranged from physical illness and posttraumatic stress to a broad array of personal crises created by long periods of wartime separation from spouses, friends, and families.[31] As of May, 1946, 595 of the 1,031 women receiving military hospital benefits were veterans of World War II. An additional 9,203 women received pensions for service-connected disabilities. In this group, 4,426 were classified as psychoneurotic, and 4,636 were considered disabled for physical and "general medical" causes.[32] Among one group of 95 WACs surveyed in 1947, 33 percent complained of "continuous tension," and 23 percent reported suffering from "nervousness" in their daily lives.[33]

The veterans' system was poorly constructed to help solve these problems. While the American military proved adaptable to women as the war progressed, lawmakers in general and the VA in particular clearly lagged behind in crafting policy for women. In part, this was the product of an absence of political pressure to do so. The comparatively small number of female veterans worked against public focus on their postwar dilemmas. Unlike the attention lavished on the difficulties faced by men just out of the service, no critical mass of public outrage appeared to coalesce and demand action on Capitol Hill. Additionally, gaps in veterans' laws specifically addressing women was a result of a compendium of mistaken assumptions. Lawmakers concluded that because women had not been officially assigned combat duties and because few had been wounded, there was no particular need to address their rehabilitation. Similarly, because few women in the military had civilian spouses, laws addressing male dependent benefits became an afterthought. Under the educational provisions of the GI Bill, married women veterans with dependent spouses were not paid an allowance, a situation that was not addressed until 1972.[34]

Additionally, because fewer than 2 percent of WWII veterans were female, the VA did not keep separate statistics for them or employ separate subagencies to address their particular needs.[35] A document produced at the end of the war and titled "Veterans Benefits as They Pertain to Women in the Army" illustrates this significant blind spot in federal policy. The only issue it addressed that pertained specifically to female veterans was their exemption from reporting to Selective Service for reclassification after being discharged from the army. Otherwise, the remaining information follows in the same boilerplate language that simply describes the basic features of the GI Bill. There is little indication in any of this information that women veterans merited additional thought.[36]

In the years following the war, some reforms were made to incorporate women veterans into general federal policy. In 1946, Omar Bradley appointed former WAC Lt. Col. Winifred Stilwell to the VA to craft programs designed to meet women's specific needs.[37] In Congress, Rep. Edith Nourse Rogers (R-MA) became an important advocate of female service members as she worked in concert with Stilwell to amend the Servicemen's Readjustment Act and federal legislation stretching back to the First World War to include hospitalization coverage, domiciliary care, and burial benefits.[38]

Despite the work of people such as Rogers and Stilwell, gaps in the law remained. For years after the war, women who had initially volunteered to serve in the Women's Auxiliary Army Corps did not receive the benefit of employment security that the GI Bill guaranteed.[39] In other cases, disparities were created by a lack of attention within the VA system itself. Veterans' Administration counselors rarely gave women the same attention they paid to male veterans. VA staffers did not actively seek out female veterans or follow up on questions asked by women. Consequently, many women fell through the institutional cracks.

This same institutional bias was replicated in many of the major private organizations that assumed responsibility for veterans' affairs after 1945. Neither the American Legion nor the Veterans of Foreign Wars created a separate body to address the concerns of its female membership. Ladies' auxiliaries were present but were essentially relegated to adjunct roles in support of the vast male-veteran majority. The problems they addressed tended toward those traditionally consigned to American women: fund-raising for local scholarship contests, school-lunch programs, and the problem of juvenile delinquency, among others.[40] The first all-female American Legion post was given a temporary charter in Minneapolis in August, 1945. Initially, the Four Branches Post 303 was composed of 16 women veterans. Later, 68 women veterans applied for a second temporary charter in Chicago.[41]

Lacking the necessary support from established institutions, women veterans created alternative means to nurture their reassimilation, albeit on a dramatically smaller scale. By the late forties, the more established VFW and American Legion chapters were joined by groups organized under names such as the "WAC Veterans Association." In Philadelphia, where the first group of women assembled in 1948, their initial membership numbered only eight.[42]

As they began to grow, groups of women veterans also shifted their emphasis from the traditional supporting role embraced by ladies' auxiliary organizations to more direct leadership contributions. Newer veterans' groups welcomed women. The upstart American Veterans Committee (AVC), largely composed of younger World War II service members, openly included women in leadership positions and made a point of illustrating their neglect by the older veterans' organizations.[43] Mainstream organizations such as Philadelphia's Helen Fairchild American Legion Post 412 also struck out in newer, more proactive directions. Composed of women veterans of both world wars, it sponsored nursing students and provided support for sports, social events, and professional development. In many important ways, the Helen Fairchild Post became a mentor for young career women and served as a bridge between them and the generations of professionals who had come before them.[44]

Social obstacles to a female veteran's assimilation ran concurrent to these institutional difficulties and often made them worse. Women exiting World War II, regardless of whether in uniform, lived within the confines of a significant double standard in American society. In general, the country recognized the contributions women made on the home front and abroad. There was no new point of departure, however, in reconstructing the postwar social status of American women. Rather than grant them special recognition for services rendered in defense of the nation, an acknowledgment that would have redrawn the playbook of social standards, the conventional wisdom in America after 1945 recast them according to the norms that had guided the country long before World War II.

This was a deliberate decision shaped by a public consensus about the need for women to ease the transition from war to peace. After August, 1945, the nation craved a sense of stability and normalcy, which had been deferred for nearly a generation since the start of the Great Depression.[45] In this context, women became the glue holding peacetime America together. Their missions were manifold. They were expected to serve as a civilizing influence on men who returned from the war. They were expected to serve as a brake against the social breakdown that had begun to plague the United States, where divorce rates, socially transmitted diseases, and teen pregnancy were on the rise.[46] They were expected to maintain the core of newly reunited families, where a third and fourth child were becoming increasingly common. A *Newsweek* article from October, 1945, sums up the general expectation that women veterans "have plans for quick conversion from martial to marital life."[47]

The climate of the late forties was more antifeminist and invested in the need for a more "womanly" American female. Popular publications such as *Collier's, Life,* and the *Saturday Evening Post* settled on themes that advocated domesticity rather than the old cross-gender concepts of work and family that had been promoted during the war.[48] Veteran Hollywood actresses such as Joan Crawford and Katherine Hepburn found it necessary to soften their screen personas to be relevant in this postwar environment. Attitudes regarding women's military service also reflected the change. When asked whether young women should be required to take a year's military training after the war, 71 percent of Americans said "no."[49]

There was precious little latitude granted to women veterans in this America. The female soldier had, by definition, challenged social convention by adopting a dramatically different role in U.S. social history. Most had done so not as a superficial attempt to mimic military values but as a full-fledged effort to incorporate the attributes of discipline, leadership, and dedication to a cause that made veterans distinct from their civilian peers. Having won many hard-fought battles to advance in the military hierarchy, women had separated themselves from their female peers. If they intended to maintain this distinction, they risked alienating themselves from an American society that was becoming increasingly removed from the idea of the independent woman.

American society held a special anxiety for women veterans. In 1945, one author expressed concern that women "won't be fit companions for men" after their wartime service was complete. Others argued the opposite case with the same bias in mind, making the point that service had extended "feminine horizons" and made women more fit homemakers. From this perspective, military experience would prove invaluable for the practical skills it gave women who could work while their husbands reentered the job market.[50] The most optimistic of the postwar commentators blithely predicted that "GI Jane got the equivalent of trade school, boarding school, travel, and a workout at a health farm in a few hectic months."[51]

In real terms, the separation created by military service translated into a variety of problems unique to women veterans of World War II. One involved her mental burden in making a clear transition out of uniform. During the war, rates of mental illness were higher among female service members. The most common difficulties were produced by adjusting to life away from home.[52] Once she began the transition back to civilian status, the female veteran faced a situation unlike that of her male counterparts. Posttraumatic stress disorders began to appear, a sometimes unavoidable consequence of women's proximity to violence, suffering, or the unfamiliar rigors of military life. However, because of their official noncombatant status, the public did not immediately grant them the same degree of sympathy that male veterans enjoyed. Moreover, because women had not faced conscription but rather volunteered for military service and promoted this service by attacking a host of military and civilian taboos, they received limited support from the public once posttraumatic stress disorders began to appear in their ranks. In a sense, because women broke with traditional societal protections that had shielded them from such problems in the past, they were "blamed" for the risks they assumed in World War II and the subsequent problems that began to affect their postwar lives.[53] As a result, therapy became a process dependent upon the individual rather than the extensive network of counselors, community members, and family that male veterans enjoyed.

A sense of alienation permeates the writings of women veterans after the war. The frustration evident upon their return from overseas is almost palpable. One ex-WAC complained in 1946 that "We had kind of a wonderful picture of peacetime America—fresh oranges, ice cream, milk, kids, our own home and peace. The America we've come back to isn't the rosy one we dreamed about."[54] Many reflected upon the difficulties of making the transition back to the most basic elements of civilian relationships. One female veteran surveyed in 1947 said, "My concept of 'friendship' took a radical twist while in the service. I had friends in the service who meant as much to me as my family did—in a way your best friend in the service is your family; to share the burden's of one's problems with and to work with. I now regard all friendships as superficial and I realize I will never again have friends like those in the service, full realizing that, even so, it was because of the conditions under which we lived and worked that brought us together so."[55]

Consequently, many women found themselves emotionally separated from their peers and the remainder of civilian society. As for the men who came home from their duty stations scattered all over the globe, their peacetime lives evolved around devising strategies to cope with their newly won civilian status. Unlike men, however, their own reassimilation was at best a social afterthought in the heady days of the late forties. At worst, it was met with skepticism and hostility from a country that was ready to re-create the social past in order to better preserve the American future.

Work was one means for GI Jane to come home again. Employment offered her the chance to apply the practical skills she had learned in the service to a booming postwar economy. More importantly, for a women who had recently departed the military, work offered a chance both to carve out her civilian identity in a new profession and to create her own economic autonomy with a stable, independent income.[56]

A mixed message greeted women veterans returning to the workforce after World War II. It appeared that the postwar American economy would be a different place for them in general. In some cases, this was because they expected that the doors that wartime production necessities had pried open would remain unlocked. Anyone with common sense could see the massive, pent-up demand for products and services that awaited the labor force after 1945. In another sense, women formulated their postwar expectations out of necessity. According to the Department of Labor, women constituted 17.6 percent of the heads of households in the nation at the conclusion of the war.[57] Even the Veterans' Administration contributed to this new sense of economic opportunity. As early as May, 1944, VA administrator Frank

Hines claimed that a new role for women in the workforce had already begun: "The right of the individual woman to work should be recognized and provided for. After the experience of the last four years it would be extremely unfair to treat women as a reserve group to be called upon during war only."[58]

Unfortunately, initial postwar trends proved less than encouraging. As hostilities drew to a close in the latter half of 1945, women who had provided the superstructure of the wartime economy were turned out of their jobs in droves. Between the Fourth of July and Christmas, nearly four million left the labor force. Many were displaced by returning veterans who had been guaranteed their old positions by the GI Bill. Other left willingly, with families and husbands their first priority for the new peacetime. Throughout the Smokestack Belt, factories, manufacturing centers, and shipyards once swarming with women began to empty of them.[59]

Despite this, millions of women remained behind, some out of necessity and some out of determination to make their mark in a new vocation. A *Wall Street Journal* poll recorded after the war that 75 percent of working women wanted to remain employed. So they did, in numbers far beyond what had been the prewar norm. By 1947, women, who were eighteen million workers strong in the American economy, constituted 28 percent of the labor force.[60]

Portions of this giant engine welcomed them with open arms. In the low-paying positions offered in textile manufacturing and the garment industry, women remained and grew in numbers as returned veterans abandoned the work in search of a better standard of living. Overall, by 1949, the number of women employed in manufacturing increased by 50 percent. The burgeoning service sector also offered opportunities. As it struggled to keep pace with the insatiable consumer demand, businesses incorporated vast numbers of new female employees. Those who were occupied in "clerical and kindred work" doubled in the five years that followed the war. Sales personnel, as well as what the census described as "operatives and kindred workers," also saw significant increases. While the majority of this growing white-collar element were men, the proportion was narrowing. By 1947, 40 percent of salespeople in the United States were female, compared to 28 percent before the war.[61]

Women's progress in organized labor was checkered at best. During the war, as industry after industry struggled to find workers to keep assembly lines moving, women joined trade unions by the hundreds of thousands. In some parts of the country, the increase in female membership was dramatic. The United Electrical, Radio, and Machine Workers in New York saw the proportion of women in their union grow from 2 percent to 17 percent during the course of the war.[62] Overall, nearly 3 million women had joined unions by 1948. The ranks of the Congress of Industrial Organizations (CIO) swelled by 1.5 million female members. Approximately 1.3 million were part of the American Federation of Labor (AFL). The largest number of memberships occurred in the garment trades (600,000), the auto industry (300,000), and textile and hosiery manufacturing (200,000).[63] By the end of the decade, women had begun to appear in leadership positions in some union locals.

However, union membership did not automatically protect upward mobility for women. In most jobs, their salaries lagged substantially behind those of men. Benefits packages rarely included provisions specific to female necessities, such as maternity leave. Moreover, in many cases, union membership did not even guarantee basic job security. Once the war ended, many unions began active campaigns to purge their ranks of female members, asserting seniority provisions in their collective-bargaining agreements to facilitate the process. The efforts of the United Auto Workers toward this end are well documented by historians.[64] As a result, total female participation in the auto, steel, and other heavy industries slipped significantly after 1945. The same was true of the trade unions in the construction industry.

Opportunities for women in professional occupations improved somewhat in the postwar economic climate. According to the Labor Department, the war had curtailed the graduation of as many as half of the students who had been engaged in science programs, a number that accounted for approximately 90,000 bachelor's degrees and 5,000 doctorates. The overwhelming majority of these students were men whose academic careers had been cut short by military service. Consequently, and not surprisingly, women began to supplement the ranks of male professionals just as they did with respect to assembly-line workers in the industrial sector. In order to keep pace with federal military contracts, particularly those that funded research and development costs, would-be employers reached out to women with advanced training. According to a 1948 Women's Bureau bulletin, "A southern school which had never before had any calls for women graduates in chemistry before the war reported 353 openings in 1944." Similarly, at a 1944 meeting of the American Chemical Society, one female chemist was interviewed by seventy-one companies for potential employment. Peacetime trends seemed encouraging. Although male veterans were returning to graduate and professional schools in droves in 1945 and 1946, women who were already in the university pipeline had a significant head start on degrees that sometimes took nearly a decade of study to complete. As these women graduated, they were snapped up by the consumer industry as well as companies that were focused on Cold War defense contracts. A postwar survey of nineteen colleges and universities around the country indicated a 29 percent rise in the number of women receiving degrees in math and science. At these same institutions, the number of master's and doctoral degrees awarded women saw a 31 percent increase.[65]

Women veterans negotiated this postwar economic environment by taking advantage of major alterations in the postwar American economy, the tools granted them by federal law, and the qualities and skills each had honed while in military service. While many gladly surrendered their accomplishments for family and children, a significant portion used their veteran's status as a springboard for a different future.

A small contingent decided to make the military a career. Thousands of women in uniform stayed on and took advantage of the precedents created by wartime changes in policy. By 1945, significant portions of the American military were heavily dependent on female service members. When Japan surrendered, more than half of the personnel in the Navy Department in Washington were women. While these numbers obviously diminished once demobilization took hold, the peacetime premium placed on basic logistical functions from medical care to the processing of personnel records maintained openings for women in military vocations. The changing nature of the modern military also held open doors for female service members. New technologies made no distinction as to gender. As military specialties began to incorporate increasing numbers of personnel who were air-traffic controllers, chemists, cartographers, "geodetic computers," or typographers, distinctions between males and females outside the combat environment mattered less with each passing year.[66]

For the majority of women veterans who left the military behind, significant changes in the nature of the American job market augmented employment opportunities. Historian Doris Weatherford makes the important observation that the very nature of women's service during World War II placed them in a very advantageous position once the postwar boom began. By doctrine, most servicewomen had performed logistical duties that were designed to free men for combat assignments in Europe and the Pacific. By definition, this placed them at the forefront of an enormous defense establishment maintained by the precise organization of what Weatherford calls "billions of facts, recorded individually."[67] Without this work, the war effort would have ground to a halt, buried under a mountain of carbon paper. More importantly, this work, by its very nature, prepared women to enter the ranks of corporate America, an organism as large and profoundly complicated as the Department of War and one that craved administration in a postwar economy that was increasingly dependent on information rather than steel or coal. Women veterans were, in many respects, far ahead of their male peers when entering an economy that was becoming dominated by a white-collar workforce.[68]

Other, more specific vocations beckoned. Growth in the U.S. health-care industry offered numerous opportunities for female veterans. The Labor Department estimated that the Veterans' Administration and other federal agencies would require as many as an additional eight thousand nurses to care for disabled military personnel after the war. Health-care work in the civilian sector was even more lucrative. As the postwar era proceeded, benefits packages in labor contracts incorporated ever-increasing provisions for preventive care and outpatient treatment. Consequently, private and publicly managed clinics and offices mushroomed around America, requiring larger professional staffs each year. The same was true of the health-care needs associated with the baby boom. In households that were better able to afford pediatric care, demands for nurses and doctors to assist with the millions of new births exploded around the country. The same was true of openings for health-care providers in the rapidly expanding elementary- and, later, secondary-school systems that needed resident nurses to care for students. According to one survey, the number of registered nurses in the United States grew from 506,050 in 1949 to 847,531 by 1962.[69]

Generally, it appeared that female veterans wanted to apply their military skills to the civilian job sector. A 1946 survey of recently discharged women, one of many conducted by the U.S. Employment Service (USES), reflects a consensus built around the idea of the practical application of military training. Typical of the women who had served, they were a well-educated group. Of eighty-seven job applicants interviewed, more than half were high-school graduates. Nine had attended college. More than 40 percent had received trade education, nursing certification, or other professional training before the war. More than half had done the same work in the military and had augmented it while in uniform, performing tasks in a list of occupations that ranged from photographic processing to physiotherapy. Most of those women wanted the same types of occupations they had held during the war. When they applied for assistance through the USES, the majority who were professionally trained by the military sought those same jobs in the civilian sector.[70]

Many prospective employers were attracted by the high quality of women veterans as job applicants. They respected the skills that women demonstrated in a broad variety of vocations. They admired the self-confidence and discipline in evidence when women started work in both small businesses and larger corporations. In many cases, the connection between male boss and female employee was the result of joint veterans' status. Men who had served with women while in the military were ready-made converts to the idea that the American female could easily transcend older, prewar stereotypes governing the workplace. With the mind-set firmly in position, they eagerly sought women veterans out of practical necessity. In the hothouse climate of the postwar American economy, where new enterprises struggled to survive in a crowded marketplace, the competence of individual workers was often the quality that determined a business's success or failure. Incorporating women of proven ability seemed a common-sense decision, one that could benefit both the job applicant and the entrepreneur.[71]

Not every part of this story resulted in a happy ending, however. The vast majority of men who started businesses after the war, whether veterans or not, had little or no contact with female service members during the war. Most of the GIs exiting World War II did so having been segregated from the female military population by doctrine, ironically after having been freed for overseas duty by the very same women who applied for positions in their new business ventures after the war. Men who stayed behind to manage war plants on the home front generally treated all female labor in the same context: as an expedient necessary to win the war. Once massive layoffs of women began in the summer of 1945, it was rare for employers to make a specific distinction between women veterans and their civilian counterparts.

Underemployment and unemployment plagued women veterans in the forties. According to one account published after the war, "In one voice, the girls of the WAC, WAVES, SPARs, and Marines complain that prospective employers completely disregard their two or three years' experience in the services. Some employers even count it against them, the women veterans believe. One veteran reported that when she applied for a position as physiotherapist, at work she had done before and during service, the employing doctor was shocked to learn that she had been in the army."[72]

Veterans' employment placement services created few options for women. Although female veterans theoretically enjoyed the same counseling services available to men through USES, the Veterans' Administration, and the Selective Service System, the help they received in practice was spotty at best. In rare cases, offices such as the Veterans' Service Center in New York created committees specifically to assist female veterans as they competed for postwar jobs. However, as a rule, these offices rarely went beyond the most superficial review of benefits available to women veterans. Many women who left the service were unsure about the exact procedures necessary to secure the support due to them according to state and federal law. Consequently, applications from women for business and farm loans, which were key supports to prospective veteran entrepreneurs, lagged far behind those from male veterans. The same bias appeared with respect to individual job placement. Employment counselors tended to reserve higher-paying white-collar jobs for male veterans and consistently denied them to both civilian and veteran women after 1945.[73]

After the war, union membership offered women who were interested in securing a good job few options. Generally, organized labor throughout the country governed the workplace according to the seniority rules established in collective-bargaining agreements. By definition, this arrangement left women hired for the duration of mobilization highly vulnerable to layoffs, and unions created practically no contingencies for this prospect. In the aircraft industry, which dominated places such as Washington state, the Aeromechanics' Union simply advised all of its members who had fewer than four years' seniority to seek other employment. As a result, even the more powerful unions like the United Auto Workers largely ignored the problems of women who were laid off after 1945. More importantly, most of the women in military service had no union seniority to count on at all. When the time came to assert the employment provisions of the GI Bill against the seniority system dictated by union contracts, the female veteran was, more often than not, excluded from the union shop.[74]

On balance, women veterans who chose to work were able to carve out a place for themselves in the American economy. Certain professions, such as nursing, were ready niches for their talent. The health-care industry as a whole seemed to offer similar opportunities. Their acumen in administration also offered a boon to corporate America, which was invested in quantifying, understanding, and marketing to the postwar boom. Here and in the burgeoning service economy a woman could also find a place.

Nevertheless, finding a job on par with what they had done in the military was rare. Civilian management was characteristically reluctant to promote women into the higher echelons of the business world despite their well-proven ability to handle responsibility. Pay rates remained skewed according to gender, even when specialization and seniority were coequal. In many cases, the forties were a decade that was defined by frustratingly slow professional and economic progress.

Nevertheless, women who had served in the war joined millions of their civilian compatriots in the American job force, a number that grew as the forties progressed. Old standards that dictated participation began to fall by the wayside in the wake of both social and economic change. By 1949, more than half of the working women were married, an unheard-of proportion a generation earlier.[75] The quality of their work had also changed. Augmented by their wartime experiences, this generation began to challenge the status quo because they were motivated by the knowledge that what they could accomplish was based on tangible results, not on airy ideals.

This attitude was most firmly rooted in the community of female veterans who entered the job market armed with the knowledge that they could perform not only for the sake of profit, advancement, or professional recognition but also when people's lives counted on their competence. In an era when the public's expectations for the future were on the rise, these women stood in the vanguard of a generation that would increasingly test acceptable norms in the workplace.[76]

If they could not find a means of assimilating at home or at work, female veterans had the option of going to school. Tens of thousands joined the GI generation in their journey from the barracks to American college campuses. According to one study, by July, 1946, eleven thousand women had taken advantage of the educational and training benefits available under the GI Bill.[77] Some did so with the desire to advance the skills they had carried with them into the military or acquired while in uniform. Others embarked upon new careers and explored new interests.

A few schools changed their structures to accommodate female veterans. Institutions such as the New Jersey College for Women (Rutgers) developed a special program for women veterans, combining advisement with course selection to complement study in the liberal arts, social sciences, and professional programs. At Rutgers, tuition was restructured to meet the limits required by the GI Bill. The college took special pains to accept credit for courses taken through the U.S. Armed Forces Institute. Some programs in "professional service training" were also compressed into a single year's duration.[78]

Many faculty were equally accommodating. As was the case with veterans in general, after a brief period of wariness, professors lauded these new students for their aggressive approach to learning as well as the maturity and forthrightness they brought to the classroom. Even so, like their male counterparts, some difficulties left over from the war sometimes strayed into the picture. One professor of writing commented that the work of a former WAC made it "plain that something had got twisted in her mind. She was genial and pleasant enough on the surface, but underneath something *had* happened."[79]

Women's colleges remained largely ambivalent toward female veterans. A few of the editorialists writing in the *Journal of the American Association of University Women* saw women entering college as a brake against the millions of GIs who were flooding into American higher education, in some cases enrolling in traditionally women's colleges.[80] However, schools such as Smith or Bryn Mawr did little to actively cultivate the female veteran population. Rather than reach out to this viable and well-funded constituency, they preferred instead to fall back upon the exclusive segment of American society that had sent their daughters to them for schooling for the better part of a century.

On the whole, mainstream American universities and colleges followed suit with the more exclusive women's institutions. Few of them initiated outreach programs designed to bring female veterans to their campuses. Most of them concentrated instead on the rush for those men who clamored for entry and, with federal dollars in hand, were veritable manna from heaven for college presidents who had endured the cash-strapped Depression era. Consequently, women veterans existed on the periphery of educational policymaking, where they were at best addressed as part of the larger contingent of former soldiers, sailors, and marines who were entering academia and where any recognition of their own unique wartime experiences was notably absent. In the end, the responsibility for a woman veteran's educational success or failure fell largely upon her own shoulders.

What did women gain as a result of their service in World War II? On the surface, the substantive rewards were obvious. Women joined men in reaping the benefits of the deluge of gender-blind state and federal laws that greeted them when they returned home. Although blatant disparities in certain benefits remained unaddressed for decades, women, like their blue-collar male counterparts, were recipients of an unprecedented amount of assistance that they used to construct a new template for the American dream. If class and racial barriers began to shift for men after 1945, the same could be said of the gender status quo in the United States in the forties.

Less tangible but perhaps more important was the degree of self-confidence that military service fostered within women veterans. This quality proved to be crucial at a time when specific institutional attention to their needs was rare and social obstacles to change remained strong and, in some cases, a regressive part of everyday life. Lacking the support created by official policy, private-sector initiatives, or a well-integrated network of veterans' organizations, women were forced to rely on their own initiative to a much greater degree than men who were leaving military service.[81]

CHAPTER 4

The core combination of ability and self-confidence allowed women veterans to successfully challenge and conquer social and economic convention. Their departure from the status quo was extraordinary and easily measurable in the manner in which they treated family and careers. According to contemporary scholarship by D'Ann Campbell, 45 percent of nurses and 27 percent of women in other military fields never married, a startling figure when compared with the 5 percent of women overall in their generation who chose the same path.[82]

This was a striking rejection of contemporary norms and a preface for a future in which professional careers would increasingly compete for the time of American women. It was also remarkable to the extent that it was a personal decision to invoke both social and economic change. Far from being the product of public policy or a broad public consensus, female veterans bore the burden of postwar reform themselves. In doing so, they strengthened the value of the individual in American society and inspired the next generation of American women to expand the boundaries of achievement even further.

CHAPTER 5

Minority Veterans
Come Home

It's now you've heard my story, there's one thing I can't see,
How you could treat a human like they have treated me;
I thought I fought on the islands to get rid of their kind;
But I can see the fight lots plainer now that I am blind.
— *Woody Guthrie, "The Blinding of Isaac Woodard"*

Americans of all races answered the call to arms in 1941. Participation in the war was a reflection of their outrage, their patriotism, and a collectively held desire to see the conflict through so that peace could someday return to the country. World War II was a "good war," as much a fight against the doctrine of Nazi racial superiority as the threat of world oppression.[1] Military service emphasized this common bond. Young men entered service with the same confidence in their physical skills and eagerness to use these tools against the enemy. New recruits suffered the same anxieties and fears in the transition from civilian to soldier regardless of race. They wrestled with the same regimentation of time, language, dress, and behavior. They managed to eventually digest military food. They learned to shape long days and short nights around the rhythm of military life. They learned about the qualities of leadership and the value of competence in the face of danger.[2] Americans of all races earned the same degree of pride that came from overcoming the obstacles prepared by the military in the course of training and in the conduct of the war. In many respects, World War II became an interracial event that served as a common cultural marker for a generation of Americans.

However, military service also highlighted the racial problems that were part of the American status quo during the war years. In this environment, merit and service were rendered meaningless by bigotry. Overseas, minority soldiers also experienced unheard-of tolerance among far more cosmopolitan European cultures. African American veteran Nelson Peery explained that "The Negro troops got a taste of racial equality in foreign lands. As they came home, that had to be beaten and lynched and terrorized out of them before they would go back to building levees and picking cotton."[3] It was almost impossible for black veterans or any of their counterparts in the American military to placidly accept a prewar social role that would set aside such experiences.

It was the friction between this common bond of service and the discrimination persisting after the war that was the starting point for social reforms afterward. As Peery put it, "war is an experience that leaves one with a sense of responsibility: the veteran never forgets the meaning of force or loses his sense of organization."[4] World War II became the launching pad for the modern civil rights movement. Its ranks were populated and stiffened by the same veterans who had sacrificed their lives and their youth for a better America. When they returned, their expectations began on that basic point.

Of all of the minority groups who served in the U.S. armed forces during World War II, African Americans were the largest, participating in numbers that exceeded by far their proportion in American society. Approximately 2.4 million registered for service during the conflict. More than 1 million eventually served in uniform in every theater in which U.S. forces deployed to fight. The group comprised 16 percent of all American enlisted personnel at a time when blacks made up only 10 percent of the population. Fewer than 2 percent became conscientious objectors during the war.[5]

African American representation in the officer corps reflected an impressive diversity of educational backgrounds and vocations. In her memoir of service in the Women's Army Corps, *One Woman's Army*, Charity Adams Early catalogues the prewar jobs held by members of her training platoon, a list that included not only beauticians, cooks, maids, and textile workers but also law students, teachers, and social workers. Many had never held a job. Quite a few had only high school or college to mark their life experience outside the home. All of them wanted to serve.[6]

For the most part, black service members were assigned to the logistical units that supported combat formations in Europe and the Pacific. Here they became an integral part of America's victory, providing all the component parts necessary for a modern military structure to prevail in a twentieth-century war. While thousands were consigned to backbreaking work in labor battalions and graves-registration units, many African Americans were able to accumulate skills far in advance of their prewar vocations. Thousands received advanced training in engine mechanics, carpentry, communications, and hundreds of other specialties with civilian applications. Even before 1945, military service created among these GIs different and better expectations for a postwar America.[7]

When the all-black units were able to contribute, their combat performance was, for the most part, impressive. On the ground, soldiers of the 761st Tank Destroyer Battalion performed extremely well against heated German opposition in France, Belgium, and Luxembourg. In the air, the black airmen of the 99th Fighter Squadron amassed eighty-eight Distinguished Flying Crosses in combat over the skies of Western Europe.[8] Perhaps even more importantly, manpower shortages near the end of the war ended the official policy of segregation out of necessity. At the conclusion of 1944, the German offensive in the Ardennes saw ad hoc units of mixed races perform effectively in bitter fighting.[9] Taken together, the achievements of African Americans on the front lines and in support of the war leaves little doubt as to their contribution toward victory.

At the end of the war, demobilization was a cause for hope and a frustrating reminder of existing discrimination. Because most black troops had not held combat assignments, they were unable to accumulate the discharge points granted to recipients of citations or medals for valor or wounds and rapidly fell behind the units that were redeploying to the United States. Ironically, some of the very logistical skills that had been assigned to the segregated units during the war made them essential to demobilization. Soldiers and sailors, whether they were truck drivers or stevedores, remained at their posts to facilitate the great migration of military personnel home. Despite this essential service and despite the performance of all-black units at war's end, the War Department refused to revoke the policy of segregation in the new peacetime environment.

The America that black veterans returned to barely resembled the home they had left behind. Upheaval, particularly in the South as a result of the war, was the rule of the day. In this region, more than 20 percent of the farming population had left the land seeking employment in war plants and shipyards that were springing up like mushrooms in the countryside. In the manufacturing sector of this new economy, employment grew by 50 percent during the war, while wages saw a 40 percent increase.[10] For African Americans in particular, the war offered an unheard-of bounty in the booming defense industries. Hundreds of thousands took the opportunity for not only economic mobility but also a chance to leave behind the Old South as well. Black workers began to appear in noticeable numbers in Portland, Oregon; Los Angeles; and San Diego for the first time as the shipping industry clamored for skilled and unskilled labor. Similar increases were also registered in the older industrial centers around Chicago, Detroit, Philadelphia, and Baltimore.[11]

Many black veterans entered this environment eager to take advantage of the new opportunities. For them, this meant leaving the South behind. In 1945, three-quarters of a million African American veterans lived in the South, primarily in Texas, Louisiana, Mississippi, Alabama, Georgia, North Carolina, South Carolina, and Virginia. A year after VJ Day, approximately 10 percent of these veterans had already left the region for better pastures in the North and West. As one veteran recalled, "Many veterans in the South came back determined not so much to change things but to get the hell out of here."[12] Most black veterans (31 percent) polled at the time cited better jobs as their primary goal after the war. In the first two years of the postwar period, only 15 percent returned to their old occupations.[13]

Migration also seemed the best way to pursue opportunities other than employment. For these veterans, movement north and west was a means to enjoy the civil rights that World War II had enshrined in a national cause.[14] For the individual in the postwar era, it was time to balance the real chances for reform at home against the potential freedoms to be found in the future. John Egerton describes the postwar years as a crossroads for the South as a whole: "It was time for the South to decide whether it was going to be a backward-looking feudal society or a modern and progressive democracy. Idealism certainly pointed the South toward a democratic future, but realism and tradition stood in the way."[15]

Freedom was not a small idea. It had been the keystone of the Allied cause when Franklin Roosevelt first articulated the meaning of the "Four Freedoms" in January, 1941. "Freedom of speech," "freedom of worship," "freedom from want," and "freedom from fear" became rallying cries that bound Americans to the world in the bleak, early days of the war. In 1943, Norman Rockwell's paintings of the Four Freedoms brought these concepts to life in homes throughout the country. Later, the same emphasis on freedom was codified in the charter of the new United Nations. After the war, during the Nuremberg war-crimes trials, the victorious Allies offered the world a sense of the penalty for threatening freedom.[16]

The link between freedom and service was made abundantly clear to African Americans at the close of the war. In a speech delivered in March, 1945, Veterans' Administration head Frank Hines explained the Four Freedoms as they applied to returning black service members. According to the VA administrator, they would mean (1) freedom from discrimination in the administration of the law, (2) freedom from inequality in education, (3) freedom from inequality in expenditures for health, hospitalization, and rehabilitation, and (4) freedom from obstacles and prejudices that prevent equal work opportunity and pay.[17] Hines was addressing a series of concerns that was already beginning to appear in the ranks of returning African American veterans. A black sailor articulated the feelings of many in a letter to the National Association for the Advancement of Colored People (NAACP) in May, 1945: "We as Negro enlisted men in the U.S. Navy are deeply concerned with the problems we have to face in a post-war America. The problem that seems to give us most concern is that of jobs and economic opportunities for Negroes in the post-war world. We fully realize this problem is but a part of the bigger problem for jobs and economic security for all. Yet as Negroes we are forced to face facts since we have been 'the first to be fired' and even more tragically 'the last to be hired.'"[18]

There was good reason for concern, specifically with respect to the Veterans' Administration itself. After the war, the VA basically refused to use federal policy to override state law when considering veterans' claims. In a letter to Jesse O. Dedmon, secretary of veterans affairs for the NAACP, Hines expressed a desire to let state segregation laws stand untouched by federal pressure. Responding to the NAACP's protests that, for example, certain states allowed real-estate transactions to be based on race, Hines noted that "It would be no favor to a veteran to promulgate regulations so loose as to induce him to become burdened with an illegal contract or deed, with resultant loss and disappointment."[19]

Lacking the VA's support, black veterans sought out other official venues. By the conclusion of the war, civil rights leaders understood that the law could increasingly be placed into the service of equality. The courts were one such starting point. In the early forties, the accumulation of judicial appointments made by FDR, a number that included legal minds such as Hugo Black and William O. Douglas, was beginning to have an impact on the interpretation of American law and progressive causes. The federal judiciary of the postwar years began a trend that reinforced civil rights issues through landmark decisions such as *Smith v. Allwright* (1944), in which the Supreme Court struck down Texas' white primary system.[20] The *Smith* decision would be as important to voting rights as *Brown v. Board* (1954) would later be to school desegregation.

Precedents established by federal policy during the New Deal and the war could also be used to further the cause of civil rights. During the thirties, the Roosevelt administration's concessions to race, specifically in the "no discrimination" clauses contained in the Works Progress Administration and the Public Works Administration, became rudimentary building blocks for desegregation and federal oversight of the process. In 1941, the same was true with respect to the victories that A. Philip Randolph scored, which led to the creation of the Fair Employment Practices Commission.

However, rather than assuage demands for change, these concessions only provoked greater expectations and highlighted the ongoing discrimination that African Americans faced. While some war plants integrated, others, most notably in aircraft manufacturing, did not. Discrimination against African Americans in uniform continued unchecked. This was particularly appalling to Northerners, who were first exposed to open segregation when stationed in military bases in the South.[21] Citing a report by Thurgood Marshall and William H. Hastie, Walter White, writing in August, 1943, after the shooting of a black military policeman by a white police officer triggered rioting in Harlem, offered a prophetic statement about the future of American race relations: "Civilian violence against the Negro in uniform is a recurrent phenomenon. . . . It may well be the greatest factor now operating to make 13,000,000 Negroes bitter and resentful and to undermine the fighting spirit of three-quarters of a million Negroes in arms. Yet, no effective steps are being taken and no vigorous, continuing and comprehensive program of action has been inaugurated by the state or federal authorities to stamp out this 'evil.' . . . To address a Negro soldier as 'nigger' is such a commonplace in the average Southern community that little is said about it. But the mounting rage of the soldier himself is far from commonplace. . . . In such a climate resentments grow until they burst forth in violent and unreasoning reprisal."[22]

To civil rights leaders, it seemed likely that the Truman White House would lend its support to furthering the cause of equality.[23] The president joined much of the country in expressing his dismay and outrage at the arrest and blinding of army veteran Isaac Woodard by police in Batesburg, South Carolina. Civil rights leaders took heart at the president's outraged realization of the continuing abuse of black veterans returning from Europe and the Pacific: "But my very stomach turned over when I learned that Negro soldiers, just back from overseas, were being dumped out of army trucks in Mississippi and beaten. Whatever my inclinations as a native of Missouri might have been, as President I know this is bad. I shall fight to end evils like this."[24] Truman's creation of the President's Committee on Civil Rights by executive order and with the assistance of his attorney general in prosecuting civil rights cases seemed to indicate that the movement had finally gained an important ally.[25]

With this belief, the NAACP fairly bombarded the VA and War Department with demands to use their power to ensure the fair treatment of African American veterans. In many cases, this applied to the institutions themselves. If Veterans' Administration health care was a national lightning rod and source of scandal after the war, the situation for black veterans was measurably worse. In 1945, the NAACP reported that seventeen VA hospitals in ten states did not accept black veterans except in emergency cases.[26] One subsequent demand, made in July, 1945, was for minority appointments within the Veterans' Administration to ensure that minority interests were represented by "qualified Negro doctors, nurses, specialists, and administrators." Moreover, according to surveys the NAACP conducted, black representation was minuscule even in northern branch offices of the VA. African Americans constituted only 22 of 800 VA employees in Maryland. In Chicago, they composed 16 percent of the staff of the large regional VA office. More than three-quarters of these employees were occupied in typing, clerical duties, and the office messenger service.[27] The NAACP also pressured Washington for the creation of a "veterans' employment service" to address the needs of veterans where the state-run U.S. Employment Service (USES) would not.[28] In Congress, it sponsored a 1945 bill that would make it a federal crime to assault a GI. Although the measure passed in the Senate, the so-called GI Assault Bill died in the House of Representatives.[29]

The most successful federal program for African American veterans was the GI Bill. Its provisions for business loans, education, job training, and health care were color blind as a matter of policy and useful tools to begin the process of creating economic and social opportunities after the war. Both the army and the NAACP heavily promoted GI benefits among returning black veterans as the war wound down. *The Buffalo,* the newspaper of the segregated 92nd Division, printed a special October, 1945, edition that outlined each of the specific benefits offered by the program. NAACP pamphlets available in demobilization centers also broke down the exact provisions contained in the law and offered, with each booklet, a discounted membership application.[30]

The GI Bill gave African American veterans a means to abandon their past economic and social status for something better. This opportunity resonated with a generation that had far greater expectations of the future than before the war. A 1947 Roper poll asked Americans in general, "Do you think your son's opportunities to succeed will be better than, or not as good as, those you have had?" Nationally, 62.1 percent responded that future opportunities would be better. However, when asked, 75 percent of African Americans answered in the affirmative.[31]

This hope was constrained by an important degree of pragmatism. Many black leaders with long memories could recall their failure to win meaningful political or social concessions after embracing the patriotic cause and closing ranks with the American mainstream during the First World War. Many were equally skeptical about the chances for progress given the ongoing resistance to the Fair Employment Practices Commission and the seemingly immovable obstacles to change in much of the country that persisted after 1945.[32]

Still, progress began to materialize in significant areas once peacetime took hold. One of these was in education. Like their white counterparts, the African American veterans saw in education a tangible chance for upward mobility. Like their counterparts, the black veterans enjoyed a substantial subsidy for tuition and living expenses if they chose to attend a technical school or a university. Not surprisingly, the traditional black college system was as overwhelmed as the rest of higher education in America. In 1941, black college enrollment was 37,203. By 1947, it had skyrocketed to 73,174. In a study comparing fall-semester enrollments between 1946 and 1947, black colleges recorded the largest percentage of increase of all institutions in the country (26.05 percent), more than doubling the national average for schools nationwide (12.52 percent).[33]

Traditionally black colleges also differed from their mainstream counterparts to the extent that their lack of facilities for the onrush of students was much more severe. Most of them lacked deep bases of alumni support common in many white institutions. Most existed in some of the poorest parts of the country. Nor did they have equal access to state or federal funds for additional construction and renovation of the buildings, labs, and physical plants necessary for day-to-day operations.[34] Professional journals complained bitterly about overcrowding and shortages of textbooks and basic equipment. By one estimate, fewer than 10 percent of black colleges had library resources adequate for undergraduate education. Most crippling of all these difficulties was the lack of qualified faculty. According to a 1946 edition of the *Journal of Negro Education,* it would be necessary for black colleges to increase their faculty rolls by 15 to 20 percent to keep up with postwar demand.[35] Rather than becoming a starting point for black colleges, the postwar years highlighted the dilapidated conditions that characterized African American higher education.

Yet, the students continued to come, their hope for a better future overwhelming the conditions that greeted them. Foremost among these new arrivals were black veterans. In 1947, African American veterans dominated the new classes of black colleges in Texas (47.1 percent), Delaware (49.7 percent), and North Carolina (54 percent). In 1948, the *Journal of Negro Education* conducted a study of black college enrollments in seventeen Southern states between 1946 and 1947. It revealed that black veterans constituted 40.5 percent of new students.[36] The result of this trend, in terms of simple numbers, is impressive. The total number of bachelor's degrees awarded by black colleges more than doubled between 1940 and 1950 from 5,707 to 13,108.[37]

More important were the long-term pressures these conditions created on American education in general. Motivated by the terrible conditions for study that existed on their side of the segregated national educational system, black students in increasing numbers petitioned for admission to traditionally white institutions. This was particularly the case in graduate and professional programs, where the disparity of quality between medical and law programs led students to challenge racially segregated admissions' policies. The basic fact that black veterans with test scores in hand and federal dollars awaiting them through the GI Bill made the case for integration unavoidable.[38]

The contrasts experienced by black veterans in college were equally profound in the American workplace. Postwar trends were abundantly clear. Wartime mobilization significantly changed the structure of African American participation in the labor force. Farms suffered in the wake of opportunities offered in the modern economy. Contemporary census data indicate that the number of men employed in agriculture declined by more than half between 1940 and 1952 (43.3 percent to 19.2 percent). Similarly, the number of women in this sector of the economy decreased by more than two-thirds (21 percent to 6.2 percent).[39] While the highest percentage of African Americans who were working remained as private household workers (56 percent) and common laborers (22–25 percent), additional pressures were building for greater economic mobility in postwar America from a segment of the population no longer content with menial work at the lowest economic rung. One South Carolina veteran captured the sentiments of many when a VA official suggested that he work as a laborer: "I was a staff sergeant in the Army . . . traveled all over England . . . sat fourteen days in the English Channel. I wasn't going to push a wheel barrow."[40]

In many cases, veterans were at the forefront of this discontent and in many cases directly at odds with the VA's handling of employment benefits and placement. VA attention to the employment needs of black veterans was at best erratic. In most states, job counseling, the management of training programs, and veterans' benefits were functions of state agencies. In much of the country, few black employees were to be found in either the U.S. Employment Service or the Veterans' Administration. In Tennessee, where 35 percent of all men entering military service during World War II were African American, only four were employed by the VA in 1946.[41] In Georgia, the administration of veterans' benefits was also segregated by race. African American veterans were required to use the rear entrance of the USES branch office in Columbus.[42] Work placement, when it was accomplished, followed predictable racial lines. In Arkansas, 95 percent of the placements made by the U.S. Employment Service for black veterans were for service and unskilled jobs.[43] Those with significant work skills—the electricians, plumbers, and draftsmen trained by the military—found few advocates when they attempted to break into trade unions. Although the construction industry cited a shortage of about 1.5 million workers in 1945, a National Urban League study of twenty-one cities uncovered open opposition to racial integration by the International Brotherhood of Electrical Workers and the United Association of Plumbers and Steamfitters.[44]

Hopes that Omar Bradley might address these problems once he became VA administrator were short lived. Grappling with issues of national policy, he showed little interest in challenging the status quo in the bureaucracy of either the VA or other organizations such as USES. He refused, for example, to reverse local policies that segregated VA hospitals. In a letter to Rep. Adam C. Powell (D-NY), Bradley claimed, "I should like to say that the practice of acknowledging *geographical difficulties* in the question of segregation or non-segregation of Negro patients does not stem from a desire to perpetuate the practice of segregation nor is it out of deference to the wishes of non-veterans." Instead, Bradley advocated gradual integration. He argued for allowing all veterans, regardless of race, into newly constructed VA hospitals.[45] Unfortunately, the slow pace of construction and accumulating congressional resistance to new spending after 1947 largely stymied even this modest proposal.

Federal action was thin gruel for a generation of former soldiers, sailors, and marines who were intent on making a better life. Rather than await decisive action from the confines of Washington, D.C., and impatient with the prospect of allowing the legal system to slowly unravel the problems of segregation, many African Americans began to act locally after the war. The numbers that illustrate the postwar growth of the NAACP speak volumes. Between 1940 and 1946, membership in the organization soared from 50,000 to 450,000. By 1948, the NAACP counted fourteen thousand branches in the country. The most rapid growth occurred in the South. This region alone accounted for 79 percent of new units chartered between 1946 and 1950.[46]

Black veterans led a significant portion of this resurgence. People who were important to the civil rights movement in the forties, Amzie Moore, Aaron Henry, and Medgar Evers, were all veterans before they became advocates for equality.[47] In many cases, their experience in the segregated military served as a catalyst, motivating them to do something about racial discrimination. Moore claimed after the war that he did not understand segregation until his army experience. His breaking point came when he tried to deliver lectures to black soldiers emphasizing the value of the Four Freedoms while understanding how his audience was being treated in the United States.[48] Many black veterans were galvanized by their own personal attempts to claim the legal rights they had fought to preserve. Mississippi law included provisions that exempted veterans from that state's poll tax. No mention was made of race in the official language, something that many country registrars would find out to their dismay after 1945. When Aaron Henry came home, he attempted to register, citing state law, and was refused three separate times. After a white veteran accompanied him and presented his own exemption certificate, the official finally relented. Henry became the first African American in Coahoma County to vote in a Democratic primary.[49]

Civil rights activism quickly became intertwined with references to the war and service. In a May, 1945, speech titled "When GI Joe Comes Home," NAACP Secretary of Veterans Affairs Jesse O. Dedmon said before the Maryland State Conference of NAACP Branches, "During the past month we have seen the cessation of hostilities on one of our major battle fronts but we must be mindful of the fact that only one-half of the victory has been attained. Our whole-hearted support is behind the war effort. We have not hesitated in our efforts to secure full citizenship rights for all. We have repeatedly urged the use by the War Department of badly needed Negro nurses on a non-segregated basis; we have continued to protest the segregation of blood plasma by the American Red Cross; we have investigated many cases of mistreatment of Negro soldiers solely because of race and color."[50] In a separate letter to Gov. Thomas Dewey of New York, Walter White, secretary of the NAACP, wrote that same year, "Returning victorious from our battles against fascist doctrines of racial inequality, the Negro veteran finds himself barred from decent housing in New York State by the passive continuance of segregation in all housing facilities."[51]

The 1946 elections served as a peacetime rallying point for these sentiments. During the course of the campaign season, an estimated six hundred thousand black Southerners registered to vote, triple the number who had done so in 1940.[52] Thousands of veterans banded together to lead both registration drives and later attempts to vote in primaries and the general election that November. Others began to lobby for reform candidates in local and state contests. In January, 1946, one hundred African American veterans marched on the courthouse in Birmingham, Alabama, to demand the right to vote. Wearing their old uniforms and carrying their discharge papers, they were organized by the Veterans Committee of the Southern Negro Youth Congress and led by Capt. H. Terrell, a former army chaplain. Most of the veterans who attempted to register were rejected by state officials for their failure to "interpret the U.S. Constitution." In reality, they were refused because of their inability to respond to arcane questions arranged by the board of registrars to disqualify them.[53] Despite this, the United Registration Committee of Birmingham continued to lobby for change, loudly proclaiming that "Men who faced bullets overseas deserve ballots at home." Insurgent veterans' political organizations also began to appear in Georgia, Louisiana, Tennessee, and Arkansas. Declaring anticorruption as their cause, they attempted to unseat established political machines that dominated local politics.[54]

As resistance to reform continued, violence and protests multiplied throughout the long, bloody year that followed the war. A scuffle between James Stephenson, a recently discharged navy veteran, and a clerk in a Columbia, Tennessee, appliance store quickly escalated into rioting in February, 1946. A young veteran by the name of Maceo Snipes was abducted and murdered by four white men after voting in the July 17 primary in Taylor County, Georgia. At least five black veterans were killed in clashes with the Birmingham, Alabama, police during the year.[55] As early as May, the National Negro Council of Washington told Truman that it was "imperative" to send troops to protect the voting rights of black veterans.[56] Not content to wait for lawmakers to act and openly doubtful that they would, many veterans' groups began to organize for the sake of self-defense. Quite a few returnees from the war came home with weapons either captured on the battlefield or secreted from American armories. More importantly, these veterans knew how to organize and coordinate their actions, making the prospect of violence even more volatile. In Bennetsville, Georgia, African American veterans armed themselves and began patrolling the streets after the appearance of the Ku Klux Klan in their town.[57]

At points, local action rose to the level of national notice. In early 1946, black veterans traveled to Washington for three days of hearings to contest the seating of Mississippi Sen. Theodore Bilbo. Similarly, the Veterans' League of America demanded the resignation of another Mississippi legislator, Rep. John Rankin, chair of the House World War Veterans' Legislation Committee, charging that Rankin's "lynch-law psychology" prevented him from adequately addressing the problems of returning black veterans.[58] While neither of these efforts succeeded in the final analysis, they did serve notice to the country that postwar America would be a different place if these former service members had anything to say about it.

Black veterans transformed the civil rights movement and the debate over the future of African Americans in two key ways. In one important respect, ex-GIs gave credibility to advocates of equality. The desire of African American veterans to attend college and move beyond their prewar station in life resonated with an American public that had much the same ambition.[59] More to the point, black veterans made excellent litigants as the NAACP Legal Defense Fund pursued desegregation through the state and federal courts in the forties. They proved to be an invaluable resource to lawyers attempting to establish a link with juries and courts that would determine the success or failure of the case for equality.[60] Representing a gold standard of citizenship, veterans were a group that both symbolized the mainstream of America and had also contributed to the greater good. These veterans, so the arguments would state, were not passive actors expecting special treatment from the law. They were citizens who had earned the right to receive due recognition of their sacrifice for the public welfare. In short, they were perfect weapons to wield against the "separate but equal" provisions that existed in laws and restrictive covenants around the country.[61]

Fueled by anger, outrage, and hope, black veterans also gave reformers the added strength of their motivation. They were prepared to attack—in large ways and small—what they saw as injustice in the economic sector and within the larger audience composed of America's mainstream society. No standing institution or practice was safe. When African American members of the Jesse Clipper American

Foreign Legion Post in New York protested their exclusion from the American Bowling Congress, they were allowed to integrate into the legion's league.[62] Thousands of similar actions followed throughout the forties, providing community activists and national organizations with a critical mass of energy. As time passed, this effort snowballed and created an expanding spectrum of expectations that mirrored those of the larger American society.[63] In the process, the modern civil rights movement was born.

Hispanic Americans constituted a relatively small percentage of the national population in the forties but made a major contribution to the war effort nevertheless. Clustered primarily in the southwestern United States, they represented a group largely isolated from the remainder of society, segregated from other Americans in public education, housing, and employment.[64] Latinos occupied the lowest possible part of the socioeconomic ladder. The median income for Mexican Americans at the start of the war was $980 per year, slightly more than half that for whites ($1,925). Instances of disease, from dysentery to tuberculosis, as well as high infant mortality and low literacy rates collectively illustrate a story of grinding poverty and an ongoing struggle for basic survival.[65] When the country did turn its attention to Hispanic Americans, it was usually in a negative context. For mainstream American society, the so-called zoot-suit riots in Los Angeles in the summer of 1943, in which hundreds of servicemen terrorized Chicano youths throughout the city, symbolized a dangerous, deviant element of society.

Hispanic American military service in World War II belied these stereotypes. Although the Department of War kept exact records only about how many men and women of Puerto Rican descent served, estimates of Latino participation in uniform range from approximately 250,000 to 500,000.[66] As many as 250,000 of these service members were Mexican nationals, who were allowed by a mutual agreement between the United States and their home country to enlist in the American military. Approximately 14,000 of this group eventually saw combat.[67] Hispanic Americans were present primarily in National Guard units from the Southwest that were called to active duty during the war. Thousands served in the 36th Infantry Division (Texas) and the 158th Regimental Combat Team (Arizona). Others populated regular formations that had been reconstituted for the conflict, such as the 30th Infantry Regiment of the 3rd Infantry Division and the 313th Infantry Regiment of 79th Infantry Division. Unlike African Americans, Latinos faced no restrictions on where they could serve. They could be found in both combat and noncombatant specialties.

The nature of this service is defined by the performance of the Hispanic Americans in combat. In many units, they developed a reputation for taking risks under fire and braving extreme danger despite the peril they placed themselves in. In many cases, this reputation was well deserved. Throughout the war, Latinos suffered casualty rates disproportionately higher than that of the vast majority of service members. Mexican Americans accounted for 10 percent of Los Angeles's population, for example, but suffered nearly 20 percent of the city's casualties during World War II. According to historian Henry A. J. Ramos, not a single Hispanic American serviceman was ever reported to have deserted, and not a single Mexican American in uniform was ever charged with cowardice or treason.[68]

However, the war itself offered more than danger to Latinos. Much of it was meaningful and contributed not only to their training, education, and self-confidence but also to their world view. Service broadened the vistas of the Hispanic American service members, catapulting them out of the American Southwest to points all around the globe. They were exposed to the world in its European and Asian forms, and they experienced a variety of cultures that were far removed from the dusty towns and dilapidated city neighborhoods in the United States. A few met up with a number of Latin American soldiers stationed abroad, including 25,000 Brazilian soldiers who served with the Allies in Italy and Mexican aviators who were stationed in the Philippines in late 1944.[69]

The booming American economy of the forties offered Hispanic Americans the prospect of advancement. During the war, with large and small businesses clamoring for workers as the military draft sank its teeth into the manpower pool, America opened its borders to Mexican labor as part of the bracero program. As a result, approximately 300,000 Mexicans legally migrated to farms, factories, and manufacturing centers scattered throughout the United States, accompanied by additional hundreds of thousands who entered the country illegally in search of work.[70]

After the war, the same demand for willing labor, legal or otherwise, persisted and even grew in some regions, particularly as the Sunbelt states began their postwar boom. In California, Arizona, New Mexico, and Texas, the construction industry cried out for both skilled and unskilled labor as the suburbs and commercial districts spread beyond cities and towns. For the more ambitious, the GI Bill offered all Latino veterans who qualified a means to enter the ranks of small-business owners, receive vocational training, or move to the unheard-of frontier of college.[71]

The unanswered question for many Hispanic American veterans was whether they could successfully gain access to these new opportunities and the new veterans' programs that supported them. As was the case with the African American returnee, Latino veterans enjoyed few intermediaries to ensure that local or federal authorities would observe their legal rights. Cooperative programs created by the VA or the Retraining and Reemployment Administration rarely reached them. Neither the American Foreign Legion nor the Veterans of Foreign Wars demonstrated much interest in lobbying for the rights of this one constituency. Latino membership in both organizations was small, when it existed at all, and members were usually sequestered in segregated posts. It was commonplace for the Veterans' Administration to openly discriminate against Hispanic American veterans when administering medical and education benefits and to ignore their protests.

Such treatment and the lack of available recourse, either formal or informal, motivated Latino veterans to organize on their own. In March, 1948, more than seven hundred met in the Lamar School Auditorium in Corpus Christi, Texas, to discuss the creation of an organization that would represent their immediate needs as well as their dreams for postwar America. What resulted became known as the American GI Forum. Its first president was Héctor García, a thirty-four-year-old physician who had served as a major in the Army Medical Corps.

The state of Mexican American life in Corpus Christi encapsulated the frustrations and impatience that caused hundreds, and later thousands, of veterans to flock to the American GI Forum. Living conditions could best be described as horrible. As late as 1948, public-health authorities in Nueces County, which encompasses the city and its surrounding area, classified 34 percent of residences as substandard. Mexican American death rates from tuberculosis were twice the state's average. Dysentery caused nearly eight times as many deaths as in the rest of Texas. Latino veterans seeking treatment for themselves and their families through veterans' medical programs were often stymied by VA officials or shunted aside into segregated hospitals.[72] The education of Mexican American residents fared little better. According to a 1944 Texas study, 47 percent of Mexican American students received no schooling at all. For those who did, school districts were commonly segregated, with white schools receiving the lion's share of taxes for books, facilities, and extracurricular activities.[73]

These issues shaped the basic platform of the forum from its creation. What Hispanic veterans demanded was not preferential treatment but the normal rights guaranteed American citizens by law—in other words, the same rights they had fought to preserve during the "good war." Their ultimate objective was direct integration into mainstream society. Wartime service in uniform became the simplest and strongest means toward that end.

The methods that the American GI Forum used to attain these goals were an interesting amalgam of broadly expressed themes devoted to nationalism and patriotism, combined with local organization within the Mexican American community. The forum was quick to stress the widely accepted values represented by its veteran membership. In public functions, speeches, and parades, it made great efforts to display uniforms, decorations, and the American flag as constant reminders of Latino contributions during the war. The need to preserve and, more importantly, advance the cause of democracy was a constant refrain on banners and in the speeches delivered by Héctor García from 1948 onward.[74] The name of the organization itself, the American GI Forum, was a deliberate invocation of the war to sixteen million other citizens who shared the same touchstone. At the same time, this overt stress on Americanism and patriotism insulated the forum from the anti-Communist crusades that attacked any type of dissidence during the McCarthy years and effectively silenced many Latino groups.

In the meantime, the forum devoted substantial efforts to develop leadership in the Spanish-speaking community of Texas. It created "ladies' auxiliary" sections and a "Junior GI Forum" to organize the younger children of veterans. These parts of the organization, particularly in the case of Hispanic American women, were critical to raising money and creating links within the community. The forum enjoyed an important degree of cohesiveness, thanks to the significant contributions of its Latina membership.[75]

Concerted action followed these organizational campaigns. García began to present the VA with specific evidence of its failure to process in a timely manner benefits claims made by Mexican American veterans. He offered well-documented cases of three hundred veterans who had enrolled in school in September, 1947, but had not received tuition and stipend checks until the following January. He presented detailed examples of others who had had their medical pensions cut by the VA despite the fact that it had received statements in support of the claims from treating physicians.[76]

In 1949, a conflict over the interment of a Mexican American soldier's body returned from the Philippines propelled the American GI Forum into national prominence. Felix Longoria was an army private who was killed while serving in the Philippines near the end of World War II. However, when his body was returned home to Three Rivers, Texas, it was placed in a segregated section of the town cemetery. The Three Rivers funeral director refused to allow the Longoria family access to his chapel for fear of provoking local white residents. Armed with this information, Héctor García and the forum membership began an extensive lobbying campaign on behalf of the family as well as the Mexican American residents of South Texas. Cables reached both the state capitol in Austin and the Texas delegation to Congress in Washington. Print journalists from around the state flocked to Three Rivers to solicit statements from both García and other town fathers accused of discrimination. It was Lyndon Johnson who broke the deadlock when he arranged for Longoria's burial in Arlington National Cemetery on February 16, 1949.[77]

From these contests over individual rights in the Corpus Christi area, the forum spread its activities throughout the state to include legal challenges to school and jury segregation. Forum organizers besieged Texas state lawmakers as well as Gov. Beauford Jester's office with demands for redress in the state capital. By 1951, it was able to successfully sponsor the creation of a new Texas antidiscrimination law. Between 1950 and 1960, state authorities would hear nearly one hundred formal complaints regarding educational inequities.[78]

From Texas, these activities spread throughout the Southwest. New Mexico acquired its first forum chapter prior to the Korean War. By 1957, there were additional chapters in thirteen states. Membership was made deliberately simple for those interested in joining. All a prospective member needed was twenty-five cents for the initial fee. Official chapters were composed of the first twenty veterans who registered their names for an official charter. Eventually, by the late fifties, the forum began to penetrate into the Midwest, with chapters forming in Michigan (1956), Illinois (1957), Indiana (1957), and Wisconsin (1958).[79]

The American GI Forum was at the core of Hispanic American community activism after World War II. It was one of the predominant organizations spawned by the Latino "GI generation," a group that also included the Mexican American Serviceman's Association, the Latin American Ladies' Club, and the Mothers of World War II. The forum was central to a series of campaigns dedicated to abolishing legal discrimination in Texas and, after 1949, other states in the union. Over the longer term, its primary contribution was the development of a political constituency that asserted its rights within the framework of the law and was demonstrably willing to hold politicians accountable if they were ignored.[80] In his biography of Lyndon Johnson, Robert Dallek points out that the Texas senator, for all his interest in the issue of civil rights, could also not politically afford to alienate 20 percent of the state's electorate, particularly when it was mobilized around an issue such as Felix Longoria's burial. The 1949 conflict in Three Rivers would establish the GI Forum as an unavoidable actor on the national political stage, one that persists in importance.[81]

In areas outside politics, the forum provided a gathering point for the Hispanic American community, one where cohesiveness could be expressed through support for practical issues like health and education. Perhaps more importantly, the forum also lent a legitimacy to the open discussion of cultural identity, one that could incorporate both the patriotic themes left over from the war and the issues of *la raza* that remained from the "old country." In military service was an enclave for a broader spectrum of social and cultural standards. This open celebration of identity in its old and distinctly Latin American forms set a significant precedent for the next generation of Latino and Latina leaders in the sixties.[82]

Japanese American GIs constituted a tiny component of America's military forces during World War II. Their arrival in the historical narrative is also relatively recent. Yet, by any measure, their history is a study in both national cruelty and individual perseverance that supersedes either quantitative measurement or place in the national timeline.

The early months of the war were extraordinarily hard for Japanese Americans. In the days and weeks following Pearl Harbor, tens of thousands of issei (Japanese-born immigrants) and nisei (their American-born descendants) were the target of open hostility on the part of the general public. In the continental United States, this suspicion and anger translated into a policy of internment. For the remainder of the war, most issei and nisei were forcibly relocated to camps hundreds of miles in the interior of the United States. Segregation, enforced by the U.S. military, became a galling new reality to the isolated pockets of Japanese Americans on the mainland.[83]

The situation was much different on the Hawaiian islands, where, in 1940, people of Japanese descent accounted for 37 percent of the area's population.[84] At the time of the attack on Pearl Harbor, many Japanese American ROTC cadets enrolled at the University of Hawaii were hastily mobilized for local defense. Still others served as members of the National Guard and the newly formed Hawaii Territorial Guard. It was a common and often incongruous sight in the days following the Japanese assault to see nisei service members guarding checkpoints and important installations all around Oahu. When the Japanese attack began, a young Daniel K. Inouye immediately departed for the local Red Cross station, where he served as a volunteer teaching first-aid classes. He did not return home for five days.[85] Despite this unblemished record of service in the midst of the hectic days of December, Japanese Americans were summarily removed from military units stationed in Hawaii in January, 1942.

From that point, when Japanese Americans faced internment on the mainland and segregation on the islands, World War II became an ongoing crusade intended to reestablish their legitimacy in the United States. Prejudice and suspicion were met with concerted efforts to volunteer and participate in war mobilization. In Hawaii, former Japanese American members of the Territorial Guard joined the Varsity Victory Volunteers, a civilian adjunct of the Army Corps of Engineers. For most of 1942, the group served as a labor battalion, providing muscle for backbreaking tasks such as road construction, work in rock quarries, and the creation of barbed-wire obstacles against the expected Japanese invasion. In their rare moments of spare time, the volunteers made three mass donations of blood and purchased $27,850 worth of war bonds. When American pilots who were shot down during Doolittle's raid on Japan were executed, they raised $10,000 and presented it to the army for "Bombs on Tokyo."[86]

Japanese Americans also clamored to be allowed to serve in uniform. When the bombs fell on Pearl Harbor, many were already in active-duty units as conscripts, noncommissioned officers, and officer cadets. In February, 1942, they experienced one of the more bizarre twists of federal policy when the War Department decided to classify all Japanese American males of draft age as 4C (enemy aliens) but kept those already in uniform because of antidiscrimination provisions in the Draft Act of 1940.[87]

Despite this, the Pentagon decided in 1943 to accept nisei volunteers into the U.S. military. Although plans for Japanese American service were modest at best, military officials soon found themselves besieged with volunteers.[88] In his memoirs, Inouye relates the scene when word came from a colonel in charge of ROTC: "As soon as he said that we were now eligible to volunteer, that room exploded into a fury of yells and motion. We went bursting out of there and ran—ran!—the three miles to the draft board, stringing back over the streets and sidewalks, jostling for position, like a bunch of marathoners gone berserk. And the scene was repeated all over Oahu and the other islands. Nearly 1,000 *niseis* volunteered the first day alone, and maybe because I was in better shape than most of them and ran harder, I was among the first 75."[89]

More than thirty-three thousand of these men eventually served in every major theater of operations in the war. Japanese Americans participated in the Pacific campaigns in the Solomon Islands, Saipan, and Iwo Jima, as well as in Burma and China. In Europe, they saw action in Italy, France, and Germany. Some, possessing valuable and rare linguistic skills, served as military specialists. One nisei, for example, landed on Iwo Jima as an interrogator for the 4th Marines. Others went to war as part of complete units, most notably the 100th Infantry Battalion and the 442nd Regimental Combat Team. The latter performed its duties with particular distinction in the mountains of Italy and, later, during the invasion of southern France and Germany. The 442nd's record is remarkable given the fact that it accumulated 9,486 casualties during the war—more than 300 percent of its original strength. Moreover, by the end of the war, the regiment had earned an incredible 18,143 individual decorations, including a Congressional Medal of Honor, 47 Distinguished Service Crosses, and 342 Silver Stars, making it one of the most highly decorated regiments in American military history.[90]

For these men, wartime service was the crucible of their devotion to America. Military service in which acts of heroism were common-place became the ultimate test of loyalty to a nation that had disdained them. This point appears frequently in correspondence to relatives back in the States, some of whom remained interned behind barbed-wire fences for the duration of World War II. One nisei soldier wrote to his family, "if you cut off my arm it will bleed the same as a white man's would." Conrad Tsukayama, who served with the 100th Infantry Battalion, recalled, "We were all Hawaiian at heart. The basic *ohana* spirit came from the Native Hawaiian people, an ethnic group filled with genuine aloha, the magic ingredient that brought together the hearts of all the oppressed immigrants' sons. We carried this spirit of the 100th even more intensely after Pearl Harbor because we had been singled out as 'Japs.' In a society in which all minorities struggled to gain acceptance, we were determined to prove to the world that we were indeed loyal Americans."[91]

As the war record of the 442nd and individual nisei soldiers became part of the public record, the debate at home over Japanese Americans began to change. Their treatment in the public domain grew more positive. Stories recording the bravery of Japanese American soldiers appeared in *Time, Life, Collier's,* and the *Saturday Evening Post* and ex-tolled the virtues of the nisei soldier fighting for democracy. When the 442nd returned home, President Truman greeted the newly arrived regiment in an official ceremony at the White House on July 15, 1945, only days before he traveled to the Potsdam conference to meet with Stalin and British prime minister Clement Atlee.

A great deal of this acclaim was genuine, a reflection of the truly heroic nature of the Japanese Americans' performance in battle. A portion of it, however, was also the product of calculation and efforts by the Office of War Information to demonstrate the truly democratic nature of the war. Highlighting the niseis' performance in this context became part of a deliberate campaign to illustrate "antiracism" in the contemporary United States.[92] For many veterans, the lack of sincerity of this campaign undercut much of the genuine support they received from the public.

The same muddled message persisted as Japanese American veterans made their way home after the war. Some Americans expressed an earnest desire to see them receive fair treatment. Former officers of the 442nd, most of them the original white leadership that served in the regiment, made public appearances up and down the West Coast to applaud the war records of nisei veterans. Testimonials were also made by Secretary of the Interior Harold Ickes, by Lt. Gen. Mark Clark, commander of the U.S. 5th Army in Italy, and by Gen. Joseph Stilwell, who saw service with Japanese Americans in the Pacific war. The objective of these efforts was to pave the way for not only veterans but also all of the interned Japanese to return home after the war. To this end, and not without a little irony, the nisei veteran became a symbol for agencies like the War Relocation Authority to reverse years of propaganda directed against Japan.[93]

Public acceptance of returning Japanese, veterans or otherwise, was mixed at best and a problematic exercise in general. Even before the war, the nisei and issei Japanese occupied a social place in America that put them in what one historian calls a "twilight zone" between the white majority and other, longer established minorities. While many achieved comparatively high levels of education and employment, for example, this did not automatically confer greater social status. On the other hand, the disdain of the majority white culture also did not automatically win acceptance of Japanese Americans into African American and Latino cultural niches. It was not for want of trying, however. Perhaps the most notable characteristic of Japanese American resettlement after the war was the deliberate effort on the part of the War Relocation Authority, private charities, and the nisei themselves to attempt integration in individual communities all around the United States rather than the reconstruction of their prewar social enclaves on the West Coast.[94]

For their own part, Japanese American veterans felt the same sense of restlessness that affected millions of their former comrades in arms. Fresh out of the army, Katsugo Miho observed that coming home was like "learning to walk again."[95] Like their nisei and issei compatriots who remained behind in the States, a significant number of Japanese American veterans expressed little desire to return to the old places or standards of living. Many had no interest in returning to farming on either the plantations of Hawaii or the truck farms of California, Oregon, and Washington state.

This generation was also prepared to challenge constraints other than geography or employment. For the nisei, an important dilemma was how best to bridge the gap between their parents' generation and mainstream American culture. At points, this problem involved friction over relatively small issues of language, dress, and behavior. In others, the desire for assimilation created enormous conflict over long-established practices. The institution of marriage was one. In Hawaii, by the second year of the war, one in five nisei brides married a non-Japanese. One in ten married a Caucasian.[96]

As these delicate and complicated issues were addressed, daunting problems confronted Japanese American veterans immediately upon their arrival home. Unlike the other minority groups prevalent in the United States during World War II, the Japanese saw their material possessions systematically confiscated by the federal government. Millions of dollars of business property, residences, agricultural land, and equipment were never recovered by their original owners. Conservative estimates place the total amount at $400 million.[97] The final disposition of 28.8 million pounds of personal property kept in storage by the federal government for the duration of the war presented returning veterans with a bureaucratic nightmare. A 1946 War Relocation Authority publication recorded only a small portion of the items that required the attention of those interned: "Much of the routine work consisted of advice and correspondence on insurance matters and in the preparation of income tax returns, reports of assets and applications for special licenses under foreign funds' control regulation, claims of evacuee depositors against Japanese-controlled banks being liquidated by the government, applications by citizens for the return of property surrendered under alien enemy control proclamations, and various types of legal instruments, including powers of attorney, leases, bills of sale, deeds, mortgages, wills, affidavits, and depositions."[98]

Added to this thicket were claims made by former real-estate agents, insurance brokers, and other professionals to regain their licenses, local businesspeople and farmers who faced boycotts from local communities disgruntled about the prospect of the Japanese Americans' return, unpaid back taxes, and defunct mortgages. One state refused to grant sales-tax permits without special army and navy clearance.

Accompanying these burdens were the widespread housing shortages and rampant inflation that dominated postwar American life.[99]

As they searched for a new place in this America, nisei veterans and their families settled into a pattern that ran contrary to that seen in the remainder of the country. In Hawaii, they spread farther outside the Japanese community. On the mainland, they headed east, drawn by the relatively high demand for work in the Midwestern states and along the Atlantic seaboard. According to the 1950 census, California suffered a net loss of issei and nisei Japanese, while their numbers in these other regions grew. Only in Hawaii did residency retain any degree of its prewar stability.[100]

In some cases, private organizations such as the West Coast Committee on Fair Play attempted to help in the resettlement process. However, for the most part, Japanese American veterans were left to their own devices.[101] As was the case with most other veterans, the GI Bill served as an important vehicle for furthering the niseis' upward economic mobility. In turn, federally subsidized training benefited from the fact that, as late as 1940, the educational level achieved by nisei children was higher than the national average. Taken together, the extensive benefits created by the GI Bill and a cultural ethic that embraced learning were a formidable combination for nisei progress after the war.[102]

In the late forties, subsequent Japanese American participation in the U.S. workforce changed significantly. In part, this was because, as Jere Takahashi has observed, there was no option to take over the "family store" after the war. The massive loss of property after 1942 compelled thousands of issei and nisei Japanese to seek alternatives. For some, this meant staying within the confines of farm labor, where nearly one-fifth (17.1 percent) remained employed as late as 1950. Even in this vocation, boycotts and local hostility mandated a shift in new niche markets. In California, for example, many nisei farmers who had been shut out of the produce industry opened flower farms and nurseries.[103] However, progress in other areas appeared by the outbreak of the Korean War. According to census data, the number of Japanese Americans employed in professional and technical jobs doubled from 3.2 percent to 6.7 percent between 1940 and 1950. The number of those employed in clerical and sales work also increased, from 11.0 percent to 15.2 percent.[104]

Even when armed with these important successes, many Japanese

American veterans found assimilation to be a difficult process, strewn with persistent ignorance and bigotry. In Los Angeles, nisei veterans who attempted to buy homes found, because of restrictive real-estate covenants, that property was available only in slum areas that were ineligible for either VA or private mortgages.[105] The experience of George Otsuka, a veteran of the 442nd who settled in Texas after the war, speaks volumes. Otsuka had participated in the famous mission to rescue a cut-off unit of the Texas National Guard in France—the so-called Lost Battalion—in 1944. However, when he returned to the United States and attempted to buy a farm in his new home state, he was rebuffed by local lenders. Otsuka complained to the *Houston Press* in August, 1946: "What I would like to know is[, is] this our answer for rescuing the 'Lost Battalion' of your proud 36th Division in the Vosges Mountains in France? Is that your answer for the terrific casualty [*sic*] we suffered to rescue those men of the 36th?"[106]

Returned Japanese American soldier Richard Setsuda, a businessman before the war, was advised by a U.S. Employment Office in Seattle to immediately apply for unemployment benefits upon returning home because their were no jobs for niseis.[107] The experience of Mitsuo Usui on a Los Angeles bus illustrates the ambivalence that sometimes greeted Japanese veterans upon their return to the States: "Coming home, I was boarding a bus on Olympic Boulevard. A lady, sitting in the front row of the bus, saw me and said, 'Damn Jap.' Here I was, a proud American soldier, just coming back with my new uniform and paratrooper boots, with all my campaign medals and awards, proudly displayed on my chest, and this? The bus driver, upon hearing this remark, stopped the bus and said, 'Lady, apologize to this American soldier or get off my bus.'" She got off the bus. Embarrassed by the situation, I turned around to thank the bus driver. He said, 'That's okay, buddy. Everything is going to be okay from now on out.' Encouraged by his comment, I thanked him, and as I was turning away, I noticed a discharge pin on his lapel."[108]

As for African American and Latino veterans facing the same obstacles, Japanese American veterans organized to protect themselves and promote their rights. Even before the U.S.S. *Waterbury Victory* returned the bulk of the 442nd veterans home to Hawaii in August, 1946, for final demobilization, veterans' groups associated with nisei service began springing up all around America. In Honolulu, the 442nd Veterans Club was created on February 7, 1946. One month later, the Nisei Veterans Committee held its first meeting in Seattle. On February 7, 1947, Yoshizo Harada became the first commander of the all-nisei VFW Post 8995 in Sacramento, California. The Veterans of Foreign Wars recognized other nisei posts in San Francisco and Los Angeles, while their American Foreign Legion counterparts appeared in Denver and Detroit. Additional nisei veterans' clubs were organized in Portland, Oregon; Chicago; Cleveland; and Minneapolis. Besides serving as a fraternal meeting place for returning Japanese Americans, these groups became heavily invested in local charities.

The Nisei Veterans Committee sponsored youth baseball, basketball, and football leagues with the express purpose of integrating their children with others from the white and African American portions of the community. The same intent appeared in blood drives, scholarship competitions, and camping outings. As part of its tenth-anniversary reunion, the 442nd Veterans Club invited Earl Melvin Finch, a Mississippi resident who had reached out to the unit during its stateside training in 1943 for a tribute and keynote address. Overall, these activities served two important and overlapping functions. In one sense, they continued efforts to integrate the Japanese American into the larger American social structure. Concurrently, they also created a public face for Japanese American service that was now extending beyond the war and into peacetime normalcy.[109]

For the returning nisei soldier, the Japanese American Citizens League (JACL) became a focal point for nisei and issei advocacy after the war. Originally founded in 1930, the JACL had tested the constitutionality of internment for the duration of World War II. After 1945, it involved itself more in the problems of racial discrimination. One of its first actions was the formation of the Anti-Discrimination Committee (ADC) to directly address many of the inequities that had begun to appear in peacetime America. As the forties moved forward, both the JACL and the ADC lobbied lawmakers at the state and federal levels on issues such as property reclamation, the naturalization of issei Japanese, and the problem of social equality that still plagued members of the Japanese American community. The JACL's primary lobbyist in its Washington, D.C., office was Mike Masaoka, a veteran of the 442nd Regimental Combat Team. In testimony before Congress in 1951, Masaoka spoke not only for Japanese Americans but also for many other minority veterans: "I think that we persons of Japanese ancestry who served in the army, both in the Pacific and in Europe, did so because we had faith in the long-time and ultimate triumph of fair play and justice in the American way, and so we saw beyond the watchtowers of our concentration camps and we saw the kind of America that we have got to have, and we saw the kind of world that we have got to have. And so, the sacrifices of the men who died was [*sic*] not in vain, and I think our record is pretty well known. No other unit in American military history, for its size and length of combat, won as many decorations or suffered as many casualties."[110]

Like their counterparts in the NAACP and the American GI Forum, veterans in the JACL and the ADC pursued recourse via legal means, battling through the court systems for their inclusion into mainstream American society. This strategy succeeded in repealing a California law that banned Japanese fishing rights and resulted in awards made in some evacuation claims against the state. The ADC and JACL were also successful in shaping the McCarran-Walter Immigration Act (1952) that granted issei Japanese the right to be naturalized citizens.[111]

In the end, most Japanese American veterans left the service proud of their country and determined to continue their contribution to public affairs, an attitude they shared with African American and Latino service members. However, of these three groups, their experience was distinct. Where World War II opened doors for groups traditionally disenfranchised by American law and American social mores, for niseis the conflict created daunting obstacles. No other minority bore the force of such a concentrated campaign to isolate them from the social and legal mainstream.[112] The tenacity with which they combated these barriers, both on the home front and on the battlefield, became a testament to human endurance and the indomitable will to prevail.

The postwar life of Daniel K. Inouye defines this journey. Badly wounded toward the end of the war, Inouye spent twenty months recuperating in military hospitals before finally being discharged in 1947. Utilizing his GI Bill benefits, he graduated from the University of Hawaii in 1950 and the George Washington University Law School in 1952. After serving for a year as deputy public prosecutor in Honolulu, Inouye next turned his sights on local politics. It took some convincing, considering the fact that Republicans had had a hammerlock on Hawaiian politics for most of the century. However, it was a friend, Dan Aoki, a former 442nd first sergeant and president of the veterans' club, who framed the issue in the blunt language of a soldier and convinced Inouye to run: "You've got the right combination—a war hero, a fresh face. If we want the vets to come into the Democratic party, we've got to give them somebody they care about, one of their own. You." He was followed by other former 442nd and 100th Battalion soldiers such as "Spark" Matsunaga and Masato Doi, veterans who had the same credentials for an increasingly influential constituency.[113]

In 1954, Inouye won his first election to the Hawaiian Territorial House of Representatives. It was a victory that served as a stepping-stone for future triumphs in the fifties. When Hawaii was granted statehood in 1959, Inouye became its first congressperson. In 1962, he moved on to the U.S. Senate, where he has remained a living example for his generation and those who have followed.

World War II did a great deal to break apart the enormous racial barriers that separated the various components of American society. Historians have reflected at length on the impact of the war on the American South when it brought together the overlapping and sometimes conflicting issues of patriotism and citizenship. In one important sense, the war pulled this isolated part of the country back into the American mainstream. Mobilization for a truly national effort returned the South to the core of the United States as millions of Northerners were sent to the massive military training facilities located there and with the additional millions of civilians who arrived in the region in search of wartime employment. As James Patterson, David Kennedy, and other historians have noted, parochial, small-town America began to melt away in the process. In the most segregated part of the nation, efforts to be "both American and Southern" began to fade into the past.[114]

Even when it clung to tradition, the South opened the door for cultural change. Time spent in uniform was, and has always been, a deeply revered tradition, in many ways the ideal illustration of Southern virtue. World War II served, in a very important way, to reinforce this regional attitude regarding conflict and military service. A 1941 Gallup poll notes that 88 percent of Southerners believed the defeat of Germany to be more important than American neutrality, the highest figure for any place in the United States. Once the demand for volunteers began, Southern states responded with a single-minded purpose.

In Alabama, more than one-third of the adult male population served in uniform during the war.[115]

Once they became part of this standard, minority veterans entered a very distinctive circle in Southern society. Military service invested them with a great historical tradition. The sheer numbers of minorities made this service too large to dismiss. Approximately 24 percent of Alabama's veterans were African American, and similar numbers occurred in Georgia (21.5 percent), Florida (22.7 percent), and Louisiana (27.6 percent). Nearly four in ten of Mississippi's veterans (38.5 percent) were black.[116]

As time passed, it became apparent that the debate over the minority contribution to civil society was not limited to the southern region of the United States. The refusal of minority veterans' groups to be treated separately from the *national* mainstream of America and their constant demand for recognition for the universal service performed by all citizens in the war were deliberate efforts to finally pry open a door that military service had first breached. This desire stood at the heart of the NAACP's "Double V" campaign and the integrationist programs promoted by the American GI Forum and the various nisei organizations that appeared after 1945. All of them were built upon a basic sentiment articulated by American Legion commander George N. Craig in May, 1950: "We who knew hardship and danger, together learned that in the final showdown, it is not a man's color, place of birth or church affiliation that counts, but only his personal merit and courage. We learned that it was not an American's name or origin that told the story but his human quality."[117] In crafting the concept of national citizenship and the ongoing perfection of American democracy, these veterans sought a means to place minorities into mainstream white society.[118] To this end, they argued, military service—and the ultimate sacrifice it entailed—settled any lingering questions about the civil legitimacy of the minority groups themselves.

As they built this case, military service also allowed minority veterans to advocate ideas that were both conservative and progressive. Throughout the late forties, whether the groups originated from an African American, Latino, or nisei membership, a common emphasis was placed, on the one hand, on family, religion, and patriotism, while the issues of educational equity, voting rights, and civil rights entered into the discussion at the same time. Veterans' status established both the desire and the ability to pursue the rights of citizenship. Henry A. J.

Ramos, an author who has dealt with the Latino history of the postwar years, refers to the impact World War II had on Mexican Americans but does so in terms that could be applied to all minority veterans: "It made them conscious that as citizens of the U.S. who had proved their loyalty and valor in the defense of American principles, they could and should fight to exercise all of their rights to nationality and citizenship which until now had been denied."[119]

A consistent theme in contemporary newspapers and periodicals was the issue of simple, fair treatment. Whether the story was published by the *Chicago Defender* or the *Pacific Citizen,* the emphasis remained on the contradiction of dedicated, patriotic service to the country and the absence of real civil rights.[120] Minority veterans' organizations took the concepts of social stability and national security embedded in World War II and extended them into more elaborate social rights. The constitution of the American GI Forum, for example, refers to both the rights granted to veterans by the GI Bill and the larger rights they expected to enjoy as equal members of civil society.[121]

Working in tandem, conservative and liberal agendas reinforced the status of minority veterans at the national level. Public-service projects developed into major enterprises for all veterans' groups, whether they were the work of large organizations such as the American Foreign Legion or smaller local and regional institutions that represented minority service members. Toy drives at Christmas, sponsorship of the March of Dimes and the Boy Scouts of America, and blood drives all became common devices by which these groups could demonstrate their ongoing contribution to the greater good. Meanwhile, these services created breathing space for minority veterans to segue toward more controversial initiatives such as improvements in public education, antidiscrimination law, and, finally, desegregation. All were portrayed as extensions of the conservative definition of citizenship they had defended during the war, when they collectively served the larger social good.[122] By crafting such a rhetorical and practical vehicle for their reform efforts, minority veterans' groups were able to sidestep much of the reactionary pressures of the postwar era, whether these were composed of McCarthyite forces in Washington or Southern segregationists.

Judging the final extent to which minority veterans advanced in American society is a problematic proposition. Clearly, in terms of the law, their status has changed for the better. The GI Bill was ground-breaking to the extent that it addressed universal rights with regard to service and without regard to race or ethnicity. Moreover, with each advance registered by minority veterans' groups in local, state, and federal courtrooms, integration into American social and economic life has grown. In terms of politics and public policy, the trend seems to reflect the growing clout of a well-organized and disciplined part of the polity. This has translated into the direct electoral representation of old unrecognized constituencies, as was the case with Daniel Inouye, and the emerging recognition by established politicians such as Lyndon Johnson that they could ignore an important bloc of votes only at a substantial cost to their future careers. Economically, it appeared that the future of minority veterans would be an improvement over that of their parents. Combined with the postwar boom, the additional training and education offered by federal law created unprecedented opportunities for upward economic and social mobility.

However, many barriers remained to claim their time and frustrate their progress. In too many cases, enforcement of the GI Bill was spotty at best. Greater representation at more levels of government did not overcome the biases reinforced by majority rule. Economic progress occurred more unevenly for some minority veterans, particularly African Americans and Latinos, than others. Perhaps most importantly, social barriers to change remained the least tangible, but the most resistant, obstacles to final integration into the national mainstream.

One thing that is clear is that all of the energy, hope, and work invested by this part of the GI generation set important social, political, and legal precedents that were a springboard for the next generation of American minorities. Minority veterans not only redefined their own basic rights within the United States but also re-created the boundaries of tolerance in the country as a whole. To a large extent, what would become possible for a more controversial time and a generation in the sixties and afterward was the product of the foundation they built.

CHAPTER 6   *The Veteran and the*
                   Postwar Film

Tell me I have led a good life. Tell me I'm a good man.
                   —*James Ryan,* Saving Private Ryan

War has always been an excellent topic for the movies. It is epic in scope, violent by nature, and, in many cases, the perfect context to resolve the moral conflict between good and evil. War is a life-and-death struggle that captures the ultimate level of human drama, overshadowing the normal spectrum of emotions while elevating them at the same time. War takes hate and gives it a sharper edge. War takes love and imbues it with a greater urgency. By highlighting the visceral elements present at the core of any one person, the war film has been uniquely able to connect with movie audiences.

An additional ingredient of the success of war films has been their ability to move beyond emotion to mirror the rational elements of contemporary conventional wisdom. *All Quiet on the Western Front* (1930), for example, captures the broadly held cynicism regarding war after 1918. *Failsafe* (1964) reflects the Cold War anxieties that were apparent in the wake of the Cuban missile crisis. In the eighties, the *Rambo* series was popular for its unrepentant glorification of the soldier-as-hero at a time when Ronald Reagan began his reconstruction of American nationalism. In each case, the war film has placed history at the service of the present, reshaping the past to fit the standards, biases, and expectations of the current day.

In more recent times, the film industry in general and war films in particular have increasingly displaced conventional historical scholarship as a primary means to inform the general public about the past.[1] The movies offer modern audiences a shortcut in an era that is characterized by its impatience with detail and enamored of imagery over substance. Many are the anecdotes offered by teachers who cite films rather than books to draw a connection with modern students. As the written word has declined, dependence on visual media has grown and, with this trend, the relative influence of the film as part of present-day discussions of history.[2]

Steven Spielberg's *Saving Private Ryan* illustrates each of these trends. Reviewers writing in 1998 devoted considerable attention to *Private Ryan* for its "realism," specifically Spielberg's re-creation of the landings at Omaha Beach. The depiction of death and the wounds suffered by the troops landing in the first wave is extremely graphic and unprecedented in its violence. Great efforts were made to emphasize an almost documentary-like approach to the opening scenes. Cinematographer Janusz Kaminski painstakingly crafted a visual atmosphere of pitched combat in part by stripping off the lens coatings of modern cameras to reinforce the feel of the technology that was available in the forties. The results are devastating, almost overloading viewers' senses with the shock of the action they are witnessing. The dominant topic surrounding the discussion of *Private Ryan,* almost completely overshadowing its main plot, is the film's shattering depiction of violence, a quality that both veterans of the Normandy landings and modern audiences have found jarring. In this respect, Spielberg's work set the standard for the war film in the late nineties, one that continued in *Black Hawk Down* (2001) and *Windtalkers* (2002).[3]

Much has also been made of Spielberg's interpretation of the Second World War in *Saving Private Ryan*. For some reviewers, the film is a thinly veiled effort to refight Vietnam in the guise of an earlier conflict. There is some justification for this view. Moral ambiguity appears everywhere in the movie. Surrendering German troops are gunned down by army rangers on Omaha Beach. Acts of humanity are sometimes punished by tragedy. Private Caparzo (Vin Diesel) dies after attempting to save the life of a French child. Tom Hanks's Captain Miller is killed by the same SS trooper he spares earlier in the film. In many respects, the moral clarity that one might expect in a retro film such as *Saving Private Ryan* is simply not present.[4]

With regard to war in general, Spielberg also represents an interesting facet of the baby-boomer generation. Notable in the commentary that followed the movie was the use of World War II as a surrogate for a generation that did not possess its own honorable cause. In 2002, one writer noted that the "historical legacy of the boomers was not to be a new Camelot, of which they'd dreamed since their youth, but the Lewinsky White House."[5] *Saving Private Ryan*'s open veneration of the World War II generation has become, according to this school of thought, a way for their children to compensate for lives spent in relative comfort and without a compelling cause to rally around.

Interestingly, *Saving Private Ryan* has had a noticeable impact on the public's enthusiasm for history, particularly topics devoted to the Second World War. After the film's release, Tom Hanks, the movie's leading actor, became a major advocate of and fundraiser for a $100-million World War II memorial on the Washington Mall. Although the memorial was controversial, it placed the discussion of history and remembrance into the national news cycle for months. Sales of histories of the war, always popular in the mass market, boomed in concert with the public's newfound fascination with World War II. Tom Brokaw's *The Greatest Generation* occupied bestseller lists for lengthy periods of time, as did its sequel, *An Album of Memories*. Stephen E. Ambrose's more traditional histories, *Citizen Soldiers, Band of Brothers*, and *The Victors* became staples in the large bookstore chains and remain so to this day. This story came full circle in 2001, when Tom Hanks, in partnership with Stephen Spielberg, produced the award-winning HBO series *Band of Brothers*.

Yet, for all its devotion to both modern technology and modern topics, *Private Ryan* is dependent for much of its content on a past age of war films, one more representative of the late forties than the late nineties. One writer, Richard T. Jameson, remarks in *Film Commentary* that *Private Ryan* has "succeeded in restoring WWII and its decade to the continuum of the American experience."[6] Absent from the film is much of the overt cynicism and political commentary apparent in the post–Vietnam War films of the seventies.[7] Gone too is the muscle-bound nationalism that Sylvester Stallone's *Rambo* series attached to the genre in the eighties. In their place is *Private Ryan,* which is, to a significant extent, a throwback that utilizes conventions familiar from the war movies of the forties. The army ranger unit, with its broad band of ethnicities (an Italian, a Jew, a Southerner, and an unrepentant Brooklynite) and its unsentimental, stoic, apolitical leadership, embodied in Tom Hanks's Captain Miller, mirrors comparable collections of men who populated the screen during the Second World War. The same group followed Dana Andrews in *A Walk in the Sun* (1946).

In the forties, John Garfield made a career as the same Everyman as Hanks's Miller. That American audiences have accepted these characters is perhaps more a commentary on the moviegoers themselves than on the films. By 1998, the controversy that surrounded Vietnam had diminished, muted by the passage of time and changing national demographics that marked the arrival of a new generation born after the conflict in Southeast Asia, the changing priorities and perspectives of its "boomer" predecessors, and the passing from society—and subsequent veneration—of those who had fought the Second World War. *Private Ryan* offers this audience a "degree of conventionality that contemporary Americans identified with the topic of war."[8] Later movies have emulated this approach. One reviewer characterizes as "Pure John Ford" Ridley Scott's approach to the nature of the American soldier in *Black Hawk Down,* which he describes as "sons who did not dream well but fought well."[9]

What begs further examination is the exact nature of the model created by the war films of the forties. How were they able to connect with their audience? A cursory glance at the better-known pictures of the war years conjures up titles such as *The Fighting Seabees* (1944) and *Back to Bataan* (1945). After the war was won, the movie industry moved beyond some of the more simpleminded exercises in patriotic propaganda. Hollywood was forced to consider the substance of its product once millions of veterans returned home and began to fill seats in movie theaters. Did this new audience influence the methods of making war movies as well as their subjects?[10] Was this new public more sophisticated in its understanding of war and its representation on film?[11]

One of the most important film topics of the immediate postwar years was the veterans' homecoming. The issue dominated public debate in late 1945. Observing the American people in the aftermath of victory, Edward R. Murrow commented that peace had been accompanied by public fear about the immediate future.[12] The overt hostility between the United States and the Soviet Union that marked the beginning of the Cold War prevented any real sense of relief that warfare had actually concluded. Instead, atomic deterrence loomed over nearly every aspect of American life. As Paul Boyer notes in *By the Bombs' Early Light,* the surreal prospect of extinction accompanied the jubilant celebrations of 1945.[13]

Economic conditions reinforced this sense of anxiety. In the late summer of 1945, Americans worried that another Great Depression was around the corner. Their concerns were not based upon idle speculation. Faced with the cancellation of billions of dollars in War Department orders, American industry responded by drastically reducing production. Mass layoffs followed.[14]

Social uncertainty further compounded this situation. One explicit dilemma faced by contemporary Americans was the impact the war had wrought regarding gender roles and sexuality. Wartime mobilization had essentially dismantled older, prewar conventions that determined work and behavior. In 1939, 86 percent of respondents to a Gallup poll answered "no" when asked whether married women should enter the workforce. Three years later, that number had declined to 13 percent.[15] Throughout the country, women appeared in previously restricted areas of the industrial and service sectors. Accompanying these changes was the concurrent disruption of the American family, which had been provoked by the absence of millions of fathers lost to the draft and millions of mothers entering the workplace. Rearing a generation of children without a complete household became a widespread problem. So too did maintaining the institution of marriage itself.[16] Sexual promiscuity by American troops stationed throughout the world was commonplace during the war, as was an alarming increase in venereal disease. Meanwhile, the term "war widow" took on new meaning as women entered into liaisons with men while their husbands were overseas. Divorce rates immediately after the war and throughout the remainder of the decade were consistent with the times. The number of Americans who married and divorced increased from 31 percent between 1928 and 1931 to 40 percent between 1948 and 1950.[17]

Very little of the Hollywood film industry escaped these trends. Among the leading men culled from the ranks of returning veterans were Van Heflin, Clark Gable, Mickey Rooney, Robert Taylor, Jimmy Stewart, and Robert Montgomery. Directors Frank Capra and John Huston had both served by making films for the War Department. So too had thousands of screenwriters, camera operators, set designers, and others who worked behind the scenes. Many, like Jimmy Stewart, had seen actual combat. In January, 1946, one writer commented that "Some wartime sobriety clings to the movie colony [Hollywood] even now that the war is well over."[18]

Films reflect this newfound sobriety. The period after 1945 saw the emergence of the so-called problem movie. These are the pictures that chronicle the social difficulties that were present everywhere in the country. Some are relatively benign in character, focusing on the housing shortage and inflation. Others, works that contemplate racial discrimination, marital infidelity, and anti-Semitism, represent a much darker side of American society.[19] Overall, the popularity of these movies was a boon to Hollywood's bottom line. The year 1946 saw the film industry gross $1.7 billion.[20]

The veterans' homecoming was a problem of particular interest. Many films focus on the veteran who is coping with a physical or emotional disability caused by the war. One of the earliest entries in this category, *I'll Be Seeing You,* was released on Christmas Eve of 1944. In it, a young marine veteran of Guadalcanal, who is plagued by physical injuries and a psychiatric disorder, comes home. Other subsequent films follow the same theme. At an early point in *Pride of the Marines* (1945), the wounded in a navy hospital look to their futures with unrepressed cynicism. One states plainly, "I'll tell you guys something funny. I'm scared. I wasn't half as scared on the Canal [Guadalcanal]. If a man came along—anybody—and told me I'd have a decent job the rest of my life, I'd get down on my knees and wash his feet."[21] In *Till the End of Time* (1946), the character Terry Kincheloe has had both legs amputated but refuses to wear his prosthetics or leave his old room in his parents' house upon returning from a military hospital. Another veteran in Kinchloe's ward, physically untouched by combat, nevertheless carries the burden of the war within him: "Okay, I'm back from the war. I'm lucky. I've got two arms, two legs, and two eyes, right? Nine out of ten of the fellows coming home are going to be in the same shape: normal. Then what's burning me up? I'm edgy. I feel out of things. You know why? Because I've been scrounged. I'm robbed out of three and a half years. Somebody stole my time."[22]

The most profound homecoming movie of the period is *The Best Years of Our Lives.* Topping a list of popular and notable films in 1946 that also includes *Henry V,* the film revolves around the return of three servicemen: a pilot (Dana Andrews), a soldier (Frederic March), and a sailor (Harold Russell). Each man, it is made clear, is anxious to return home to the sense of normality that he had craved throughout his overseas deployment. Each one, as it quickly becomes apparent, will face a difficult adjustment to the new America that awaits him. The three veterans discover that they have changed even more than their much-dreamt-about hometown. March returns to his position in the local bank and is dismayed to find his fellow employees fixated on their pursuit of the postwar boom. The honor he had witnessed in the infantry seems sadly missing. At home, his children have grown up and are no longer dependent on his advice or his authority.[23] Andrews, a decorated pilot, is haunted by his memories of the war. Unskilled in civilian work, he is forced to return to his old job as a soda jerk in the town's pharmacy. In the meantime, he watches his marriage, made in haste early in the war, crumble. His nightmares of past air missions and waking flashbacks to the times spent in the nose of a heavy bomber reveal a young man deeply disturbed by the war and his role in it.

The most compelling character in *The Best Years of Our Lives*, however, is played by Harold Russell. As the young sailor Homer, he represents the veteran who has lost the most during the war. In what is one of the most heartbreaking scenes of the movie, Homer returns home, and his family and fiancée witness for the first time the grievous wounds that cost him both of his hands. Russell's Homer captures both the mental and physical obstacles that awaited veterans and, although matched with the formidable March and the popular Andrews, is the most powerful figure in the entire film.

The choice made by Samuel Goldwyn to cast Russell in the *Best Years of Our Lives* was an important risk that propelled the film from mediocrity to greatness. Russell was an army veteran who had lost both hands in a training accident at Camp Mackall, North Carolina, during the war. His appearance in an army training film initially attracted Goldwyn not only because of Russell's earnestness but also because of the credibility he would lend a project that was attempting to convey the troubles faced by veterans after the war.[24] Russell's Homer is the focal point of the movie. He embodies the ambivalent status of the veteran as both a victim of and a threat to society. The vivid depiction of his wounds, a shocking image even for modern audiences, immediately separates Homer from the rest of the characters. More important, however, is the undercurrent of anger and awkwardness that is constantly present in the early parts of the film. Homer's dread of returning home and his desire to abandon his girl and his family for the company of other veterans mark him as a badly damaged person under the skin, a man who is unsure of and perhaps even apathetic about his future role in society. *The Best Years of Our Lives* largely sidesteps these larger problems with a conventional ending. Homer's fiancée, Wilma, is able to win Homer back from his doubts. Their marriage essentially solves the question of his future.[25] Even so, the first two-thirds of the film leaves behind a powerful afterimage.

American critics and audiences applauded *The Best Years of Our Lives* for its artistic value and its realism. It earned the New York Film Critics' Award for best film of 1946 and swept the Oscars that year, winning awards for best picture, director, actor, supporting actor, screenplay, and score. The new head of the Veterans' Administration, Omar Bradley, personally thanked Samuel Goldwyn for producing the film and had it shown to federal workers to "help them realize what these veterans mean to the people of this country."[26] Harold Russell's Oscar for best supporting actor is perhaps the best measure of the film's ability to capture its audience. Russell, a former paratrooper, had no acting experience whatsoever when the movie was shot. He was chosen nonetheless because he embodies the purest means by which *The Best Years of Ours Lives* builds a bridge between itself and the viewers, by allowing art to imitate life. One editorial writer commented in 1947 that Russell "revealed, as none but a crippled veteran could have done, the spiritual agonies and possible triumphs of the mutilated."[27] His casting—and the risk it implied—were not lost on contemporary observers, who lauded Goldwyn for his efforts to depart from the film industry's more predictable artistic standards.[28]

On a much broader level, *The Best Years of Our Lives* also touches a nerve with regard to the ambivalence that millions of veterans felt toward the country upon their return home. Their remembrance of America had sustained them during the war. In the postwar years, it stifled them.[29] Could they achieve what one author has recently described as "the hurtful and ruthless relegation of those brave deeds to a private past?"[30] Could they successfully make the leap that Dana Andrews's character makes near the conclusion of the movie, in the nose of the junked bomber, and leave both the war and home behind?

This dilemma occupied a generation for years. Artistically, the broad social and economic problems following the war also provided the foundation for a new genre of filmmaking that appeared in American cinema during the late forties—a method that became known as film noir.

Film noir, according to one recent history of Hollywood, is "a disturbing world—a world of treachery, entrapment, mistaken identity, psychopathology, greed, lust, betrayal, and finally murder. Dimly lit, set in nightmarish locations, these films featured a cast of amoral or corrupt characters: drifters, patsies, cold-blooded femme fatales, and sinister widows."[31] It is a reflection of a distinct postwar movie genre in which dramatic content shifts from outside events to the inner tensions that permeated postwar America.[32] Film noir flourished at a time when moral absolutes were becoming increasingly difficult to identify or sustain. The genre was also highly popular with postwar audiences because, to a great extent, its subjects reflect events that were familiar at the time. Moreover, because it bolstered declining box-office receipts, it was equally popular with the major movie studios.[33]

The catalyst of the environment depicted in film noir was World War II. As one author describes it, America's postwar urban culture "developed at hothouse speed, with all the attendant hothouse permutations, glorious, freakish, stunted, and delirious."[34] Crime was an important yardstick by which to measure this new milieu. Although most major crimes declined during the war, with murders dropping significantly from 8,329 in 1940 to 6,675 in 1944, the country itself grew more accustomed to operating at the periphery of the law.[35] By 1945, Americans were used to dodging wartime regulations in many small ways, from black-market purchases to tax evasion.[36] Public discontent with sometimes heavy-handed government regulations, embodied in disdain for agencies such as the Office of Price Administration, often transformed the black marketeer into a folk hero.[37]

Once the war was over, crime rates rose alarmingly for the remainder of the decade. Crimes against both people and property rapidly escalated throughout the forties. Between 1945 and 1950, burglary, larceny, aggravated assault, and robbery all saw double-digit increases.[38] To many people, these years fulfilled the dire predictions made by pundits like Willard Waller, who claimed that service experience would prepare veterans for crime. Citing statistics from the post–Civil War period, Waller predicted a veteran-led crime wave.[39]

This event did not materialize in the forties. However, the perception that veterans could easily be associated with the criminal element lingered in the popular imagination. Traditionally, the criminal has always been cited as the polar opposite of the good citizen. By definition, many of the attributes adopted by lawbreakers are antisocial. Their treatment of the rule of law, life, and property all represent a rejection of conventional norms.

Disturbingly consistent in this comparison are the distinctions one might make between the civilian and the veteran. In order to become effective as combatants, veterans were required to selectively abandon the moral and legal constraints that had guided their lives before the service. Military service cultivated youth, aggression, and intolerance, hardly attributes of the social order. At worst, military service meant picking up a weapon to take a human life. At the very least, it involved disposing of the basic elements of life that made it stable and civil. The unanswered question that lingered was whether this human being, once exposed, could make a successful return to the lawful status quo.[40]

These perceptions became part of the foundation of film-noir movies. One of the most common portrayals of the veteran in film noir is as the perpetrator of crime. In this instance, he becomes a person whose wartime scars both prevent assimilation back into society and place him on the margins of legal behavior. In *Act of Violence* (1949), the disabled veteran finds refuge in the off-kilter environment of postwar America, particularly within its criminal element.[41] Robert Montgomery's character Gagin, in *Ride the Pink Horse* (1947), is a former soldier who is referred to throughout the movie as "the man with no place."[42] Criminality granted structure or, in some cases, allowed the veteran to vicariously experience the same danger he had witnessed in combat. In some cases, film noir depicts this transition as essentially seamless. The *House of Bamboo* (1955) depicts former GIs as the core of a notorious gang in postwar Tokyo. In film noir, therefore, crime becomes a haven for the returning veteran.

The most ominous portrayal of the veteran in film noir is as a murderer. Throughout the genre, the war is seen as the agent that strips away not only the veteran's commonality with civil society but also the basic elements of his humanity. Combat has rendered the ex-soldier immune to the psychological consequences of killing, and peacetime has unleashed this finished product on an unsuspecting

TABLE 1. Characteristics of the Criminal and the Good Citizen

The Criminal	The Good Citizen
lawlessness	conformity
freedom	constraint
violence	peace
danger	safety
cruelty	kindness
cynicism	idealism
guilt	innocence
autonomy	commitment
integrity	compromise
spontaneity	deliberation
sassy repartee	polite speech
subculture	dominant culture
adventure	routine
courage	timidity
life	spiritual death
youth	age
masculinity	femininity
mean streets	home
broads	old bags
strength	weakness
wise guys	saps

Source: Nicole Rafter, *Shots in the Mirror: Crime Films and Society* (New York: Oxford University Press, 2000), p. 152.

public. Robert Ryan's role as the bigoted killer in *Crossfire* (1947) set a new standard for the portrayal of the veteran. Ryan's character brutally beats another man to death for no reason other than that he is Jewish. The connotation, particularly given the widespread knowledge of the Holocaust, combined with the callousness of the act, is a chilling commentary on the significant danger the veteran supposedly posed to his contemporaries. Variations on this theme resurfaced in numerous noir movies of the period. In *Gun Crazy* (1950), military training rather than combat provides the catalyst for a murder spree.

The veteran, played by John Dall, finds his urge to commit homicide encouraged and focused by his military service. Dall's character is a sociopath: an asset to his country while he is in uniform but a mad dog once released from the confines of the military.

This suspicion that the veteran was a threat to social good was somewhat ironic given the fact that crime in America evolved after 1945 to take advantage of the veteran. The various frauds perpetrated upon unsuspecting soldiers are as old as time. However, after the conclusion of the war, they tended to focus upon the veterans' benefits. According to the American Legion, more than eight hundred different scams were unleashed upon veterans, a list that includes the phony processing of government claims, fake home and auto loans, and retail fraud. There were many instances of "counseling experts" charging one hundred dollars to assist veterans in processing their Veterans' Administration claims, something the VA was already doing for free. In 1945, one in five complaints fielded by the Better Business Bureau came from veterans with these problems.[43]

Art often imitated life in this case. One of the most often-portrayed victims in film noir is the veteran. The soldier recently returned from the war is depicted as exhausted and depleted by its brutality and encumbered by physical and mental disabilities. In *The Blue Dahlia* (1945), the character Buzz Wanchek is a navy veteran who has been discharged with a steel plate in his head. His injury leaves him prone to blackouts and fits of rage. Throughout the movie, he negotiates his life in almost constant confusion and becomes the main suspect in a murder investigation. In *Somewhere in the Night* (1946), the veteran is the victim of service-related amnesia. This character is desperate to avoid conflict but repeatedly finds himself a victim of it. The down-on-his-luck veteran is a recurrent theme in movies such as *Among the Living* (1941), *Dead Reckoning* (1947), *The High Wall* (1947), *The Crooked Way* (1949), *Thieves' Highway* (1949), *The Strip* (1951), and *The Garment Jungle* (1957). Humphrey Bogart's returning veteran in *Key Largo* (1948) sees an obvious injustice in the gang that is occupying the hotel of his army buddy's widow, but he is initially too disillusioned to involve himself. Money is also a constant problem leading the veteran toward trouble. In *Kansas City Confidential* (1952), when the character Joe Rolfe, who has been unjustly arrested for his role in a robbery, overhears a police officer remark that "He won a Bronze Star and Purple Heart," Rolfe acidly retorts, "Try buying a cup of coffee with them."[44] Assailed by forces he can neither understand nor control, Rolfe is forced to seek his own justice. The clear message throughout *Kansas City Confidential* and other films like it is that there is no safe haven for the veteran in postwar America.

Film noir became, according to Bruce Crowther, a "dark mirror" held up to reflect an American society much changed by the Second World War.[45] Its common narrative threads—pervasive fear, paranoia, deception—were derived from and extended by an era made uncertain by social upheaval and a burgeoning crime rate no longer checked by wartime mobilization. The threat this new, alien environment posed to the returning soldier, both on screen and in reality, is the link that establishes film noir's credibility and its attraction to audiences. Conversely, the prominent threat posed by the veteran himself as a perpetrator of crime reflects the other half of the concern of film-noir audiences that soldiers could not be remade into safe citizens. Whichever role the veteran plays, his status, like that of his counterpart in *The Best Years of Our Lives*, is an ambivalent quantity on the screen.[46]

World War II changed both the manner in which audiences saw war films and their demands for realism. In part, this was the result of a deliberate effort to mobilize public support for the war through the movie industry. Starting in 1942, Hollywood worked closely with agencies such as the Office of War Information and the War Activities Committee to produce feature war documentaries designed for public consumption. This cooperative effort drew on some of the best artists then at work in America. John Ford established the precedent for the war documentary with *The Battle of Midway*, which was released in August, 1942. Darryl Zanuck produced *At the Front* in 1943. That same year, John Huston directed *Report from the Aleutians* and then *With the Marines at Tarawa* in 1944. A young Army Air Corps officer named William Wyler, who would win an Oscar for best director with *The Best Years of Our Lives*, chronicled the twenty-fifth mission of a B-17 bomber crew in *The Memphis Belle* (1944).

The style in each of these works is remarkably consistent. Each emphasizes vivid, up-close depictions of combat as it unfolds before the camera. Many directors, Ford first among them, pioneered the early use of color film to reinforce the action. Most were successful in exposing audiences to the war and illustrating the danger, fear, and tension involved in fighting. Bowsley Crowther, the *New York Times* film critic, commented in 1946, "Maybe the average movie-goer didn't see all of them; maybe he missed, for various reasons, all but five or six. But whichever and however many of them he happened to see, his knowledge and comprehension of the real thing was sharpened thereby."[47] As a result of these films, even before the war ended, the average member of the movie audience gained an important understanding of at least the visual reality of the war. Their expectations changed accordingly, as did their tolerance for the traditional Hollywood product.

Once veterans began to reoccupy movie-theater seats, the expectation that Hollywood would make more than a passing attempt at realism grew even stronger. As soldiers and sailors stationed overseas, they had loudly expressed their preferences for entertainment to the celebrities traveling with the USO. Military audiences liked the singing troupes and comedians who performed for them. The Andrews Sisters were particular favorites, as were comedians like Joe E. Brown and Bob Hope. Movie actors who cultivated the image of the action hero received different treatment. John Wayne and Humphrey Bogart, the toughest characters dominating the industry, generated responses that varied between silence and open hostility. Wayne was openly heckled by troops on his tour of European bases during the war.[48]

By 1945, Americans' understanding of war had drastically evolved outside of the theater. The world war took the country into combat on nearly every continent of the globe. Its prosecution exposed citizen soldiers to horrors unprecedented in human history, from the death camps in western Germany to the funeral pyres that existed in cities throughout Japan.[49] Veterans' hospitals and rehabilitation facilities were filled to capacity in the years after 1945, indications of the price the country had paid—reminders that remained for decades.[50]

More importantly, once peace was declared in August, 1945, it was not clear to most Americans that world conflict would cease. The status of occupied Germany remained unresolved and became a growing point of friction between the Anglo-American alliance and the Soviets.[51] The public fractures that began to appear among the erstwhile allies in the war against Hitler soon developed into full-blown animosity. By 1947, a new Cold War had emerged. In many respects, it was a conflict easy to understand within the confines of public discourse in America.[52]

To the extent that this fight would become another war against oppression, the transition from one totalitarian dictator (Hitler) to another (Stalin) was comparatively simple.

Much of the remainder of the Cold War was less certain. The manner in which this next conflict might be fought alarmed Americans. In 1945, many of them had seen cities reduced to rubble by a thousand heavy bombers. Bill Mauldin, a popular writer who had fought in Italy, described the country as if "a giant rake had gone over it from end to end, and when you have been going along with the rake you wondered that there is anything left at all."[53] Stories of this destruction were commonplace among returning veterans. Yet, the atom bomb took this concept and exponentially multiplied it. One single bomb might now destroy as much as thousands had before. In the aftermath of Hiroshima and Nagasaki, civil society understood in an abstract but horrifying way that the next time total war was practiced, it could be the last war.[54]

What constituted an enemy in this new Cold War was even more problematic. On battlefields around the world, guerrilla warfare soon became an appendage of the larger global standoff. In Greece, Turkey, the Philippines, Malaya, and a dozen other locations, the line between a civilian and a military combatant blurred.[55] At home, the nature of what characterized the enemy changed as well. Breaking news of spy rings and atomic espionage shocked the nation and opened up to scrutiny previously sacrosanct institutions like the Department of State. For nearly a decade after the Second World War, the junior senator from Wisconsin, Joseph P. McCarthy, rode a wave of real security concerns and outright paranoia.[56] By the late forties, it seemed as if the clear, bold lines of demarcation between good and evil or friend and enemy were beginning to disappear.[57]

As this environment changed, so too did the war film of the period. Notable is a declining focus on the larger goals of war. Gone are the almost constant allusions to the basic purposes and high-minded ideals of a crusade that are found in the World War II–era pictures. Replacing them are overt references to the fact that a larger strategic vision has been lost or is, at worst, an impediment to success. Robert Mitchum's colonel in the Korean War film *One Minute to Zero* (1952), for example, complains bitterly about the intrusion of the United Nations into his decision making. Politics, once the foundation of certainty, is now the adversary of decisiveness. In a related sense, the combat films of the late forties and early fifties openly question the motives and capabilities of those placed in charge. The difference between an incompetent officer and the enemy has diminished, although both fundamentally represent a threat to the Americans around them.[58] In *The Caine Mutiny* (1954), the mental stability of the commander both galvanizes and divides the junior officers, who are subordinate to him. In *Attack!* (1956), the commanding officer is executed by his own men because his ambition and incompetence have become a threat to his unit.[59]

As the grand vision of war diminished as a viable subject of the combat film, it was replaced by the story of the soldiers themselves. War movies became efforts to depict the lives of the average combat soldier. *The Story of GI Joe* (1945), a biography of war correspondent Ernie Pyle, became a tribute to the infantryman, dwelling not on his heroism but on his endurance. "The GI," Pyle (Burgess Meredith) intones, "he lives so miserable and he dies so miserable."[60] Films produced at the conclusion of the war, like *The Story of GI Joe* and *They Were Expendable* (1945), increasingly reflect upon the human cost of war, where suffering has become a common denominator.[61]

Throughout the remainder of the forties, war films derived their dramatic content from the toll war took on the mind and body. In *Battleground* (1949), the snow-shrouded forests of Belgium become an enemy equal to the Germans. The frostbite created by plunging temperatures and the cloud cover that holds back supplies become basic elements in a life-and-death struggle. Sometimes danger is subtle. One of the more poignant moments in the movie occurs when the Mexican American soldier (played by Ricardo Montalbán) enjoys his very first snowfall and is killed by a German rifleman for the brief pleasure of it. The *New York Times* has called *Battleground* "a smashing pictorial recreation of the way that the last one [WWII] was for the dirty and frightened foot-soldier who got caught in a filthy deal."[62] Another reviewer notes that the film is able to "preserve the ever-present unintentional humor that characterizes the American GI."[63]

One of the most popular war pictures to finish out the decade uses the idea of endurance as one of its most important narrative devices. *Twelve O'clock High!* (1949) presents a study of men forced to confront both the periodic physical danger of bombing missions and the continuous mental strain interspersed between them. Endurance in this case becomes a yardstick that measures leadership, bravery, and cowardice. Gregory Peck's General Savage is introduced to his new command after the breakdown of its former commander. His challenge to them is not directed so much against the German enemy as at their own fears. The complacent pilot, Gately, who bears the brunt of Savage's contempt for his laziness, redeems himself by enduring the physical pain of an injury in addition to the punishment of bombing runs. Receding into the background all the while is the actual point of the "strategic" bombing campaign. War is reduced to the struggle each man faces within his aircraft and his mind. In its climax, *Twelve O'clock High!* becomes something of a cautionary tale. Savage's failure to complete his final mission—because of his own collapse—is a pointed commentary that even the strongest of men could not stand the strain of combat or the totality of war.[64] *Twelve O'clock High!* drew considerable critical acclaim in 1949. One writer has commended the film for its "rugged realism and punch."[65] Peck garnered an Academy Award nomination for best actor, one of four nominations the film received, and Dean Jagger won the award for best supporting actor.

Between 1945 and 1950, the combat film changed to suit the altered nature of its new audience. During World War II, according to historian Jeanine Basinger, movies provided a means by which the audience could "watch the war together, celebrate its satisfactory completion, reenact its combat, and come together in their understanding of it."[66] Artistic preference and the wartime need to present positive imagery largely determined the content of what was presented to the public. However, almost as soon as the war was over, this emphasis was forced to contend with a new audience containing sixteen million veterans, an audience that was tempered by experience. In order to maintain relevance and box-office receipts, the very nature of the post-1945 war film changed. Some, such as *Sands of Iwo Jima* (1949), retain the characteristics of the previous time period. Many others represent a different trajectory, one that incorporates the veterans' widely held understanding of war with the existing conventions of the combat movie. During its depiction of the battle of Bastogne, *Battleground,* an enormously popular film in 1949, includes twenty actual veterans of the 101st Airborne who were on temporary assignment from the army.[67] Overall, the final product of these movies is a hybrid of past art and present reality and a distinctly new genre of filmmaking.

Americans welcomed the new peace of 1945 with a sense of relief and a lingering uneasiness about how much had been sacrificed to achieve victory. Measured in dollars and demographics, these changes appeared obvious in the sprawling boomtowns scattered over the nation's landscape. More worrisome to the country, however, were the more subtle shifts in a society that was welcoming millions home from a former global battlefield.

The veterans who returned were different men. They were a harder generation when they came home. Bill Mauldin noted at the time that their sense of humor had changed. The GI, he wrote, "can grin at gruesome jokes, like seeing a German get shot in the seat of the pants, and he will stare uncomprehendingly at fragile jokes in print which would have made him rock with laughter before."[68]

Clearly, the viewing audience in theaters had changed. As was the case with work, politics, and the household, the wartime experience altered the manner in which Americans entertained themselves. The public that emerged after August, 1945, had had a portion of its civility excised by the sacrifices of service and the necessities of combat. It was a public that was impatient with the escapist fantasies that dominated the movies of the thirties. Instead, audiences were attracted to films that reflected the sense of pragmatism prevalent in America and offered some recognition of the price paid to ensure the country's survival.

In order to retain the marketability of its movies, Hollywood compensated for this new audience. The industry produced pictures that revolved around the subject of veterans and the war. Some, to be sure, struck a lighthearted tone. But the movies that attracted the public's attention and held it were those best able to replicate the hardships of the wartime experience and the sense of alienation that accompanied many Americans into peacetime. Through its critical and commercial successes, *The Best Years of Our Lives* established a precedent that other movies emulated for the remainder of the forties.

As depictions of war and the veteran evolved, so too did the redefinition of realism in film. The superficial patriotism prevalent in movies made during the war diminished in the wake of more introspective examinations of the human condition. The renaissance enjoyed by Dashiell Hammett and Raymond Chandler in the film-noir productions of the forties and the inclusion of the veteran in these films are interesting commentaries on the fusion of prewar literary realism with a postwar vehicle to make the genre relevant to movie audiences.

CHAPTER 6

Ambiguity thrived in the war films of the forties. Whether they dealt with the prosecution of war or the recovery from it, the pictures of the era are suffused with a sense of ambivalence regarding what is normal. William J. Prior, writing in 2000 on the morality of war, noted that soldiers see reality from many different and sometimes conflicting perspectives. They act as human beings who are attempting to effect their own survival when fighting. They are also members of a unit tasked with a mission to take action against the enemy. By virtue of their citizenship, soldiers are also members of their own particular nation and captured by its legal and social expectations. Lastly, soldiers at times represent a cause greater than themselves, their unit, or their country, one that encompasses a larger moral objective such as the liberation of a people from oppression.[69] Each of these four perspectives coexists with the others. At points, one holds sway over the other three as the situation permits or demands. The higher moral cause might mean very little if survival is at stake.

What Prior recognizes is a truism of history. War is an ugly, often very contradictory event. Ambiguity did not appear as a result of Vietnam. Nor did ambiguity in war films suddenly emerge as a result of war films about Vietnam. This sensibility existed long before the genre took hold in the recent past.

Reviewers of *Saving Private Ryan* have missed this point. The film is not a vehicle for baby-boomer sensibilities. It is truly a throwback to the forties but in ways more important than the technical methods utilized or the multiethnic cast of characters constructed. *Saving Private Ryan* takes a long step backward toward the past by including the lack of moral surety that is present in a great many of the homecoming, film noir, and war films of the postwar era. It would be a mistake to characterize Spielberg's use of modern special effects as simple pandering to the tastes of younger audiences. Instead, the very potency of the depiction is an appeal to the reality of the event and the collective memory of those who served in it.

Retreads

When the invasion of the south came, of course everyone was interested, but it never occurred to us that we Americans serving in Japan in the Army of Occupation would ever get involved. For me, it was a typical Sunday night in Japan. I was at home with my family. It had rained all day. My wife was giving the kids a bath prior to putting them to bed, and I was reading a book and nursing a drink when the call came for me to report at once to headquarters! The wife wanted to know what the call was about. "Something must be wrong with next week's training schedule," I answered. "I'll be back as soon as I can." (Which happened to be eleven months later.)
—*C. W. Menninger, 24th Infantry Division*

It was easy to fall into a comfortable routine. New priorities came with new births, new jobs, new mortgages. Every day started with the coffeepot, the commute to work, small headaches over numbers and deadlines. The tempo continued at home with the changing of diapers, the celebration of birthdays, baseball games, and marking a child's growth in pencil on the inside of a door jamb. Time passed. The war passed into another lifetime.

But life changed. The war came home again. Obscure names such as Seoul, Suwon, Taejon, and Pusan traveled across newspaper headlines to mark its progress. One day a letter appeared in the mail marked with barely remembered terminology. Soldiers who had passed time in armories each month or on lists as inactive reservists suddenly found themselves on the sharp edges of another war.

It was an unsettling realization for many. After Pearl Harbor, GIs had said farewell to family and friends with a sense that national survival was at stake. Friend and enemy appeared in sharply drawn contrast. In 1950, the same call to arms reappeared but this time in lines drawn with much less clarity. The war against Communism dominated the American dialogue, but it was a conversation with more shades of gray and very little agreement over how it might end.

In another important sense, GIs had also matured by the time they went off to their second war. In 1941, "normalcy" was something associated with hard times: the Great Depression and American stagnation. In 1950, "normalcy" expressed the postwar boom. Rather than abandoning it, veterans at the outbreak of the Korean War looked upon the status quo as something to cherish. In part, this motivated the soldiers who deployed to northeast Asia. Fighting against Communism was a means of preserving their newfound way of life.

O n June 25, 1950, North Korean Communist forces boiled across the 38th parallel and brought war to a generation of Americans who had finally begun to enjoy the fruits of peace. As the desperate battles on the peninsula unfolded, America was wrenched from its domestic priorities and forced to contemplate a much darker alternative future. In December, 1950, a Gallup poll revealed that 55 percent of respondents believed the United States was already involved in World War III.[1]

Korea was able to whipsaw America out of postwar complacency because the war so badly exposed the nation to its lack of preparation. Unlike the collapse of China to Communism or the Soviet Union's explosion of its first atomic bomb a year earlier, in Korea, American citizens fought and died for want of better doctrine or support. This price propelled Korea past more abstract discussions regarding atomic parity with Moscow or the distant civil war fought between the Chinese. Korea brought the Cold War home in earnest.

The conflict highlighted an American military that had declined drastically since 1945. In the five years following Japan's surrender, the army alone shrank from more than 8 million men in arms to just 591,000 in 1950.[2] The postwar American military suffered from a number of overlapping assumptions that collectively gutted its ability to perform its strategic mission. Some of these were old standards, particularly those that addressed the "peace dividend" and the desire to shift federal spending priorities to domestic issues. Another assumption was rooted in Harry Truman's honest desire to make the military more efficient, something he had pursued as a senator during World War II. Under this philosophy, the president asked the Pentagon to do more with less, unsuccessfully proposing armed forces' unification to reduce redundancy and improve military procurement.[3] Lastly, there was a belief prevalent in the forties that the United States had entered an era of "push-button" warfare, wherein the gigantic leaps made in military technology during World War II had rendered conventional conflict obsolete. This assumption was rooted in the belief that air power, coupled with atomic weapons, would prevail in all future clashes among nations. Even where gaps in readiness appeared, this school of thought clung to the basic faith that American know-how could close them with ease.[4]

In the meantime, as political debates raged in Washington and attention toward matters of national security drifted from the public domain, the human element that made up the American military suffered and soldiered on. All of the service branches took major budget cuts in the late forties. By the outbreak of the Korean War, total appropriations for defense amounted to only $13.2 billion.[5] Force reductions followed out of necessity. Between 1948 and 1950, the total number of army divisions was reduced from twelve to ten. In order to keep even this number of divisions, army planners were forced to reduce the authorized strength of major maneuver units (e.g., battalions, brigades, divisions) by one-third.[6] As ground forces declined, so too did those at sea. The total number of major surface ships in the navy dropped from 1,194 at the end of World War II to just 267 in 1948.[7]

For the average service member, however, the declining military budgets translated into an almost obsessive focus on the bare essentials. The army was forced to pare down spending to accommodate food, clothing, and medical supplies. Other priorities were placed on hold. When, in 1947, the U.S. Army Ordinance Department requested $750 million for essential ammunition, training, and equipment, the Bureau of Budget immediately cut the figure to $275 million. Consequently, essential work was not accomplished. Troops did not train in basic skills such as marksmanship. For want of fuel, units could not conduct large-scale exercises. Major weapons systems fell into disrepair because spare parts and replacements were unavailable. This wretched state of readiness was perhaps best illustrated in the desperate search for working equipment once the Korean War broke out in June, 1950. Some of the armored vehicles dispatched to American ports for deployment were actually taken from concrete pads, where they had been on display at the Ft. Knox Armor School in Kentucky.[8]

One of the most notorious examples of this institutional problem was situated close to Korea. Although few contemporary observers outside the U.S. military were aware of it, the Eighth Army in Japan was a far cry from a combat-ready formation when the war erupted. For five years, it had served as an occupation force, slowly losing the combat edge it possessed as draftees and replacements depleted the ranks of veteran soldiers in uniform. Duty in Japan was a relatively easy affair, with too little attention spent on training and too much on the amenities offered by the Japanese people. The military employed Japanese civilians to take over many of the daily tasks that had normally been performed by the lowest-ranking privates—laundry, housekeeping, shoe shining. Leonard Korgie, assigned to the 34th Infantry Regiment of the 24th Division, has offered an account of life in Japan that was typical of the time: "Occupation duty was heaven. I was troop information and education NCO at Sugamo Prison, where Japanese war criminals were held. My unit did very little military training. Life away from the prison consisted mostly of athletics, clubs, nightly dances, theater, and Japanese girls. Although in those days alcohol made me sick, there was always plenty to drink. GI money and cigarettes went a long way on the black market."[9]

Pampered by this relationship, the Eighth Army lost its sense of urgency. As Cold War tensions escalated, a large proportion of American forces settled into a comfortable routine. By the army's own account, the overall quality of the troops stationed on the home islands was alarming. Almost half (43 percent) of service members fell into the two lowest categories of the army aptitude test. Overall, the divisions assigned to the Eighth Army were nearly 7,000 men short of their assigned wartime strength.[10]

The story is much the same with regard to the Eighth Army's tools of war. Most of the weapons and equipment in stock were of World War II vintage and worn out. New weaponry was in chronically short supply in the maneuver battalions. The Eighth Army was authorized 226 modern recoilless rifles in the summer of 1950 but actually had only 21 on hand when called to deploy. In 1950, of the 13,780 two-ton trucks carried on the Eighth Army's property books, arguably the logistical backbone of MacArthur's ground forces, only 4,441 were in running condition.[11]

MacArthur took remarkably few steps to alleviate this situation before the war. Ensconced in the luxury of the Dai Ichi Insurance Building in the center of downtown Tokyo, the supreme commander rarely visited units in garrison or the field. Personnel problems were attributed to the poor quality of peacetime recruits and draftees. Otherwise, MacArthur dabbled in Japanese politics, indulged in searches for Communist conspiracies on the home islands, and rather transparently floated trial balloons for his own entry into American presidential politics.[12]

Despite this inertia, some attempts were made to fix the problems that plagued the Eighth Army. As part of Operation Roll-Up, MacArthur authorized the cannibalization of equipment left behind on World War II battlefields scattered all over the Pacific. Thousands of rusted, damaged vehicles were claimed in this manner and shipped to the Eighth Army to be reconditioned by Japanese contractors. In 1949, more than 200,000 tons of ordinance supplies were shipped to Japan from Okinawa alone.[13]

One of MacArthur's key subordinates in the Eighth Army, the hard-charging Lt. Gen. Walton H. Walker, attempted to institute a rigorous company- and battalion-training program in the year before the war. However, this effort to breathe life back into the foundation of the American military force in Northeast Asia came far too late to improve its readiness.[14] Nor was Walker able to overcome the conventional wisdom among some Americans stationed in Northeast Asia that bordered on arrogance and eerily echoed the attitudes of many European colonial powers on the eve of World War II. Alerted to the fact that the invasion of South Korea had begun, Lacy Barnett, a medic assigned to the 34th Infantry Regiment, remembers: "When word reach us in Japan on that rainy Sunday, the first reaction by many members of my unit was 'Where is Korea?' The next reaction, 'Let the gooks kill each other off.' Among the majority of men there was absolutely no fear or thought that the United States would become involved in the war. During the next few days it was business conducted as usual."[15] The same assumptions persisted even after U.S. forces arrived in South Korea. When Task Force Smith made contact with the North Korean People's Army in early July, 1950, many soldiers assumed that the invasion would stop once it confronted Americans.[16]

CHAPTER 7

Taken together, these overlapping failures were a recipe for disaster. As American forces reeled back from the Communist North Korean onslaught, shrill calls began to emanate from MacArthur's headquarters, demanding reinforcements from U.S. forces stationed around the world. The problem was that no such strategic reserves existed. With the possible exception of the 82nd Airborne Division stationed at Ft. Bragg, North Carolina, the army was already at the bottom of the replacement barrel by the end of July, 1950. The same held true for the other branches of the American military. Personnel shortages would bedevil the American defense establishment throughout the war. After a year of fighting, the Defense Department reported a 500,000-soldier shortfall. In 1951, the navy placed its need at 8,000 officers and 43,000 enlisted personnel. The air force estimated its shortage to be as high as 120,000 service members.[17]

Major changes followed in the wake of this strategic reality. Recognizing the dire nature of American readiness, Truman recalled George C. Marshall to head the Defense Department. This decision was a profoundly important one on the part of the president. During the great struggle to mobilize the nation in World War II, Marshall had crafted much of the military institution that defeated Germany and Japan. The crisis of 1950 demanded exactly the same expertise. Unfortunately, however, former Secretary of State Marshall was at the center of a political firestorm that year as a result of his involvement in the Chinese civil war and the subsequent "loss" of China to Communism. As far as the McCarthyite wing of the Republican Party was concerned, at least in its public rhetoric, George C. Marshall was barely one step removed from a traitor.[18] Despite the heated exchanges that roiled around this outstanding public servant, Truman stuck with him. It was to prove a wise choice. Marshall quickly reestablished a sense of order in the Department of Defense. Preparations for the Korean War continued with a renewed sense of purpose. While many of his decisions would prove unpopular with the general public, they were critical to America's war effort in the early days of the conflict.

One of the first measures taken by the Defense Department was a massive mobilization of American military reserves and the National Guard. In 1950, the army alone recalled 9,500 inactive reserve officers. The air force initially called 8,000 service members back to active duty. Overall, approximately 310,000 reservists and National Guard troops were placed on active duty during the war. The entire

Marine Corps Reserve was recalled for service. Four complete National Guard divisions—the 28th (Pennsylvania), the 40th (California), the 43rd (Connecticut, Rhode Island, and Vermont), and the 45th (Oklahoma)—were federalized for service in addition to two regimental combat teams, the 196th (South Dakota) and the 278th (Tennessee).[19]

Word of this mass mobilization rippled across the country, quickly reaching armories and drill halls all around the United States. Soldiers, marines, aviators, and sailors, some veterans, as well as recent draftees and volunteers began breaking gear out of their lockers and storage buildings. From the drill floors, word soon spread to immediate family members and then to the communities where these men and women worked and lived each day that war had returned. For many of these service members, Korea was their second or, in some cases, their third war. In New Mexico, soldiers of B Battery, 716th Anti-Aircraft Artillery Battalion, prepared to deploy for Korea. Their commander, Capt. Alvin Wheeler, contemplated his second conflict. His first action had been as part of the defense of Bataan in 1942.[20]

Throughout 1950, major problems soon began to appear as the reserve call-up proceeded. Mobilization proved poorly managed from the start. Initially, the Defense Department was reluctant to draw personnel from the active reserves, fearing a degradation in the quality of standing formations that trained each month. As a substitute, they sought out the inactive and volunteer reserves for individual replacements. However, even as recall notices were churned out to bring these people back into uniform, no priority was established to dictate who should be mobilized first. Compounding the confusion was the universally poor quality of military record keeping for reservists. The mothballing of millions of files after the mass demobilization of 1945 and 1946 created havoc for the Pentagon and thousands of reservists. Moreover, the decision to call upon the inactive and volunteer reserve proved to be very controversial with the general public, which failed to see the practical logic of this decision when perfectly good formations of reserve and National Guard troops stood all around them.[21]

Specific difficulties also plagued the separate service branches. Faced with an enormous shortage of combat leaders, the Department of the Army initially appealed to reserve officers to voluntarily return to active duty. Practically none of them did, which forced the army to involuntarily recall 7,862 captains and lieutenants.[22] Some marine reservists were given as little as seventy-two hours' notice to report for duty, leaving families and employers scrambling to compensate. To help fill shortages for the combat units engaged in Korea, many marines were reclassified as riflemen regardless of their occupational specialties.

Some of the mobilization notices were premature. When the 236th Marine Fighter Squadron was recalled, its members immediately began making arrangements with their families and employers. The order was later rescinded with a Defense Department disclaimer lamely offering that reservists "could apply for and probably get active duty" at a later date. Many reservists experienced significant difficulties with employers who were unwilling to accommodate the mobilization. Col. Charles W. Skeele, president of the Reserve Officers Association, claimed in September, 1950, that many employers were refusing jobs to part-time soldiers who faced the prospect of active duty.[23] Other difficulties emerged with respect to record keeping. One report noted that a physically disabled reservist was still maintained on an active personnel list. Many with existing disabilities or reasons for deferment found that they could not get off the mobilization rosters. One man with ten children was recalled to active duty. The outdated military personnel file of one nurse who received her notice from the Defense Department to report still indicated that she was single, although she was actually married with three children.

A small number challenged the legality of the mobilization. One reservist, Capt. William H. Miley, sued the army for release from his military commitment, contending that it had expired by the time war had broken out. He eventually lost his case in a Virginia federal court.[24] While a relatively minor incident, Miley's case symbolizes a large undercurrent of public resentment that centered on the war effort. Further embarrassing the military was the story of M.Sgt. Luther Bradley, who, in 1952, was convicted of accepting bribes to disqualify four U.S. Army Reserve officers from serving on active duty.[25]

As these stories began to accumulate, Congress weighed in on the issue. Bombarded by letters and telegrams from angry constituents, lawmakers began a public debate on the process of mobilization. Carl Vinson (D-GA), chair of the House Armed Services Committee, openly asked why inactive reserves were being called before others in the organized and active reserve.[26] While this political dialogue offered an outlet for concerned families as well as the reservists themselves, it also added a substantial layer of difficulty for the Pentagon's planners, who were scrambling to fill skilled positions (e.g., medical specialists) and forced to rely upon inactive personnel. Translating immediate military need into terms sufficient for the public to understand became a large, unplanned, and ongoing burden for the Defense Department at an early point in the war.

As they formed up into their assigned reserve and National Guard units, veterans soon faced additional readiness problems. If active-duty forces had fared poorly after World War II, their counterparts in the federal reserves and state National Guard systems were in considerably worse shape. Turnover rates for officers and enlisted ranks were high. Few units possessed anywhere near the manpower necessary for even basic missions. Referring to the four National Guard divisions brought into federal service in September, 1950, the army reported six months later that "training on induction was estimated to be about 30 percent of a regular army unit of comparable size." Leadership in these formations was uneven. Some officers were hardened combat veterans, whereas others were brand-new products of the Reserve Officer Training Corps. This would prove to be critical at the company and battalion levels, where equally young enlisted soldiers required the greatest amount of attention. New equipment in these formations was scarce. What was available was often "deadlined," or nonoperational, for lack of maintenance or because it was simply worn out. Col. Alexis B. McMullen, president of the Air Reserve Association, complained before a House armed services subcommittee that although three-quarters of air force officers were reservists, only 1 percent of the fiscal year 1949 budget had been dedicated to that part of the service.[27]

Despite all of these obstacles, the reservists and National Guard members facing deployment simply carried on. They untied knots in the system and resolved a hundred small headaches. They trained newcomers and retrained some of the old hands who had fallen behind. They improvised and made do, in many cases like their older brothers had ten years earlier. In a matter of months, they were ready for war.

They began to say goodbye to their loved ones as well. Once the practical matters of mobilization were addressed and dispensed with, the realization dawned that families were being left behind. Lt. Leslie E. This reflected in a March, 1952, issue of *Parents' Magazine* that "Life was moving along. The children were having new experiences I couldn't share and we got to draw further apart."[28] Interestingly, another self-help industry emerged after 1950, more muted and unlike the one that had appeared five years earlier. This time, the problems addressed were those experienced not by returning veterans but by tens of thousands of family members—spouses and children—who remained on the home front in an undeclared war.

Neither family members nor reservists were reluctant to express their discontent about the situation. This was particularly the case when the Defense Department began to levy the mobilized National Guard divisions for individual replacements in 1951. The 31st Division, made up of Alabama and Mississippi National Guard personnel, had 4,300 members taken from it to serve as individual active-duty replacements bound for Korea. This was a particular blow to many who joined because recruiting promotions had emphasized "fighting for your buddies" and the communities around local armories. The idea that guard members were simply cogs in the military replacement system stripped away the entire character of state service. The levy system proved highly unpopular and controversial during the war.[29]

Public dissent in the affected states proved to be far from impotent. Each had its own National Guard associations that were powerful actors in state and federal politics and more than willing to flex their political muscle. It did not take long for the clamor to reach sympathetic ears on Capitol Hill. Sen. Edwin Martin of Pennsylvania, a former commander of his home state's 28th Infantry Division, took time to express his concerns regarding the sacrifice made by mobilized citizen-soldiers at the 73rd Annual National Guard Association Conference in 1951. When lawmakers like Martin took note of his constituents' displeasure at the hardships created by the war, the Defense Department followed suit. As early as October, 1950, Secretary of Defense Marshall ordered involuntarily recalled reservists home after they had completed training and been replaced by draftees and regulars.[30] The following year, this policy was extended to federalized elements of the National Guard. By 1952, many units formerly made up of home-state soldiers were being replaced by draftees and transfers from other parts of the military.

As the war ground on, it continued to be highly unpopular, not only in the states most directly affected by the reserve mobilization, but in the entire country as well. Polling data gathered from the period indicate a number of strong and consistent trends throughout the three-year conflict. When the war broke out, many Americans worried that it would escalate into a wider clash with Communist China or the Soviet Union. A large percentage (49 percent) of those who were asked in October, 1950, believed the United States should begin wartime production of military items even if this came at the expense of civilian goods. A decisive majority (73 percent) of respondents in December, 1950, approved doubling the defense budget, and a majority supported the idea of paying for this increase with higher taxes.[31]

When it came to the human cost of the war, interesting trends appeared that were much less supportive of the United States' approach to Korea. At the start of the Communist Chinese advance in January, 1951, two-thirds of Americans who were asked favored pulling out U.S. troops "as fast as possible." For much of the remaining two years of fighting, the public clearly supported measures that would return American forces. As early as February, 1951, a substantial majority (56 percent) endorsed the idea of negotiations to end the war. This included leaving the north in Communist hands if peace could be achieved. Perhaps the extreme limit of this sentiment was recorded in October, 1953, when a majority (53 percent) said that the United States should not reenter a war if South Korea provoked hostilities with the North.[32]

The Korean War clearly finished the Truman presidency and provided the foundation for Dwight D. Eisenhower's leadership in the White House. Most Americans who agreed with the characterization of Korea as a "useless war" placed that sobriquet on Truman's doorstep. His approval ratings, which were not strong in June, 1950, varied from the low to high twenties for much of the war.[33] Eisenhower, in contrast, gained enormous traction by promising to go to Korea to extricate the United States from the conflict. His status as supreme commander of the Allied forces in Europe and his later role in the formation of NATO established a basic credibility that resonated with an American public that had grown weary of war in Northeast Asia.[34]

Further, Korea left a stamp on presidential politics that persisted through the fifties and beyond. For Eisenhower, the days of open-ended commitments to far-flung places was over. From his perspective, what was necessary in the Cold War was a means of divining national security without bankrupting the nation.[35] More important was a conscious decision by his successors to avoid direct, overt confrontations with Communism, a path that would lead America on a slippery slope to another country in Asia almost as soon as the war in Korea was over.[36]

In the meantime, as the political waters roiled back and forth across the United States, reservists continued with their deployments to Korea. More often than not, replacements arrived without adequate clothing, equipment, or rations. Not much in the way of resupply awaited them as frontline units claimed the lion's share of new materiel bound for the war.[37] For the most part, the war of maneuver and dramatic advances and retreats along the Korean peninsula had also diminished. By the spring of 1951, both sides occupied a stabilized front that generally followed the 38th parallel and began to fortify their positions. As the war dragged on and mobilized reservists began to arrive, the point of fighting shifted from the defense of South Korea or the liberation of the North to a conflict defined by attrition and the ability to gain leverage at the armistice talks at Panmunjom.[38]

Many arrivals were appalled at the poor quality of maintenance in frontline units as well as those preparing to transit overseas. Air force pilots and crew members lodged frequent complaints about poorly kept aircraft and the danger this presented to aircrews. According to official accounts, between October, 1951, and April, 1952, 350 flyers were killed in accidents. Consequently, the number of crews requesting ground duty grew from 6 per month in the first half of 1951 to 44 per month in November, 1951. By April, 1952, 269 requested removal from flight status. Their de facto spokesperson for the national media was 1st Lt. Verne Goodwin, who noted that "We don't see any sense in giving our lives for a cause that even the civilians are apathetic toward."[39] It was not just the country's apathy that disturbed Goodwin and others like him. The air force that flew in Korea was dominated by reservists. According to contemporary accounts, they constituted 80 percent of the pilots who served during the war. At an average age of 31 years (compared to 22.5 years during World War II), their sense of daring did not extend to their aircraft. Demanding the bare necessities from a logistical network was common sense—and a means to ensure a safe return home.

Coming home became the primary yardstick of victory for service personnel with few other measurements to rely upon. As early as the spring of 1951, it became clear that a stalemate in the war had been reached. The battles fought between 1951 and 1953—for Pork Chop Hill, Heartbreak Ridge, and the Punch Bowl—were famous as tests of determination and endurance but not as decisive strategic events, a realization that did not enhance the popularity of the war at home or among the reservists themselves. Marching into the enemy's capital and resolutely finishing a conflict between alliances of nation-states was an obsolete concept in the new Cold War. Instead, wars over productivity, propaganda, covert operations, or clashes between proxies and third parties—conflicts with great human cost and sometimes very few tangible rewards—came to replace that scenario.[40] Stripped of its rhetoric and ideology, this new climate defined victory as a product of individual survival. Nearly a generation before Vietnam, a new standard for American military service was set.

The Pennsylvania 28th National Guard Infantry Division's mobilization for Korea is a case study in the myriad obstacles encountered by American reservists in 1950 and the solutions they created to overcome them. The unit had seen extensive service in World War II, when it had deployed to England in 1943 and, later, to the continent in July, 1944, following the Normandy invasion. Extensively engaged in combat across France, the "Bloody Bucket" division had become famous for its hard-fought victories in a costly campaign that culminated in the brutal fight for the Huertgen Forest near the end of the war.[41]

Unfortunately, once peace was secured, the division witnessed a rapid decline in its overall readiness. Most of the soldiers who had served in the war ended their relationship with the National Guard once they returned home. In rather short order, the reservoir of experienced combat veterans dwindled to a fraction of the original numbers. During its annual two-week training in 1948, out of an assigned strength of 15,781 members, the 28th Division included 10,627 soldiers who had no prior military experience. It was also a much younger formation. Of the more than fifteen thousand soldiers in its ranks, 6,998 were between 17 and 19 years of age. Old hands who were left over from the European campaigns found themselves surrounded by youngsters, many of them eager to learn but completely lacking in some of the most basic, commonsense skills of the private soldier. This problem was compounded by significant shortages in professionally trained personnel. In 1948, there was a conspicuous shortage of medics and doctors, one that sick call in the field exposed on a daily basis.[42]

Two years later, at the outbreak of the Korean War, state evaluations of individual units in the 28th Division indicated a disturbing trend regarding the formation's overall ability to wage war. Units observed during the annual two-week training cycle in 1950 revealed serious deficiencies with respect to the most basic functions they were expected to perform. Company A of the 110th Infantry Battalion from Monongahela reported 101 enlisted men present for training, but only 40 of them qualified on their individual weapons. Of the 19 men assigned to crew-served weapons, only 2 had qualified by the end of camp. Similarly, Battery C of the 108th Field Artillery Battalion, stationed in Philadelphia, reported 68 enlisted men present for training, only 38 of whom qualified with their individual weapons.[43]

On August 2, 1950, this was the general state of readiness when division headquarters received an alert from the Department of Defense that it would be called to federal service. Despite the many shortcomings revealed in annual training reports, Pennsylvania ranked in the top echelon of National Guard units prepared for deployment. One month after the alert, the 28th Infantry Division was formally mobilized for active duty.[44]

News of the mobilization spread quickly throughout the state. Small articles appeared in local newspapers chronicling preparations for the official date, September 5, on which soldiers would formally enter federal service. What is notable about the media coverage is the absence of apprehension or criticism of the event. Editorials focused upon the domestic issues of the day: the war in Korea, labor troubles, and allegations of corruption in the Truman administration. Otherwise, there is a distinct routineness to the stories that address the thousands of service members who were severing ties with their families and communities. When the day for mobilization finally arrived, the *Reading Times* carried the story on page fourteen.[45] As the war progressed, news tended to focus on other units that were called up for service, local soldiers' experiences in Korea, and the periodic report of a resident who had been killed or wounded in the fighting.[46] For the most part, the larger question of the war in the minds of Pennsylvanians appeared to follow national attitudes. Citizens of the commonwealth perceived Korean service as part of their civic duty and saw it, in the best instances, through the lens of World War II. At the very least, most citizens grudgingly acquiesced to a commitment they expected to be temporary.

Unfortunately, unlike the generally solid degree of public support for deployment, the process of actually preparing the 28th Infantry

Division for war proved to be neither smooth nor easy. During the mobilization, a number of "bottlenecks" or "misunderstandings" appeared, according to unit after-action reports. Record keeping, for example, differed significantly between the army and the Pennsylvania National Guard when it came to maintaining pay records, physicals, immunizations, and a whole host of other administrative details that determine the course of a soldier's life. In this case, the Department of Defense delegated bureaucratic responsibilities from regular army offices in Washington to the Pennsylvania Military District. However, the 28th Division's headquarters lacked the resources and personnel to begin organizing thousands of service members. Similarly, there was nowhere near the number of trained physicians and medics necessary to process or update eyes exams, immunizations, dental checks, or X rays for thousands of personnel bound for overseas duty. The absence of institutional experience hamstrung efforts to jury-rig measures to keep the system functioning. Reserve medical officers who were recalled briefly to active duty to assist in screening had no knowledge of army regulations or standards and frequently ruined many of the physicals they intended to help.

Exactly who would eventually deploy with the division was also an open question in September, 1950. Neither the state capital in Harrisburg nor the Pentagon could agree on a consistent set of standards for hardship discharges. Service members could request termination for "essential employment," "educational interference," or family hardship. However, while many cases were being rejected by the Pennsylvania Military District, they were being approved by the army.[47] The cycle of applications and appeals bouncing back and forth between the state's and the nation's capitals played havoc with unit personnel rosters.

Despite these difficulties, the Keystone Division muddled through the early chaotic weeks of September in preparation for federal service. By the fall of 1950, it was ready for movement to Camp Atterbury, Indiana. Once arrived, every single formation and nearly every guard member underwent extensive retraining for active duty. The renovation process started from the ground up, emphasizing individual skills first learned by recruits in basic training. It was not a small consideration. In October, the commander of the U.S. Army, Lt. Gen. S. J. Chamberlain, had written directly to division commander Maj. Gen. Daniel B. Strickler to hammer home the "principle of self-respect,

CHAPTER 7

self-reliance, self-defense, and offensive action." Responding to the poor quality of enlisted soldiers evident during the opening phases of the Korean War, Chamberlain wanted Strickler to avoid "a tendency to short cut" in covering fundamental skills that he had observed in stateside basic-training programs.[48]

There was also a definite need for large-scale unit training. National Guard units traditionally met in their individual armories each month. The basic unit at these monthly training assemblies was the company, a collection of roughly one hundred men who broke down into even smaller platoons and sections to accomplish their scheduled tasks. It was rare for these scattered companies to meet up with their counterparts at the battalion level. Brigade exercises, even during the two-week annual training, were practically nonexistent.

An additional shortfall addressed at Camp Atterbury dealt with combined arms training. A built-in blind spot in the National Guard system was the practice of having local units concentrate on their particular specialties. Consequently, infantry units trained at infantry tasks. The field artillery kept mainly to their own batteries. Logistical units focused on their own individual missions as a matter of routine. Aside from annual training, it was rare to see mechanics work outside the motor pool. If opportunities for battalion and higher levels of training were rare, integrating the various types of arms—artillery, armor, tactical aircraft—never happened. For reasons of safety, live-fire exercises, when they were held, were usually limited to range qualifications. Budget and time restrictions placed a significant limit on even the possibility of cross-branch training. Over time, a certain myopia settled in as the annual cycle of maintenance and logistical requirements, unit inspections, and field exercises reinforced a military institution largely segregated from its counterpart units.

As a result, the Pennsylvania National Guard was severely handicapped when the moment arrived for it to enter federal service. The last time all of its major maneuver elements had functioned together was World War II. In truth, this distinction applied well beyond Pennsylvania, as a similar lack of coordination hampered all of the major service branches in 1950. Aircraft for tactical-support missions were technically owned by the embryonic air force and jealously guarded from the army. This was a critical omission, given the American military's reliance on firepower in place of troops on the ground, a dependence driven home after Communist China's intervention during the brutal winter fighting of 1950 and 1951. Perhaps the only branch deliberately integrated in combined armed warfare in 1950 was the Marine Corps, which itself was severely hampered by budget cuts that had been enacted before the war.[49]

At Camp Atterbury, combined-arms instruction accounted for 45 percent of the overall training program in the fall of 1950. Specific emphasis was placed on the process of obtaining and controlling air support.[50] In addition to these classes, training also focused on "battle indoctrination courses," which included obstacle courses that combined the usual barbed-wire mazes and ditches with live fire from prepositioned machine guns. Infiltration and escape-and evasion-methods were reinforced as well. The overall objective of this training was to acclimate soldiers to the stress of post-1945 combat. A January, 1951, division memorandum notes that modern war would not grant the time for troops to slowly get used to the tempo of battle. It recognized that there would not be a "quiet sector" along any portion of the front to break in new units. The demands of the Korean War during the winter of 1950–1951 also indicated a desperate need for soldiers who could withstand the constant strain of combat.[51]

Unfortunately, the Department of the Army short-circuited many of these measures just as they were beginning to produce results. In February, 1951, again desperate for replacements after the Communist Chinese intervention in the war, the army summarily required a levy of draftees who were then being trained in the 28th Division. One month later, it initiated a second levy of personnel, this time including National Guard and regular army personnel assigned to the division. Altogether, six thousand troops were summarily removed from units that had been training for deployment.[52]

It was a devastating blow to an organization that had made great strides toward full readiness. The February and March levies gutted the division at the precise moment when all of the training and preparation from the previous autumn had finally begun to jell. The removal of so many enlisted soldiers caused havoc at the small-unit level, disrupting a level of performance that resulted from constant repetition and personal familiarity. By this point, the soldiers' habits and their positive and negative additions to the unit were ingrained parts of the whole. Adding fresh replacements to this situation mandated that a unit start the entire process all over again.[53] More critically, the removal of experienced officers and NCOs robbed the 28th Infantry Division of the glue that held these formations together. By April, 1951, with the addition of new draftees, the division was able to field a full complement of personnel for the first time since World War II. However, by this point, the number of veterans within the formation had fallen to only three thousand men.[54]

As commanders coped with personnel problems, other logistical knots continued to cause headaches throughout the division. Internal communications systems were incomplete and in disrepair. In May, 1951, the assistant division signal officer reported that communications maintenance was severely handicapped by shortages of spare parts and replacements. He noted that the division staff had not yet completed a complete technical inspection of communications equipment. Vehicle maintenance was in even worse shape. The division ordinance officer, Lt. Col. Chester N. Rees, reported that same month that "maintenance of vehicles throughout the division is below satisfactory standards." He cited 150 vehicles, a significant proportion of the wheeled capability of the 28th Division, as deadlined because of various mechanical defects.[55]

Despite these lingering difficulties, the division began its final preparations for deployment during the summer of 1951. In August, the 28th, the 43rd Infantry Division, and the 82nd Airborne Division at Ft. Bragg, North Carolina, began joint exercises as part of Operation Southern Pine. For the first time since 1942, the Pennsylvania Guard was able to conduct brigade-level maneuvers under simulated combat conditions. By all accounts, it acquitted itself well, overcoming the inevitable confusion that such large masses of troops created, the heat of a harsh Southern summer, and an "enemy" opposition force of well-trained U.S. paratroopers.[56]

From Ft. Bragg, the 28th Division deployed to West Germany to become part of the U.S. forces assigned to NATO. There it was broken down into components assigned to patrol the East German border or conduct unit training and refresher courses. In relatively short order, the Keystone Division became part of the Cold War front line in Western Europe.

However, recognizing that the division was only a temporary addition to NATO, the Defense Department attempted to make amends for the soldiers deployed to West Germany. Troops had the usual gamut of tours and recreational activities available to other active-duty GIs, although they were warned to avoid conflicts with locals. For boys from

Pennsylvania, many of whom had never traveled beyond the Delaware Valley, it was the opportunity of a lifetime.

Beyond these distractions, military planners also took great pains to allow deployed soldiers a chance to continue their education while temporarily in uniform. Soldiers who were assigned to the 28th Division were offered nearly three hundred college correspondence courses through the U.S. Armed Forces Institute. They also had the option of taking hundreds of additional classes through forty-eight colleges and universities cooperating with the Defense Department.[57] In devoting these resources to service members, the Pentagon recognized that military duty would go only so far in motivating the average part-time soldier. Careers that had been put on hold back home still waited. Troopers guarding the border between Western Europe and the Communist bloc kept their minds focused on their mission but could not escape the realities of mortgages, college tuitions, and promotions—issues that defied the professional civilian limbo they found themselves in. In an important sense, a trend that had been started by the educational provisions of the GI Bill of Rights created an interesting symmetry between civilian training and military service. After World War II, military service had defined educational opportunity. However, by 1951, educational opportunity was defining the value of military service.

The 28th Infantry Division remained under federal orders until 1954. During its nearly three-year term, many of the original members trained at Camp Atterbury were rotated home and replaced by draftees. By the time the unit's colors came back to Pennsylvania, only a skeleton cadre from the 1950 mobilization remained. The National Guard returned this time, but not to parades and dramatic public acclaim. Most of the soldiers quietly and carefully picked up the threads of their civilian lives. Nearly half a century would pass before the 28th Infantry Division would be called upon for another major deployment.[58]

In the final analysis, the role played by veterans in the Korean War was both broad and multifaceted. Militarily, they provided a desperately needed reservoir of manpower for American armed forces perched on the brink of their greatest defeat in the twentieth century. Further, they provided important knowledge to units that comprised young draftees immediately engaged in the war and to those preparing for deployment at places like Camp Atterbury, Indiana. Politically, the veterans' general commitment to the war effort proved critical to the Truman administration. John Cogley, writing for *Commonweal* in 1953, reflected on a basic truth in America during the war: "I suppose that never before in our history have we had a fighting army backed up by so many civilians at home who should have a true understanding of what it means to be a soldier carrying on a war."[59] This understanding served a White House that called upon a sizable part of the population to abandon the postwar boom and embrace an unexpected separation from families, higher draft quotas, and the inevitable casualties that resulted from the conflict. Although the American public heartily endorsed an end to the Korean War, particularly as it bogged down into a stalemate after 1951, the country was never rocked by the protests that bedeviled the next decade. It is arguable that the veteran population, with a "true understanding" of the nature of war, created the critical mass of public support in America's first "hot" conflict of the Cold War.

This general foundation of wartime support also resurrected a public and programmatic emphasis on veterans in the fifties. One of the ironies of the Korean War is that the Veterans' Administration had begun an economy drive almost immediately before fighting broke out in the summer of 1950. Fraud, corruption, and inefficiency were front-page news items earlier in the year. A February, 1950, *New York Times* story titled "Millions in Waste Charged in Schooling for Veterans" highlights pervasive abuses of the GI Bill's educational benefits. Investigative journalists digging into this one avenue uncovered a cottage industry that had attached itself to the Servicemen's Readjustment Act, one that took advantage of the fact that the law had set no standards for entry requirements, curriculum standards, or faculty credentials in the more than 5,600 schools created below the college level, predominantly for veterans, since 1945. Widespread exploitation led to an announcement early in the year that educational benefits would be cut off after July 25, 1951.[60]

In fact, veterans' enrollments in educational institutions had already begun to decline by 1950. From a peak in 1948 and 1949 of 1.1 million, their numbers in colleges dropped by nearly 200,000 the following year and declined to 601,753 by the fall of 1950.[61] At the outbreak of the Korean War, the majority of former GIs were largely finished with their training and appeared ready for entry into the job market. The postwar wave of college applicants had, in the minds of most lawmakers, finally crested.

Cutbacks in veterans' medical benefits followed hard on the heels of educational downsizing in 1950. The amount of revenue spent by the VA shrank significantly that year. Major health-care providers such as the Brooklyn Regional Office of the VA saw one-third of its psychiatric and social-work staff cut in March. Overall, more than 7,800 employees were laid off from the Veterans' Administration that month.[62]

Efforts to roll back veterans' benefits came to a screeching halt in June, when North Korean forces began their offensive. From that point onward, officials in the Truman administration quickly embraced a reverse course, establishing legislation to extend existing benefits to the veterans who would inevitably come out of the war. The VA announced as early as July, 1950, that contemporary insurance and disability benefits would extend to Korean veterans.[63] Vocational-rehabilitation legislation followed in December and included provisions for tuition reimbursement and living expenses.[64] The following year, Congress overrode Truman's veto and increased pensions for nonservice disabilities to $120 a month.[65]

Holes in veterans' policy remained, however. The case of David R. Arellano, a discharged marine who was refused treatment for cancer by the Veterans' Administration, became part of a national scandal in May, 1951. The reason cited by VA officials was that Arellano had not technically served in a declared war. The resulting hue and cry over the story prompted the White House to request an extension of medical and pension benefits to Korean War veterans. The measure passed by a unanimous resolution in both houses in two hours.[66]

In some cases where legislative action was rapid and captured headlines, follow-through was often problematic and failed to arrest cutbacks that had started before the Korean War. While individual benefits for education and rehabilitation improved the lot of veterans, the Veterans' Administration itself continued to decline in important ways. A Joint Congressional Economic Committee report released in 1951 recommended a reduction in hospital construction and medical care within the VA system. The following year, the federal legislature complied, and 2,250 hospital employees were subsequently released from service. Similarly, the 1952 budget for the VA's Department of Medicine and Surgery was cut by 5 percent.[67]

Veterans groups immediately protested the cutbacks. The Disabled Veterans of America characterized the reductions as "a tragic betrayal of America's fighting men."[68] The medical community soon weighed in on the issue. Daniel Blain, medical director of the American Psychiatric Association (APA), warned that the shrinking budget would result in the "throttling of medical leadership and the inability to continue the employment of consultants and attending physicians" in VA hospitals. The APA went further, warning that the entire veterans' medical-care structure would completely deteriorate in five years if the decline in funding were not halted.[69]

No groundswell of public outrage or congressional reforms awaited these claims, however. President Truman did not again convene a press conference to dramatically announce the appointment of a new head of the VA. No one arrived to fix the problems confronting this latest generation of returning veterans. Omar Bradley remained in the Joint Chiefs of Staff, and no one of his caliber appeared on the political horizon to invoke the policies he had initiated many years before.

The simple fact was that 1953 was not 1945. At the time of the Korean armistice, the American public registered not a sense of joy over a war well fought but relief over a burden that had finally come to an end. The same acclaim lavished on the GIs who returned home in the earlier decade was more muted this time around. The country recognized the need to acknowledge service but stopped at the point where it would contemplate a dramatic departure in programs or attention. This sense of ambivalence was reflected in contemporary law devoted to veterans. Most of what was accomplished for them was a simple extension of what had already been done. Where any sense of urgency appeared, it usually focused on returning the GIs to an already established normalcy and not on looking back. This desire overshadowed the Korean War and those who served in it, placing both the event and the veterans in a time largely forgotten by history.

CHAPTER 8

Legacies

Our obligations to our country never cease but with our lives.
—*John Adams*

Our perception of the late forties has grown more complex with the passage of time and the inclusion of old details rediscovered by younger eyes. As we have peeled away the layers of this decade, old assumptions about the seamless transition from war to peace have diminished and, in some cases, disappeared altogether. We begin to see the late forties for what they were, a very rocky period punctuated by strikes, inflation, fear of a second Great Depression, bitter political partisanship, racial strife, and great social uncertainty.

Ironically, as a result of this study and contemplation, our perception of the time has come to reflect the understanding of those Americans who lived through it.[1] It has come, in other words, to represent a truer normalcy that included not only the achievements of the "greatest generation," which are crucial to the story, but also its foibles and failures, which are equally critical in striking a balance for historians and readers. In the 2000 edition of his memoir, *My War,* Andy Rooney frames the issue in a very simple context: "The popular works of Stephen Ambrose have helped younger generations learn about World War II and Tom Brokaw's *The Greatest Generation,* though flawed in its basic concept, has been a huge success and it has created added interest in details of that war. (It was my feeling that *The Greatest Generation* tailored the evidence to fit Tom's theory that our generation was special. He did an extraordinarily good job of it but we won the war not because we were special or different but because we had a war to fight. It seems probable that the current generation of Americans has the same qualities Tom so admires in ours, but has not had the occasion to call them up.)"[2]

Central to both the tragedies and the accomplishments of the times were sixteen million returning veterans. It is important to understand that it was the GIs and their families who were responsible for much of the tumult that followed the war. They stampeded the Truman administration into a demobilization that proved difficult to execute and disastrous for the country's strategic position at the outset of the Cold War. Their impatience fueled the contentious debates over domestic policies and gave an early start to a remarkably bitter political atmosphere in which the likes of Joseph McCarthy and Richard Nixon thrived.

On the opposite side of the ledger, the veterans deserve equal credit for establishing the footing of a stable and prosperous America. Guardians of the country in time of war, they took it upon themselves to act as caretakers of the peace. The skills they gained through the provisions of the GI Bill fueled and sustained the postwar boom. Over the years, ex-service members became inveterate joiners and leaders in politics, at work, and in their local communities. They became coaches, fund-raisers, and advocates of causes large and small. The list of objectives most of them pursued in the postwar period is a study in mundane topics. Yet, the overwhelming majority of these men and women made a basic decision to build a better America and pass this accomplishment along to the next generation, which was arriving each year in homes and delivery rooms by the millions. For the GI generation, their families were their country.

Yet a bothersome question remained: What would peacetime normalcy mean to these veterans? Real worry emerged when the harshness of military existence blended into their new civilian lives. James Jones, reflecting on the war thirty years after its conclusion, addresses what he calls "the de-evolution of a soldier" in these terms: "Slowly, bit by bit, it began to taper off. Men still woke up in the middle of the night, thrashing around and trying to get their hands on their wives' throats. Men still rolled out from a dead sleep and hit the dirt with a crash on the bedroom floor, huddling against the bed to evade the aerial bomb or artillery shell they had dreamed they heard coming. While their wives sat straight up in bed in their new frilly nightgowns bought for the homecoming, wide-eyed and staring, horrified."[3] However, even though the violent afterimages of combat faded, slipping away as they were healed by the passage of time, they were never completely purged from memory. The war loitered in the subconscious of millions, arriving unbidden at night when they least expected or wanted it. Unlike American veterans of wars during and after Vietnam, the ugly side of the war persisted in the minds of the GI generation and among the close comrades who had fought together. The reticence of World War II veterans to talk about their personal experiences would take decades to breach. In many cases, the deaths of old soldiers in their seventies and eighties circumvented their inclination to talk.

The war also appeared in the waking dream that was America in the forties. Bolstered by the discipline and confidence that military service had either created or refined, millions of former service members inserted themselves into the basic institutions that made America work, play, and live and transformed them in the process.

Veterans of World War II redefined American normalcy in terms that would last far beyond the forties. The very relationship between military service and citizenship was altered forever. After 1945, the peacetime draft became an American institution. For the first time in the nation's history, young male members of society were required by law to sacrifice a number of years of their lives to military service for the greater good. For most, the draft involved the inconvenience of separation from family, friends, and personal plans for a short period. At other times of national crisis, as was the case during the Korean War, it might have meant a real threat to life and limb. Regardless, the ethic of peacetime military service and the concept of collective duty persisted for a generation and became, at the same time, a measurement of civil credibility and one of the greatest points of controversy in recent American history.[4]

The World War II generation of veterans also had an enormous impact on the young men who went to Vietnam. In his novel *Fields of Fire*, James Webb describes what became a rite of passage for young boys everywhere in America: the discovery of their father's old footlocker. Containing the musty, mothballed old uniforms, decorations, and mementos of war, it revealed an unknown side of a man who was already a hero to his son in many ways. The footlocker would become the first link between a new generation and the last, a connection that passed along a fascination with things military and an embryonic sense of duty to a greater cause.[5]

The grip of this allure continued as the young lives of the boomer generation moved forward. Distinct in the memoirs of Vietnam veterans such as Ron Kovic and Philip Caputo are their mention of how much the fact and fiction of World War II surrounded them. Around the dinner table, they heard the inevitable war story. In the movie theater, they bathed in the cinematic glory of John Wayne or Gregory Peck.[6] "Then," Webb writes, "after the movies, they would stand shyly at the outer fringes of the gathered farmers who had come to spend their Saturdays in the courthouse square. The men would sit in gaggles, chewing slowly on cuds of tobacco or rolling their own cigarettes, talking of their wars and scratching faded scars."[7] Immersed in the culture of the war and its memory, the baby boomers reaching adulthood in the fifties and sixties found a yardstick by which to measure themselves all ready to use. Author Robert Timberg, speaking about the war's influence on his peers in *The Nightingale's Song*, notes that "World War II, the myth as well as the reality, was probably responsible, both for those who went and those who didn't. The Vietnam generation grew up on tales of sacrifice and heroism, of long lines in front of recruiting stations the day after Pearl Harbor, of a terrible burden equally shared."[8]

Myth and reality combined to transfer the responsibility of service to the next generation of Americans. In a very important sense, the boundaries of the debate over military service that would ravage the nation in the sixties were created by this transfer of obligation. For young people reaching adulthood in the post-1945 era, a conventional wisdom unlike any in American history was present to guide one important part of the early evolution of their lives or to assign a substantial social penalty if they decided to defy it. While race and economic class no doubt contributed significantly to the controversy regarding the draft that roiled through America during the sixties, the expectations created by sixteen million veterans of World War II stood at the heart of the conflict.

Veterans of World War II also permanently changed the basic nature of the federal state after 1945. In a very real sense, the GI Bill and all the legislation that it carried in its wake created a bridge between Franklin Roosevelt's New Deal and Lyndon Johnson's Great Society. Simply put, programs of veterans' benefits represented a quantum leap in the growth of the American social-welfare state, far exceeding anything that had been contemplated at the height of the Great Depression and contributing significantly to the baseline for subsequent programs in the sixties and seventies. As it applied to health, education, work, housing, business, and a staggering array of other activities, the Servicemen's Readjustment Act of 1944 was unprecedented in its scope and scale.

Perhaps equally important, the GI Bill reduced the social stigma that veterans suffered for overt dependence on the state. The myriad of programs that flowed from Washington undoubtedly helped them to heal their wounds and create unimaginable socioeconomic progress. However, large portions of federal budgets for veterans' assistance were devoted to economic and social limbo. About 60 percent of World War II veterans chose membership in what they euphemistically called the 52-20 Club and accepted a "readjustment" allowance of twenty dollars per week while they decided what to make of their lives after the war. On average, "membership" in the 52-20 Club lasted nineteen weeks rather than fifty-two, a relatively small draw on a potentially large benefit.[9] However, a review of veterans' claims for unemployment benefits reveals a much different story. Between September, 1944, and December, 1950, more than 185 *million* claims totaling $3.2 billion were made under Title V of the GI Bill.[10] While it is clear that World War II veterans took full advantage of federal and state benefits programs to advance both their lives and their fortunes after 1945, it is equally apparent that they were more than willing to accept an increasingly elaborate social safety net constructed by government policy.

For the GI generation, accommodation became an increasingly prevalent expectation. On one level, many of these changes were definitely for the good. The utility of military service to advance the cause of civil rights was a breakthrough in the forties that energized minorities in America and led inexorably to further pressure for reform in the fifties and sixties. Similarly, the scramble set off by colleges and universities intent on capturing federal dollars, coupled with the demands made by veterans for entry into higher education, ended an atmosphere of exclusivity that had prevented many aspiring students from advancing their education.

Problems arose, however, not so much with the ends intended by some of these accommodations, but with the means used to achieve them. The willingness of colleges and universities to welcome massive new student populations opened education to an increasing proportion of the American public. Unfortunately, access came at the cost of rising student-faculty ratios, stadium seating in introductory courses, vast dorm complexes that clustered students together in unheard-of numbers, and a growing depersonalization of learning. The taffy pull that college curriculums began to reflect, with its ongoing desire to accommodate life experience, noncollege training, and utility in the job market, created flexibility at the cost of intellectual contemplation. Education, by virtue of its desire to create a more welcoming environment, became more of a commodity than a privilege after World War II. The collective result of these trends was a growing sense of restiveness and disillusionment that would later explode on college campuses in the sixties.[11]

Veterans of World War II were responsible for the creation of an additional bridge in America, one that spanned the distance between American society of the thirties and the baby boomers, who arrived after 1945. In his book *The Age of Doubt,* historian William Graebner observes that the forties placed a premium on both collective cooperation and a positive emphasis on self. Sacrifice to the greater good and self-aggrandizement became parallel and paradoxical keynotes in the decade and a permanent part of postwar American life.[12] The question scholars often debate revolves around the point at which the individual became the guiding light in America, determining the course of social interaction, economy, and politics. For the most part, historians have been willing to assign responsibility for this passage to the baby boomers, consigning the national cult of narcissism and self-indulgence to the generation that followed the war. It has become something of a historical cliché to mark the "me decade" of the seventies as the moment when the national consensus, forged by World War II, was finally overwhelmed by the pursuit of individualism.[13]

The story lacks a key element, however. While the boomers unquestionably benefited from the affluence of post-1945 America and had a multitude of expectations created by it, this knowledge required a framework, a set of reference points that could mark and measure what the future might hold. Who better than the parents of these children, the victors of war, to shepherd them to the next stage in the American dream?

After 1945, World War II veterans built a bridge between the collective and individual priorities that drove the country. Omar Bradley stated prophetically in May, 1946, that "The objective of the Veterans' Administration is and has been to meet the individual needs of ex-servicemen according to his [*sic*] own desires."[14] In Bradley's time, official policy was designed to augment the personal preferences of a generation of veterans who had served in a war and waited since the

Great Depression to pursue their long-deferred personal gratification.[15] The war succeeded in cementing this individual ambition with the legitimacy of sacrifice earned in the performance of national duty. The cornucopia of programs that followed came with a credible expectation that they were entitlements earned for a job well done. The "rights revolution" had begun.[16]

Passing the dual ethic of service and entitlement to the children born after World War II became a problematic exercise. For the baby-boom generation, the benefits of military service were established parts of life, divorced from the urgency and sacrifice that drove their fathers and mothers during the war. Suburbs were built. Doors to colleges were open. Prosperity was everywhere in the air they breathed during the fifties and sixties. The foundation of it, the service of millions of veterans, was history to them, abstract and almost archaic. The cleavage that was the generation gap was built around this disconnect between the fruits of victory and their origin.

Interestingly, today, as the country finds itself at war again, the veterans of World War II have regained much relevance to their grandchildren now in uniform. Four aircraft plunging into Manhattan, the Pentagon, and a patch of Pennsylvania farmland shoved aside the rampant, boisterous self-indulgence that defines the nineties and replaced it with a renewed focus on duty. Public service, embodied in the police, fire, and military personnel mobilized to meet the disaster, once again occupies a premium place in American life. The fundamental importance of this service to the survival of the nation has once again dawned in the public mind.

Veterans of World War II live as a touchstone for this generation. Their struggles and mistakes are no longer the abstract stuff of *Saving Private Ryan* but real-life examples for young men and women rapidly driven to maturity in a time of national crisis. The old soldiers, sailors, and marines will live again as the latest generation pursues its own definition of the American dream.

NOTES

Introduction

1. Theodore Ropp, *War in the Modern World* (New York: Macmillan, 1962), pp. 19–25.

2. Douglas Edward Leach, *Flintlock and Tomahawk: New England in King Philip's War* (East Orleans, Mass.: Parnassus Imprints, 1958), pp. 103–11.

3. For examples of this characteristic, see Warren W. Hassler, *With Shield and Sword: American Military Affairs, Colonial Times to the Present* (Ames: Iowa State University Press, 1982), pp. 3–19. This was a particular problem during the Pequot Wars, when colonies to the south of New England balked at the idea of sending expeditions to relieve the besieged Plymouth and Massachusetts Bay colonies. See Leach, Flintlock and Tomahawk, pp. 176–77. The same tendency plagued later British efforts to coordinate military campaigns between 1689 and 1763.

4. Walter Millis, *Arms and Men: A Study in American Military History* (New Brunswick, N.J.: Rutgers University Press, 1984), pp. 13–25.

5. R. Claire Snyder, *Citizen-Soldiers and Manly Warriors: Military Service and Gender in the Civic Republican Tradition* (New York: Rowman and Littlefield, 1995), pp. 80–86; see also Eleanor L. Hannah, "Manhood, Citizenship, and the Formation of the National Guards, Illinois, 1870–1917" (Ph.D. diss., University of Chicago, 1997).

6. Snyder, *Citizen-Soldiers and Manly Warriors*, pp. 80–86.

7. Bruce Lancaster, *The American Revolution* (Boston: Houghton Mifflin, 1985), pp. 343–44.

8. Forrest McDonald, *Novus Ordo Seclorum: The Intellectual Origins of the Constitution* (Lawrence: University Press of Kansas, 1985), pp. 179–80.

9. Edward Pessen, *Jacksonian America: Society, Personality, and Politics* (Chicago: University of Illinois, 1985), pp. 149–96; George B. Tindall and David E. Shi, America: A Narrative History, 5th ed. (New York: Norton, 2000), p. 313.

10. David Herbert Donald, *Lincoln* (London: Jonathan Cape, 1995), pp. 44–45.

11. William S. McFeeley, *Grant: A Biography* (New York: Norton, 1982), pp. 276–77.

12. Edmund Morris, *The Rise of Theodore Roosevelt* (New York: Ballantine Books, 1979), pp. 662–87.

13. William H. Glasson, *History of Military Pension Legislation in the United States* (New York: Columbia University Press, 1900), pp. 12–19.

14. Ibid., p. 17.

15. Ibid., p. 42.

16. Ibid., pp. 20, 44–45, 91–95.

17. Glasson, *History of Military Pension Legislation,* pp. 73–76, 78, 90, 104; William H. Glasson, Federal Military Pensions in the United States (New York: Oxford University Press, 1918), pp. 123–30; Harold M. Hyman, American Singularity: The 1787 Northwest Ordinance, the 1862 Homestead and Morrill Acts, and the 1944 GI Bill (Athens: University of Georgia Press, 1986), pp. 62–63.

18. Patrick J. Kelly, *Creating a National Home: Building the Veterans' Welfare State, 1860–1900* (Cambridge: Harvard University Press, 1997), pp. 55–57.

19. Allan R. Millett and Peter Maslowski, *For the Common Defense: A Military History of the United States of America* (New York: Free Press, 1994), p. 653.

20. William P. Dillingham, *Federal Aid to Veterans, 1917–1941* (Gainesville: University of Florida Press, 1952), pp. 54, 58–59; J. M. Stephen Peeps, "A B.A. for the GI . . . Why?" History of Education Quarterly 24 (Winter, 1984): 513–25. See also Nancy Gentile Ford, Americans All! Foreign-born Soldiers in World War I (College Station: Texas A&M University Press, 2001), and David M. Kennedy, Over Here: The First World War and American Society (New York: Oxford University Press, 1980).

21. Peeps, "A B.A. for the GI . . . Why?" pp. 513–25.

22. Dillingham, *Federal Aid to Veterans,* pp. 14–15.

23. The VFW was formed in 1913 from a conglomeration of local and state veterans' groups.

24. Jennifer E. Brooks, "From Hitler and Tojo to Talmadge and Jim Crow: World War Two Veterans and the Remaking of the Southern Political Tradition" (Ph.D. diss., University of Tennessee, Knoxville, 1997), pp. 7–10.

25. See Thomas A. Rumer, *The American Legion: An Official History, 1919–1989* (New York: M. Evans, 1990), pp. 8–56.

26. Dillingham, *Federal Aid to Veterans,* pp. 131–32, 141, 224.

27. James T. Patterson, *Grand Expectations: The United States, 1945–1974* (New York: Oxford University Press, 1996), p. 7.

28. For an excellent account of this story, see David Brinkley, *Washington Goes to War* (New York: Ballantine Books, 1988).

29. Publishers offered extensive catalogues of benefits programs available through state and federal agencies. See, for example, Charles Hurd, *The Veterans' Program: A Complete Guide to Its Benefits, Rights, and Options* (New York: McGraw Hill, 1946).

30. See Patterson, *Grand Expectations,* pp. 12–15. Patterson's book, winner of the 1997 Bancroft Prize, spends only a brief three pages on the topic. For a relatively recent example, see Eugenia Kaledin, Daily Life in the United States, 1940–1959: Shifting Worlds (Westport, Conn.: Greenwood Press, 2000). Kaledin mentions veterans exactly twice and only briefly. One explanation might be rooted in the tendency of historians to follow the most recently declassi-

fied scholars, with a few notable exceptions, and in the fact that they have also moved away from the forties in search of new documents that illuminate later periods.

31. For an example of this topic, see Anne L. Shewring, "We Didn't Do That, Did We? Representation of the Veteran Experience," *Journal of American and Comparative Cultures* 23 (Winter, 2000): 51–66.

32. For recent studies see Sarah Turner and John Bound, "Closing the Gap or Widening the Divide: The Effects of the GI Bill and World War II on the Educational Outcomes of Black Americans," *Journal of Labor History* 63 (Mar., 2003): 145–77, and Michael J. Bennett, When Dreams Come True: The GI Bill and the Making of Modern America (London: Brassey's, 1996). An excellent standard work on the subject remains Keith W. Olson, The GI Bill, The Veterans, and the Colleges (Lexington: University Press of Kentucky, 1974).

33. David A. Gerber, ed., *Disabled Veterans in History* (Ann Arbor: University of Michigan Press, 2000); Robert Klein, Wounded Men, Broken Promises (New York: Macmillan, 1981); Sar A. Levitan and Karen A. Cleary, Old Wars Remain Unfinished: The Veterans' Benefits System (Baltimore: Johns Hopkins University Press, 1973).

34. See, for example, David H. Onkst, " 'First a Negro, Incidentally a Veteran': Black World War Two Veterans and the GI Bill of Rights in the Deep South, 1944–1948," *Journal of Social History* 31 (Spring/Summer, 1998): 517–44; Henry A. J. Ramos, The American GI Forum: In Pursuit of the Dream, 1948–1983 (Houston: Arte Publico Press, 1998); Carina A. del Rosario, ed., A Different Battle: Stories of Asian Pacific Veterans (Seattle: University of Washington Press, 1999); Richard Aquila, Home Front Soldier: The Story of a GI and His Italian American Family during World War II (Albany: State University of New York Press, 1999); Jeré Bishop Franco, Crossing the Pond: The Native American Effort in World War II (Denton: University of North Texas Press, 1999); Maggi M. Morehouse, Fighting in the Jim Crow Army: Black Men and Women Remember World War II (New York: Rowman and Littlefield, 2000). See also Robert F. Jefferson, "Organization Is the Key: Wounded African American World War II Ex-GIs and the Civil Rights Struggles of the Late 1940s" (paper presented at the Veteran and Society Conference, Knoxville, Tenn., Nov., 2000).

35. See, for example, Leisa D. Meyer, *Creating GI Jane: Sexuality and Power in the Women's Army Corps during World War II* (New York: Columbia University Press, 1996). For some of the earliest and best work on this subject, see D'Ann Campbell, "Servicewomen of World War II," Armed Forces and Society 16 (Winter, 1990): 252.

36. Many of these collections appear on the Internet. One of the best is by Kurt Piehler and is held at Rutgers University. See also Charity Adams Early, *One Woman's Army* (College Station: Texas A&M University Press, 1989); Howard S. Hoffman and Alicia M. Hoffman, Archives of Memory: A Soldier Recalls World War II (Lexington: University Press of Kentucky, 1990); Frances Zauhar, Richard D. Wissolik, and Jennifer Campion, eds., Out of the Kitchen: Women in the Armed Services and on the Homefront: The Oral Histories of Pennsylvania Veterans of World War II (Latrobe, Penn.: Saint Vincent College, 1995);

Judy Barrett Litoff and David E. Smith, eds., American Women in a World at War: Contemporary Accounts from World War II (Wilmington, Del.: Scholarly Resources, 1997); LaVonne Telshaw Camp, Lingering Fever: A World War II Nurse's Memoir (Jefferson, N.C.: McFarland, 1997); Russell E. McLogan, Boy Soldier: Coming of Age during World War II (Reading, Mich.: Terrus Press, 1998); Edward M. Coffman, "Talking about War: Reflections on Doing Oral History and Military History," Journal of American History (Sept., 2000): 582–91; John Milliken Hall, ed., My Brother's Letters Home: Blutiger Eimer (28th) Division Field Artillery Officer's Letters Home (New York: Vantage Press, 1999); John Bodnar, "Saving Private Ryan and Postwar Memory in America," American Historical Review 106 (June, 2001): 805–17.

37. Mark D. Van Ells, *To Hear Only Thunder Again: America's World War II Veterans Come Home* (Lanham, Mass.: Lexington Books, 2001). Earlier examples include Richard Severo and Lewis Milford, The Wages of War: When America's Soldiers Came Home—from Valley Forge to Vietnam (New York: Simon and Schuster, 1989); Davis R. B. Ross, Preparing for Ulysses: Politics and Veterans during World War II (New York: Columbia University Press, 1969).

Chapter 1

1. Marion Hargrove, *See Here, Private Hargrove* (New York: Henry Holt, 1942), pp. 3–4. See also James Jones, WWII (New York: Ballantine Books, 1975), pp. 31–32; Gwynne Dyer, War (New York: Crown, 1985), pp. 102–28.

2. Paul Fussell, *Wartime: Understanding and Behavior in the Second World War* (New York: Oxford University Press, 1989), pp. 66–78. For an interesting treatment of mobilization, see Lorraine Bayard de Volo, "Drafting Motherhood: Maternal Imagery and Organizations in the United States and Nicaragua," in The Women and War Reader, ed. Lois Ann Lorentzen and Jennifer Turpin (New York: New York University Press, 1998), pp. 240–53; Sonya Michel, "American Women and the Discourse of the Democratic Family in World War II," in Behind the Lines: Gender and the Two World Wars, ed. Margaret Randolph Higonnet et al. (New Haven, Conn.: Yale University Press, 1987), pp. 154–67; William H. Chafe, The Paradox of Change: American Women in the Twentieth Century (New York: Oxford University Press, 1991), pp. 176–77.

3. T. Grady Gallant, *On Valor's Side* (New York: Doubleday, 1963), pp. 41–42, 99. See also Richard Holmes, Acts of War: The Behavior of Men in Battle (New York: Free Press, 1985), pp. 36–56.

4. Thomas R. St. George, *C/o Postmaster* (New York: Thomas Y. Crowell, 1943), pp. 16–17.

5. Wilbur D. Jones, *Gyrene: The World War II United States Marine* (Shippensburg, Penn.: White Mane Books, 1998), p. 8.

6. Ernie Pyle, *Last Chapter* (New York: Henry Holt, 1946), p. 130.

7. Annette Tappert, ed., *Lines of Battle: Letters from American Servicemen, 1941–1945* (New York: Times Books, 1987), p. 271.

8. S. L. A. Marshall, *Men against Fire: The Problem of Battle Command in Future War* (New York: William Morrow, 1947), pp. 56–57.

9. Dyer, *War,* p. 120.

10. Samuel A. Stouffer et al., *The American Soldier,* vol. 2, Combat and Its Aftermath (Princeton: Princeton University Press, 1949), p. 583.

11. Some contemporary civilian writers addressed the problem of veterans' expectations. See George K. Pratt, *Soldier to Civilian: Problems of Readjustment* (New York: McGraw Hill, 1944), pp. 113–15.

12. Judy Barrett Litoff and David C. Smith, eds., *Since You Went Away: World War II Letters from American Women on the Home Front* (New York: Oxford University Press, 1991), pp. 208–209.

13. Stephen E. Ambrose, *Band of Brothers: E Company, 506th Regiment, 101st Airborne, from Normandy to Hitler's Eagle's Nest* (New York: Simon and Schuster, 1992), pp. 277–81; Robert Peters, For You, Lili Marlene: A Memoir of World War II (Madison: University of Wisconsin Press, 1995), pp. 73–75.

14. Charity Adams Early, *One Woman's Army: A Black Officer Remembers the WAC* (College Station: Texas A&M University Press, 1989), p. 173.

15. Andy Rooney, *My War* (New York: Essay Productions, 1995), p. 282.

16. Stephen E. Ambrose, *Eisenhower: Soldier, General of the Army, President-Elect, 1890–1952* (New York: Simon and Schuster, 1983), p. 409.

17. Stouffer et al., *American Soldier,* p. 457.

18. Ibid., p. 534.

19. Keith E. Eiler, *Mobilizing America: Robert P. Patterson and the War Effort, 1940–1945* (Ithaca, N.Y.: Cornell University Press, 1997), pp. 427–29, 434–35; Stouffer et al., American Soldier, pp. 520–30.

20. Robert J. Havighurst et al., *The American Veteran Back Home: A Study of Readjustment* (New York: Longmans, Green, 1951), p. 67.

21. Memo, Col. H. D. W. Riley to Brig. Gen. K. C. Royale (special assistant to the secretary of war), "Transmittal of Transcript of Minutes of Meeting," Oct. 14, 1945, National Archives and Records Administration (hereafter NARA), RG 165, War Department general staff, box 327; Michael J. Bennett, *When Dreams Come True: The GI Bill and the Making of Modern America* (London: Brassey's, 1996), p. 206.

22. Memo for the president from Fred M. Vinson (Office of War Mobilization and Reconversion), July 20, 1945, in *Documentary History of the Truman Presidency: Demobilization and Reconversion: Rebuilding a Peacetime Economy following WWII,* vol. 4, ed. Dennis Merrill (Frederick, Md.: University Publications of America, 1996), p. 115.

23. Letter, Robert Patterson (secretary of war) to Andrew J. May (chair, Committee on Military Affairs), Aug. 31, 1945, NARA, RG 165, War Department general staff, decimal file, 1942–June, 1946, box 317.

24. Cable, Dwight D. Eisenhower to Robert P. Patterson (secretary of war), Jan. 15, 1946, in *The Papers of Dwight David Eisenhower: The Chief of Staff,* vol. 7, ed. Louis Galambos (Baltimore: Johns Hopkins University Press, 1989), pp. 645–46; John C. Sparrow, History of Personnel Demobilization in the United States Army (Washington, D.C.: Center of Military History, 1994), pp. 161–67; radiogram, "Advertisement to Be Inserted in 15 Leading U.S. Newspapers," Jan. 9, 1946, Walter P. Reuther Library, Emil Mazey Papers, box 4.

25. John J. Noll, "Goodbye, Olive Drab," *American Legion Magazine* 38 (Jan., 1945), p. 10; Charles Hurd, "The Veteran's Return," American Legion Magazine 38 (Mar., 1945), pp. 10–11. By March, 1945, two months before the formal German surrender, 1.5 million veterans had already returned from overseas.

26. Eilier, *Mobilizing America,* pp. 449, 450; Stouffer et al., American Soldier, p. 547.

27. Memo from Col. H. D. W. Riley to Brig. Gen. K. C. Royale, "Transmittal of Transcript of Minutes of Meeting," Oct. 14, 1945, NARA, RG 165, records of the War Department general staff, box 327.

28. Harry S. Truman, *Memoirs,* vol. 1, 1945: Year of Decisions (Garden City, N.J.: Doubleday, 1955), p. 509.

29. Letter, Maj. Gen. W. S. Paul (assistant chief of staff, G-1) to James M. Mead (chair, Special Committee Investigating the National Defense Program), Apr. 22, 1946, NARA, RG 165, War Department general staff, box 327.

30. Arthur T. Hadley, *The Straw Giant: America's Armed Forces, Triumphs and Failures* (New York: Avon Books, 1987), p. 61.

31. Theresa Archard, *GI Nightingale: The Story of an American Army Nurse* (New York: Norton, 1945), p. 178.

32. Ibid., p. 179; Alvin H. Goldstein, "Home, Boys, Home," *American Legion Magazine* 39 (Oct., 1945), p. 50; Carina A. del Rosario, ed., A Different Battle: Stories of Asian Pacific Veterans (Seattle: University of Washington Press, 1999), p. 35.

33. David Kennedy, *Freedom from Fear: The American People in Depression and War, 1929–1945* (New York: Oxford University Press, 1999), pp. 747–48.

34. Bennett, *When Dreams Come True,* p. 11.

35. Ibid., p. 16; see also David McCullough, *Truman* (New York: Simon and Schuster, 1992), pp. 480–81, 492–93, and Robert J. Donovan, Conflict and Crisis: The Presidency of Harry S. Truman (New York: Norton, 1977), pp. 116–26, 163–76, 208–18.

36. Agnes E. Meyer, "The Veterans Say, 'Or Else!' " *Collier's* (Oct. 12, 1946), pp. 16–17.

37. Ibid.; Charles G. Bolté, "We're on Our Own," *Atlantic Monthly* 179 (May, 1947), p. 29; Veterans' Administration, GI Loans: The First Ten Years, 1944–1954, VA pamphlet 4A-11, June 22, 1954, American Legion Library, Veterans' Welfare Classification, GI Bill file; Office of War Mobilization and Reconversion, Office of the Housing Expediter, The Veterans' Emergency Housing Program: A Report to the President, Feb. 7, 1946, Library of Congress, records of the NAACP, branch files, 1940–1955, box A657; Omar N. Bradley, Collected Writings: Articles, Broadcasts, and Statements, 1945–1967, vol. 3 (Washington, D.C.: GPO, 1967), p. 203.

38. "Report on the Activities of the CIO Committee on Housing," Sept. 8, 1947, Walter P. Reuther Library, UAW Office of the President, R. J. Thomas Collection, part 3, box 32.

39. Office of Temporary Controls, Office of War Mobilization and Reconversion, "Economic and Statistical Notes of Current Interest," Jan. 7, 1947, in *Documentary History of the Truman Presidency: Demobilization and Reconversion, Re-*

building a Peacetime Economy following WWII, vol. 4, ed. Dennis Merrill (Frederick, Md.: University Publications of America, 1996), p. 744; Kennedy, Freedom from Fear, p. 641.

40. William M. Tuttle, *Daddy's Gone to War: The Second World War in the Lives of America's Children* (New York: Oxford University Press, 1993), pp. 218, 220. According to statistical analysis by D'Ann Campbell, one in five veterans had children. See D'Ann Campbell, Women at War with America: Private Lives in a Patriotic Era (Cambridge: Harvard University Press, 1984), pp. 90–91. See also Anna W. M. Wolf and Irma Simonton, "What Happened to the Younger People?" in While You Were Gone: A Report on Wartime Life in the United States, ed. Jack Goodman (New York: Simon and Schuster, 1946), pp. 71–72. For an interesting contemporary examination of the American family and the war, see Therese Benedek, Insight and Personality Adjustment: A Study of the Psychological Effects of War (New York: Ronald Press, 1946), pp. 103–242.

41. Michael C. C. Adams, *The Best War Ever: America in World War II* (Baltimore: Johns Hopkins University Press, 1994), pp. 123, 132, and see also pp. 40–45; Joseph C. Goulden, The Best Years, 1945–1950 (New York: Atheneum, 1976), pp. 41–42.

42. U.S. Department of Labor, *Thirty-fourth Annual Report of the Secretary of Labor for the Fiscal Year Ended June 30, 1946* (Washington, D.C.: GPO, 1947), p. 211; U.S. Department of Labor, Thirty-fifth Annual Report of the Secretary of Labor for the Fiscal Year Ended June 30, 1947 (Washington, D.C.: GPO, 1948), p. 104; Sherna Berger Gluck, Rosie the Riveter Revisited: Women, the War, and Social Change (Boston: Twayne, 1987), p. 16.

43. Stouffer et al., *American Soldier*, pp. 468, 583.

44. William Graebner, *The Age of Doubt: American Thought and Culture in the 1940s* (Boston: Twayne, 1991), p. 9.

45. John Dos Passos, *Tour of Duty* (Boston: Houghton Mifflin, 1946), p. 244.

46. Jones, *Gyrene*, 255; J. Glenn Gray, The Warriors: Reflections on Men in Battle (New York: Harper and Row, 1970), pp. 1–14; Stanley Weintraub, The Last Great Victory: The End of World War II, July/August 1945 (New York: Truman Talley Books/Dutton, 1995), p. 45. An excellent study of the relationship between veterans and civilians in World War II is found in Gerald F. Linderman, The World within War: America's Combat Experience in World War II (New York: Free Press, 1997), pp. 300–44.

47. Janice Holt Giles, *The GI Journal of Sergeant Giles* (Boston: Houghton Mifflin, 1965), pp. 376–77.

48. William Manchester, *Goodbye, Darkness: A Memoir of the Pacific War* (Boston: Little, Brown, 1979), p. 380. See also James Jones, The Thin Red Line (New York: Charles Scribner's Sons, 1962), p. 339. Jones was pointed in his references to the postwar era: "Perhaps long years after the war was done, when each had built his defenses of lies which fitted his needs, and had listened long enough to those other lies the national propaganda would have distilled for them by then, they could all go down to the American Legion like their fathers and talk about it within the limits of a prescribed rationale which allowed them selfrespect [sic]." See also Leon C. Standifer, Not in Vain: A Rifleman Remem-

bers World War II (Baton Rouge: Louisiana State University Press, 1992), pp. 215–16.

49. Gray, *The Warriors*, pp. 203–54.

50. Stouffer et al., *American Soldier*, p. 599; Peters, For You, Lili Marlene, p. 76.

51. Ben Kagan, "The Veteran Comes Back," *Jewish Veteran* 14 (Dec., 1944), pp. 4–6.

52. For example, see Francis J. Braceland, *The Retraining and Reeducation of Veterans* (Oberlin, Ohio: Oberlin College, 1945); Alexander Dumas, A Psychiatric Primer for the Veteran's Family and Friends (Minneapolis: University of Minnesota Press, 1945); Morse A. Cartwright, Marching Home: Educational and Social Adjustment after the War (New York: Institute of Adult Education, 1944).

53. Clarice H. L. Pennock, "The GI Volunteer," *Compass* 27 (Apr., 1946), pp. 10–11; Grace Sloan Overton, Marriage in War and Peace: A Book for Parents and Counselors of Youth (New York: Abingdon-Cokesbury Press, 1945), pp. 40–45; Goulden, Best Years, pp. 37–39.

54. Maxwell Gitelson, "The Role of the Community in Relation to the Emotional Needs of the Returning Soldier," *Social Service Review* 19 (1945): 94.

55. Pratt, *Soldier to Civilian: Problems of Readjustment*, pp. 113–14.

56. Alice C. Lloyd, "Women in the Postwar College," *Journal of the American Association of University Women* 39 (Spring, 1946): 131–34.

57. Jud Kinberg, "Faults on Both Sides," *American Scholar* 16 (Summer, 1947): 347; M. T. Cooke, "The Need for Direction and Meaning," American Scholar 16 (Summer, 1947): 345; Thomas N. Bonner, "The Unintended Revolution in America's Colleges since 1940," Change 18 (Sept./Oct., 1986): 46; Robert M. Hutchins, "A Plan to Meet 'The Crisis in Education,' " New York Times Magazine 28 (June 9, 1946), p. 11.

58. Willard Waller, *The Veteran Comes Back* (New York: Dryden Press, 1944), pp. 28, 89–103, 115.

59. Dixon Wecter, *When Johnny Comes Marching Home* (Boston: Houghton Mifflin, 1944), p. 5.

60. John Kenneth Galbraith, *The Great Crash: 1929* (Boston: Houghton Mifflin, 1954), pp. 154–67, 168–94; John Kenneth Galbraith, The Affluent Society (Boston: Houghton Mifflin, 1958), pp. 108–10. For contemporary concerns about the transition to peace, see E. Jay Howenstine, The Economics of Demobilization (Washington, D.C.: Public Affairs Press, 1944), pp. 23–29.

61. Kennedy, *Freedom from Fear*, pp. 746–97; McCullough, Truman, pp. 468–69; Donovan, Conflict and Crisis, p. 108; James T. Patterson, Grand Expectations: The United States, 1945–1974 (New York: Oxford University Press, 1996), pp. 3–9; U.S. Department of Labor, Thirty-fourth Annual Report of the Secretary of Labor for the Fiscal Year Ended June 30, 1946 (Washington, D.C.: GPO, 1947), p. 5; Bennett, When Dreams Come True, p. 195.

62. Geoffrey Perrett, *Days of Sadness, Years of Triumph: The American People, 1939–1945* (New York: Coward, McCann, and Geoghegan, 1973), p. 399.

63. Richard Severo and Lewis Milford, *The Wages of War: When America's*

Soldiers Came Home—from Valley Forge to Vietnam (New York: Simon and Schuster, 1989), pp. 284, 290.

64. Robert G. Adams, army service questionnaire, Mar. 21, 1989; Edward Nedved, army service questionnaire, n.d., U.S. Military History Institute (hereafter USMHI), WWII veterans' survey, 1st Armored Division, individuals, alphabetically arranged.

65. Stouffer et al., *American Soldier,* p. 561.

66. Veterans' Administration, *GI Loans: The First Ten Years, 1944–1954,* VA pamphlet 4A-11, June 22, 1954.

67. Hurd, *The Veterans' Program,* pp. 2, 27–28.

68. David Camelon, "I Saw the GI Bill Written," *American Legion Magazine* 47 (Nov., 1949), p. 45; Severo, Wages of War, p. 286.

69. Davis R. B. Ross, *Preparing for Ulysses: Politics and Veterans during World War II* (New York: Columbia University Press, 1969), pp. 192–237. Although dated, the book offers an important breakdown of federal-policy development following the war. See also Veterans' Administration, administrator of veterans' affairs, Annual Report for Fiscal Year Ending June 30, 1945 (Washington, D.C.: GPO, 1946) for listings of the first of hundreds of separate acts of Congress passed after 1945. See also NARA, RG 147, records of the Selective Service System, 1940–, Special Monograph Studies, 1945–1953, box 1.

70. Office of War Mobilization and Reconversion, *From War to Peace: A Challenge,* Aug. 15, 1945; director of War Mobilization and Reconversion, Second Report to the President, the Senate, and the House of Representatives, Apr. 1, 1945, in Documentary History of the Truman Presidency: Demobilization and Reconversion, Rebuilding a Peacetime Economy following WWII, vol. 4, ed. Dennis Merrill (Frederick, Md.: University Publications of America, 1996), pp. 34, 191.

71. Hurd, *The Veterans' Program,* pp. 198–204.

72. Hurd's book, for example, breaks down benefits programs from federal sources as well as state by state.

73. Interview, Jan. 18, 1970, Marine Corps Historical Center, Oral History Collection, p. 406.

74. Sutherland Denlinger, "The Vets' Best Bet," *Collier's* (Apr. 27, 1946), pp. 34, 54; for an example of Erskine's efforts to strengthen local authority, see U.S. Department of Labor, Retraining and Reemployment Administration, To Organize, to Operate Your Community Advisory Center for Veterans and Others (Washington, D.C.: GPO, 1946).

75. Omar N. Bradley and Clay Blair, *A General's Life* (New York: Simon and Schuster, 1983), pp. 439–41.

76. Forrest C. Pogue, *George C. Marshall: Statesman, 1945–1959* (New York: Viking Penguin, 1987), p. 438.

77. U.S. House of Representatives, Committee on Veterans' Affairs, *Medical Care of Veterans* (Washington, D.C.: GPO, 1967), p. 189.

78. Bradley and Blair, *A General's Life,* pp. 441; Donald J. Lisio, "United States: Bread and Butter Politics," in The War Generation: Veterans of the First World War, ed. Stephen R. Ward et al. (Port Washington, N.Y.: Kennikat Press, 1975), p. 46.

79. Bradley, *Collected Writings,* vol. 3, p. 217.

80. Bradley and Blair, *A General's Life,* p. 450. See also Annual Report of the Administrator of Veterans' Affairs for the Fiscal Year Ended June 30, 1945, p. 1, NARA, RG 15, records of the Veterans' Administration, office of the administrator, library set of agency issuances and publications, 1914–1964, box 1.

81. Bradley and Blair, *A General's Life,* p. 441.

82. Veterans' Administration, Public Relations Office, "A Preliminary Advance Copy of a Report to Be Issued to the Employees of the Veterans' Administration on Operations from VJ Day to August 15, 1946," Aug. 15, 1946, NARA, RG 15, Veterans' Administration, office of the administrator, miscellaneous publications, 1928–1953, box 5.

83. For recent scholarship see David H. Onkst, " 'First a Negro, Incidentally a Veteran': Black World War Two Veterans and the GI Bill of Rights in the Deep South, 1944–1948," *Journal of Social History* 31 (Spring/Summer, 1998): 517–44. This topic is discussed at length in chapter 5.

84. Veterans' Administration, public relations office, "A Preliminary Advance Copy of a Report to Be Issued to the Employees of the Veterans' Administration on Operations from VJ Day to August 15, 1946," Aug. 15, 1946, NARA, RG 15, office of the administrator, miscellaneous publications, 1928–1953, box 5; Omar N. Bradley, press conference, "One-Year Retrospective on VA," Aug. 15, 1946, Omar N. Bradley, *The Collected Writings of General Omar N. Bradley: Articles, Broadcasts, and Statements, 1945–1967,* vol. 3 (Washington, D.C.: GPO, 1967), pp. 176, 193.

85. Bradley and Blair, *A General's Life,* p. 450. See also Bradley, Collected Writings, vol. 1, pp. 9–12, 53, 153; vol. 3, pp. 76, 120, 133, 177, 192–93, 217.

86. Severo and Milford, *Wages of War,* p. 307.

87. For an example of these appearances, see Omar N. Bradley, *Collected Writings,* vol. 3.

88. "Gen Bradley Lauds Film: Praises *Best Years of Our Lives* in Letter to Samuel Goldwyn," New York Times (Dec. 11, 1946), p. 42.

89. An excellent study of this topic is found in Paul Boyer, *By the Bombs' Early Light: American Thought and Culture at the Dawn of the Atomic Age* (New York: Pantheon Books, 1985). See also Tom Englehardt, The End of the Victory Culture: Cold War America and the Disillusioning of a Generation (Amherst: University of Massachusetts Press, 1995).

Chapter 2

1. Allan R. Millett and Peter Maslowski, *For the Common Defense: A Military History of the United States of America* (New York: Free Press, 1994), p. 653. The army and navy recorded 22.7 million medical admissions for disease and injury during the war. See Norman Q. Brill and Gilbert W. Beebe, A Follow-up Study of War Neuroses (Washington, D.C.: Veterans' Administration, 1955), p. 26.

2. James Bradley, *Flags of Our Fathers* (New York: Bantam Books, 2000), p. 219.

3. Millett and Maslowski, *For the Common Defense,* pp. 483–84; John W. Dower, War without Mercy: Race and Power in the Pacific War (New York: Pan-

theon Books, 1986), pp. 45–46, 105–106. See also Geoffrey Perrett, Days of Sadness, Years of Triumph: The American People, 1939–1945 (New York: Coward, McCann, and Geoghegan, 1973), p. 410.

4. For an excellent study of this issue, see D. M. Giangreco, "Casualty Projections for the U.S. Invasions of Japan, 1945–1946: Planning and Policy Implications," *Journal of Military History* 61 (July, 1997): 521–81.

5. "Take Up Thy Bed," *Time* 45 (May 21, 1945), p. 90; Capt. French R. Moore, "Progress in Naval Medicine," Carry On 24 (Feb., 1945), p. 15.

6. Edward M. Maisel, "Crippling the Disabled Veteran," *Nation* 161 (July 7, 1945): 9–11.

7. Devon Francis, "How We're Healing the Scars of Battle," *Popular Science Monthly* 146 (June, 1945), p. 88. Overall, the mortality rate for wounded in World War Two (4.5 percent) was nearly half the rate for World War One (8.1 percent). See Gilbert W. Beebe and Michael E. De Bakey, Battle Casualties: Incidence, Mortality, and Logistical Considerations (Springfield, Ill.: Charles C. Thomas, 1952), p. 77.

8. Paul Fussell, *Wartime: Understanding and Behavior in the Second World War* (New York: Oxford University Press, 1989), pp. 52–65; S. M. Ferree, "Readjustment of GI Joe Studied," Forty and Eighter (Apr., 1945), pp. 8–10.

9. Hans Binneveld, *From Shell Shock to Combat Stress: A Comparative History of Military Psychiatry* (Amsterdam: Amsterdam University Press, 1997), pp. 83–106.

10. Edward A. Strecker and Kenneth E. Appel, *Psychiatry in Modern Warfare* (New York: Macmillan, 1945), pp. 3–10.

11. Trevor N. Dupuy, *The Evolution of Weapons and Warfare* (New York: Bobbs-Merrill, 1980), p. 312.

12. S. L. A. Marshall, *Men against Fire: The Problem of Battle Command* (Gloucester, Mass.: Peter Smith, 1978), p. 47.

13. Binneveld, *From Shell Shock to Combat Stress,* pp. 94–95; J. R. Neill, "How Psychiatric Symptoms Varied in World War I and II," Military Medicine 158 (1993): 151.

14. John Keegan, *The Face of Battle: A Study of Agincourt, Waterloo, and the Somme* (New York: Penguin Books, 1976), pp. 274–84; Maxwell Gitelson, "The Role of the Community in Relation to the Emotional Needs of the Returning Soldier," Social Service Review 19 (1945): 93.

15. Paul Wanke, "American Military Psychiatry and Its Role among Ground Forces in World War II," *Journal of Military History* 63 (Jan., 1999): 132–33.

16. See *Annual Report of the Administrator of Veterans' Affairs for the Fiscal Year Ended June 30, 1945* (Washington, D.C.: GPO, 1945), p. 3, NARA, records group 15, Veterans' Administration, office of the administrator, library set of agency issuances and publications, 1914–1964, box 1. The rate of hospitalization for mental illness in the military was thirty times higher than for civilians. See Strecker and Appel, Psychiatry in Modern Warfare, p. 11. The army alone recorded 336,959 soldiers with "psychiatric disorders" between 1942 and 1945. See U.S. Army Medical Department, Neuropsychiatry in World War II (Washington, D.C.: Office of the Surgeon General, Department of the Army, 1966), p. 204; Megan Barke, Rebecca Fribush, and Peter N. Stearns, "Nervous Break-

down in Twentieth-Century American Culture," Journal of Social History 33 (Spring, 2000): 565–84. See also "The Health of the Veteran," Newsweek (Feb. 3, 1947), p. 53.

17. "The Army and the Deaf," *New York Times Magazine* 28 (Oct. 14, 1946), p. 78; "Worth It," Time 46 (Dec. 17, 1945), p. 88; "Army Blind School," Life 21 (Nov. 11, 1946), pp. 101–102.

18. Memo from Col. H. D. W. Riley to Brig. Gen. K. C. Royale, "Transmittal of Transcript of Minutes of Meeting," Oct. 14, 1945, NARA, RG 165, records of the War Department general staff, box 327.

19. For book references see George K. Pratt, *Soldier to Civilian: Problems of Readjustment* (New York: McGraw-Hill, 1944); Willard Waller, The Veteran Comes Back (New York: Dryden Press, 1944); Grace Sloan Overton, Marriage in War and Peace: A Book for Parents and Counselors of Youth (New York: Abingdon-Cokesbury Press, 1945); Dorothy W. Baruch and Lee Edward Travis, You're Out of the Service Now: A Veteran's Guide to Civilian Life (New York: D. Appleton-Century, 1946); Charles Hurd, The Veterans' Program: A Complete Guide to Its Benefits, Rights, and Options (New York: McGraw-Hill, 1946).

20. Milton Greenberg, *The GI Bill: The Law That Changed America* (New York: Lickle, 1997), p. 22.

21. Helen Keller, "An Epic of Courage: 'Seen' by Helen Keller," *New York Times Magazine* (Jan. 6, 1946), pp. 5, 44.

22. Bernard Frizell, "Handless Veteran," *Life* 21 (Dec. 16, 1946), pp. 74–75.

23. "House Body Defers News Source Vote," *New York Times* (May 23, 1945), p. 17; "Deutsch Insists Medical Care for Veterans Is under Standard," New York Times (June 6, 1945), p. 15.

24. "Trouble in the VA," *New Republic* 112 (Apr. 23, 1945): 545. See also Albert Q. Maisel, "The Veterans Betrayed," Reader's Digest (May, 1945), pp. 22–26.

25. "Veterans' Inquiry Attracts Bradley," *New York Times* (June 9, 1945), p. 7. Official documents corroborated print-media investigations. A survey of New York City hospitals by the War Manpower Commission in May, 1945, reveals, for example, nurse-patient ratios "far below the safety level." See letter, Edward M. Bernecker (commissioner, New York City Department of Hospitals) to L. Louise Baker (assistant executive officer, Nursing Division, War Manpower Commission), May 22, 1945, NARA, RG 211, records of the War Manpower Commission, records of the Bureau of Placement, records of the Procurement and Assignment Service, box 111.

26. Charles Hurd, "Legion, VFW Attack Treatment of Patients in Veteran Hospitals," *New York Times* (June 13, 1945), pp. 1, 11.

27. Donald J. Lisio, "United States: Bread and Butter Politics," in *The War Generation: Veterans of the First World War,* ed. Stephen R. Ward et al. (Port Washington, N.Y.: Kennikat Press, 1975), p. 43; Ralph G. Martin, "They Must Be Awfully Bitter," New Republic 114 (Jan. 7, 1946): 12–14. See also Robert Maris, "The Little Trapezes," New Republic 112 (May 21, 1945): 706–707.

28. Charles Hurd, "The Veteran: House Group Nearly Shows Its Inability to Act on Complaints over Facilities," *New York Times* (May 20, 1945), p. 21.

29. Gertrude Keough, *History and Heritage of the Veterans' Administration Nursing Service, 1930–1980* (New York: National League for Nursing, 1981), p. 4.

30. Memo, "Necessity for Immediate Action on Veterans' Administration Personnel Matters," Oct. 20, 1943, NARA, RG 165, records of the War Department general staff, box 328.

31. David Brinkley, *Washington Goes to War* (New York: Ballantine Books, 1988), pp. 107–108.

32. Report, office of the surgeon general, Commissioned Personnel Division, "Temporary Figures for Officers on Active Duty in the Medical Department, July 25, 1942, NARA, RG 211, records of the War Manpower Commission, Bureau of Procurement, Procurement and Assignment Services, general files, 1941–1946, box 8; War Manpower Commission, press release, "The Urgent Need for Doctors," June 8, 1942, p. 2, AL, Great War classification: Countries, United States, Social Conditions.

33. Letter, office of the surgeon general to all officers concerned, "Waiver of Physical Defects for Limited Service Officers," Apr. 23, 1943, NARA, RG 211, records of the War Manpower Commission, Bureau of Procurement, Procurement and Assignment Services, general files, 1941–1946, box 8.

34. Memo for General White from John J. McCloy (assistant secretary of war), Oct. 20, 1943, NARA, RG 165, records of the War Department general staff, box 328.

35. Letter, Frank T. Hines (VA administrator) to all facilities and regional offices of the Veterans' Administration, Mar. 30, 1942; and to M. E. Lapham (War Manpower Commission), Sept. 15, 1943, NARA, RG 211, records of the War Manpower Commission, Bureau of Procurement, Procurement and Assignment Services, general files, 1941–1946, box 8.

36. Clarence McKittrick Smith, *The Medical Department: Hospitalization and Evacuation, Zone of the Interior* (Washington, D.C.: GPO, 1956), p. 324.

37. Leo Egan, "Veterans' Hospitals Widely Criticized," *New York Times* (May 16, 1945), p. 36.

38. Memo for the record, Lt. Col. Carl C. Sox, Aug. 30, 1945, NARA, RG 112, records of the surgeon general, Historical Division, AMEDD records, 1947–1961, box 39; Kathi Jackson, *They Called Them Angels: American Military Nurses of World War II* (Westport, Conn.: Praeger, 2000), p. 159.

39. Committee on Veterans' Affairs, *Medical Care of Veterans*, p. 216; U.S. Veterans' Administration, administrator of Veterans' Affairs, Annual Report for Fiscal Year Ending June 30, 1947 (Washington, D.C.: GPO, 1948), pp. 4, 100.

40. Col. John B. Coates, ed., *Medical Department, United States Army: Personnel in World War II* (Washington, D.C.: GPO, 1963), p. 493.

41. Mary T. Sarnecky, *A History of the U.S. Army Nurse Corps* (Philadelphia: University of Pennsylvania Press, 1999), p. 283.

42. VA pamphlet ER-1, *Benefits for World War II Veterans*, Sept., 1947, NARA, RG 15, pamphlets, 1946–1953, box 1.

43. Albert E. Cowdrey, *Fighting for Life: American Military Medicine in World War II* (New York: Free Press, 1994), pp. 279–88.

44. Charles Hurd, "Bradley Is Sworn as Veterans' Head," *New York Times* (Aug. 16, 1945), p. 14.

45. *Annual Report of the Administrator of Veterans' Affairs for the Fiscal Year Ended June 30, 1945* (Washington, D.C.: GPO, 1945), p. 3, NARA, RG 15, Veterans' Administration, office of the administrator, library set of agency issuances and publications, 1914–1964, box 1.

46. Albert Q. Maisel, "General Bradley Cleans Up the Veterans' Hospitals," *Reader's Digest* (Dec., 1945), pp. 85–88.

47. Omar N. Bradley and Clay Blair, *A General's Life* (New York: Simon and Schuster, 1983), p. 458.

48. "Baruch Proposes New Veterans' Medical Setup," *American Journal of Public Health* 35 (Oct., 1945): 993.

49. Bradley and Blair, *A General's Life*, p. 457.

50. *Annual Report of the Administrator of Veterans' Affairs* for the Fiscal Year Ending June 30, 1947 (Washington, D.C.: GPO, 1947), pp. 3–4, NARA, records group 15, Veterans' Administration, library set of issuances and publications, 1914–1964, box 1.

51. U.S. House of Representatives, Committee on Veterans' Affairs, *Medical Care of Veterans* (Washington, D.C.: GPO, 1967), pp. 210–11.

52. Bradley and Blair, *A General's Life*, p. 458; U.S. House of Representatives, Committee on Veterans' Affairs, Medical Care of Veterans, p. 207.

53. Lois Mattox Miller and James Monahan, "Veterans' Medicine Second to None," *Reader's Digest* 51 (Sept., 1947), p. 57.

54. *Annual Report of the Administrator of Veterans' Affairs for the Fiscal Year Ending June 30, 1946* (Washington, D.C.: GPO, 1947), p. 3, NARA, RG 15, Veterans' Administration, office of the administrator, library set of agency issuances and publications, 1914–1964, box 1; "New Levels of Professional Compensation Set in Veterans' Administration," American Journal of Public Health 36 (Apr., 1946): 331.

55. "Veterans' Doc" *Newsweek* (Aug. 12, 1946), p. 62.

56. Keough, *History and Heritage of the Veterans' Administration Nursing Service*, p. 5.

57. "Lady in GI White," *Newsweek* (Nov. 11, 1946), p. 71.

58. Binneveld, *From Shell Shock to Combat Stress*, pp. 93–97, 121.

59. Kyra Kester, "Shadows of War: The Historical Dimensions and Social Implications of Military Psychology and Veteran Counseling in the United States, 1860–1989" (Ph.D. diss., University of Washington, 1992), p. 132.

60. Albert Deutsch, "New Hope for Disabled Veterans," *American Magazine* 142 (Dec., 1946), pp. 23, 127–30; Francis J. Braceland, "Essentials of Veterans' Rehabilitation," Diseases of the Nervous System 6 (Apr., 1945): 101–105; Saul Hofstein, "Differences in Military Psychiatric Work Practices," Journal of Psychiatric Social Work 16 (Winter, 1946–1947): 74–82. A mental-hygiene clinic in New York City was able to identify more than 370 different types of headaches from its examination of veterans. See "Kilroy Was Here," Time 48 (Aug. 19, 1946), p. 68. See also Wanke, "American Military Psychiatry," p. 134. For a useful overview of this issue, see Jack H. Stipe, Veterans' Administration, Social Service Division, "The Veterans' Administra-

tion Social Service Program," 1947, Walter P. Reuther Library (hereafter WPRL), United Community Services Central Files Collection, box 112.

61. Omar N. Bradley, *Collected Writings: Articles, Broadcasts, and Statements, 1945–1967*, vol. 3 (Washington, D.C.: GPO, 1967), p. 86.

62. *Annual Report of the Administrator of Veterans' Affairs for the Fiscal Year Ended June 30, 1945* (Washington, D.C.: GPO, 1945), p. 2, NARA, RG 15, Veterans' Administration, office of the administrator, library set of agency issuances and publications, 1914–1964, box 1. See also Charles Hurd, "The Veteran: Bradley's Tasks Are Many in New Job That Will Need Aid to Bring Results," New York Times (July 29, 1945), p. 41.

63. American Legion National Headquarters, "Progress Report on the Serviceman's Act of 1944," June 25, 1947, AL, Veterans' Welfare Classification, GI Bill, folder 10.

64. *Annual Report of the Administrator of Veterans' Affairs for the Fiscal Year Ended June 30, 1945* (Washington, D.C.: GPO, 1945), p. 2, NARA, RG 15, Veterans' Administration, office of the administrator, library set of agency issuances and publications, 1914–1964, box 1.

65. Francis, "How We're Healing the Scars of Battle," pp. 91–93; Walter B. Pitkin, "The Advantage of Handicaps," *Rotarian* 67 (Oct., 1945), pp. 16–18.

66. "Mind over Muscles," *Time* 46 (July 16, 1945), p. 56.

67. "Occupation to Help Get Them Well," *National News of the American Legion Auxiliary* 19 (Sept., 1945), p. 15.

68. Jack Sher, "Why Hire Disabled Vets?" *American Legion Magazine* 43 (Oct., 1947), pp. 22–23; Veterans' Administration, administration order no. 41-A, "Organization of the Vocational Rehabilitation Division at Those Field Stations Having Regional Office Activities," June 16, 1943, AL, Veterans' Welfare Classification, Vocational Rehabilitation.

69. Maisel, "General Bradley Cleans Up," p. 85.

70. Paul B. Magnuson, *Ring the Night Bell: The Autobiography of a Surgeon* (Boston: Little, Brown, 1960), p. 287.

71. Bradley and Blair, *A General's Life*, pp. 459–60.

72. Sutherland Denlinger, "The Vets' Best Bet," *Collier's* (Apr. 27, 1946), pp. 53–55; letter, Maj. Gen. George B. Erskine (Retraining and Reemployment Administration) to Robert Patterson (secretary of war), Apr. 29, 1946, NARA, RG 165, records of the War Department general staff, box 330.

73. Brinkley, *Washington Goes to War*, pp. 50–82.

74. Leo Egan, "Army Stop-gap Aids Veteran Hospitals" (*New York Times*, May 18, 1945), p. 34. See also Brian Waddell, "The Dimensions of the Military Ascendancy during U.S. Industrial Mobilization for World War II," Journal of Political and Military Sociology 23 (Summer, 1995): 81–98.

75. U.S. Department of Commerce, *Historical Statistics of the United States: Colonial Times to 1970* (Washington, D.C.: GPO, 1975), p. 1091.

76. Ibid., p. 1102; John Morton Blum, *V Was for Victory: Politics and Culture during World War II* (New York: Harcourt Brace, 1976), p. 91. See also David M. Kennedy, Freedom from Fear: The American People in Depression and War, 1929–1945 (New York: Oxford University Press, 1999), pp. 615–68.

77. *The Budget of the United States for the Fiscal Year Ending June 30, 1947* (Washington, D.C.: GPO, 1946), pp. 114–16.

78. Omar N. Bradley, speech before the Army Air Force Conference on Community Centers, Mitchell Field, New York, Dec. 5, 1945, Library of Congress, records of the NAACP, branch files, 1940–1955, box A657.

79. Clarice H. L. Pennock, "The GI Volunteer," *Compass* 27 (Apr., 1946), p. 10. See also U.S. Department of Labor, Thirty-seventh Annual Report of the Secretary of Labor (Washington, D.C.: GPO, 1950), pp. 80–81.

80. U.S. Department of Labor, Retraining and Reemployment Administration, *To Organize, to Operate Your Community Advisory Center for Veterans and Others* (Washington, D.C.: GPO, 1946), pp. 1–7.

81. Veterans' Administration, *Annual Report for Fiscal Year Ending June 30, 1950*, pp. 44, 56–57.

82. "Women to Aid Veterans," *New York Times* (June 26, 1946), p. 46.

83. Committee on Veterans' Affairs, *Medical Care of Veterans,* p. 216; U.S. Veterans' Administration, administrator of Veterans' Affairs, Annual Report for Fiscal Year Ending June 30, 1950 (Washington, D.C.: GPO, 1951), p. 33.

84. Mildred Adams, "Caring for Our Own," *American Legion Magazine* 41 (Sept., 1946), p. 16; T. O. Kraabel, "Legion Rehabilitation in 1946," National News of the American Legion Auxiliary 20 (Jan., 1946), p. 6.

85. Gaylord P. Coon, "Clinical Impressions of Psychiatric Problems Presented by Veterans," *Diseases of the Nervous System* 6 (May, 1945): 143; Helping Disabled Veterans (Washington, D.C.: American National Red Cross, 1945), p. 3.

86. Veterans' Administration, "List of Recognized Organizations, Associations, and Other Agencies," bulletin 18-C, Nov. 11, 1943, WPRL, UAW Veterans' Department Collection, Series II, box 6.

87. Winifred Zwemer, "Psychiatric Social Work in a Volunteer Clinic for Veterans," *Journal of Psychiatric Social Work* 17 (Autumn, 1947): 42–43.

88. Russell B. Elliott, "The War Veteran and His Problems," *Detroit Trust Company Quarterly* (Summer, 1945), p. 9; Detroit Council of Veterans' Affairs, Veterans' Information Center, "Record of Calls and Referrals for the Month of September, 1945," n.d., WPRL, United Community Service Central Files Collection, Series III, subject files, box 112.

89. Magnuson, *Ring the Night Bell,* p. 325; Robert Klein, Wounded Men, Broken Promises (New York: Macmillan, 1981), pp. 49–50.

90. Magnuson, *Ring the Night Bell,* pp. 331–47.

91. Interview, Jan. 18, 1970, Marine Corps Historical Center, Oral History Collection, p. 400.

92. Robert J. Donovan, *Conflict and Crisis: The Presidency of Harry S. Truman* (New York: Norton, 1977), pp. 208–13.

93. James T. Patterson, *Grand Expectations: The United States, 1945–1974* (New York: Oxford University Press, 1996), p. 145.

94. David McCullough, *Truman* (New York: Simon and Schuster, 1992), p. 523.

95. Ibid., pp. 529–31.

96. Donovan, *Conflict and Crisis,* p. 260.

97. U.S. Department of Commerce, *Historical Statistics*, p. 1114. In 1949, the federal budget rebounded somewhat to $39.4 billion.

98. Dean Acheson, *Present at the Creation: My Years in the State Department* (New York: Norton, 1969), pp. 354–61.

99. Omar N. Bradley, *The Collected Writings of General Omar N. Bradley: Testimony, 1946–1949*, vol. 4 (Washington, D.C.: GPO, 1967), pp. 82–86.

100. Ibid.

101. Charles Hurd and Robert B. Pitkin, "Where Are the Veterans' Hospitals?" *American Legion Magazine* 43 (July, 1947), pp. 18–19, 48.

102. "Veterans and Health," *New Republic* (May 20, 1946): 718.

103. Charles Stevenson, "How Bureaucracy Swindles the Taxpayer," *Reader's Digest* 54 (Mar., 1949), pp. 61–66.

104. Committee on Veterans' Affairs, *Medical Care of Veterans*, pp. 201–204.

105. U.S. Veterans' Administration, administrator of Veterans' Affairs, *Annual Report for Fiscal Year Ending June 30, 1950* (Washington, D.C.: GPO, 1951), p. 9.

106. Perry Brown, "The Growing Attack on Veterans' Benefits," *American Legion Magazine* 47 (July, 1949), pp. 14–15, 57–58, 60–63.

107. U.S. Veterans' Administration, administrator of Veterans' Affairs, *Annual Report for Fiscal Year Ending June 30, 1950* (Washington, D.C.: GPO, 1951), p. 4.

108. See, for example, VA pamphlet 10-32, *A New Approach to the Rehabilitation of the Blind at the Veterans' Administration Hospital, Hine, Illinois*, Feb., 1950, NARA, RG 15, pamphlets, 1946–1953, box 4.

109. Ibid., p. 22. See also Kester, "Shadows of War," p. 68. Kester notes that 67,336 veterans, or four-tenths of one percent of the total WWII veteran population, was classified as psychoneurotic and unable to adjust to civilian life.

110. "The Blind and the World," *Newsweek* 28 (Dec. 30, 1946), p. 48.

111. Sher, "Why Hire Disabled Vets?" pp. 21, 57.

112. For a good discussion of the postwar boom, see William E. Leuchtenburg, *A Troubled Feast: American Society since 1945* (Boston: Little, Brown, 1983), pp. 37–68.

Chapter 3

1. Omar N. Bradley, "Protecting the Mental Health of the Veteran," *Mental Hygiene* 30 (Jan., 1946): 1.

2. Ibid., p. 3.

3. Norman Frederiksen and W. B. Schrader, *Adjustment to College: A Study of 10,000 Veteran and Nonveteran Students in Sixteen American Colleges* (Princeton, N.J.: Educational Testing Service, 1951), p. xx.

4. J. M. Stephen Peeps, "A B.A. for the GI . . . Why?" *History of Education Quarterly* 24 (Winter, 1984): 514–19.

5. George Friedman and Meredith Friedman, *The Future of War: Power, Technology, and American World Dominance in the Twenty-first Century* (New York: Crown, 1996), p. 32; James F. Dunnigan, How to Make War: A Comprehensive Guide to Modern Warfare (New York: Quill, 1983), pp. 308–22; John Ellis, The

Sharp End: The Fighting Man in World War II (New York: Charles Scribner's Sons, 1980), pp. 156–59.

6. J. Hillis Miller and Dorothy V. N. Brooks, *The Role of Higher Education in War and After* (New York: Harper and Brothers, 1944), pp. 103–106; V. R. Cardozier, Colleges and Universities in World War II (Westport, Conn.: Praeger, 1993), pp. 3–18, 29, 40, 84.

7. Milton Greenberg, *The GI Bill: The Law That Changed America* (New York: Lickle, 1997), p. 36; Michael C. Behnke, "Five Decades on Campus: Snapshots of College Life in America," College Board Review 157 (Fall, 1990): 6; Thomas N. Bonner, "The Unintended Revolution in America's Colleges since 1940," Change 18 (Sept./Oct., 1986): 44; Diane Ravitch, The Troubled Crusade: American Education, 1945–1980 (New York: Basic Books, 1983), p. 9; Kenneth H. Ashworth, American Education in Decline (College Station: Texas A&M University Press, 1979), pp. 28–29.

8. James T. Patterson, *Grand Expectations: The United States, 1945–1974* (New York: Oxford University Press, 1996), pp. 562–92.

9. Walter Spearman and Jack R. Brown, "When the Veteran Goes to College," *South Atlantic Quarterly* (Jan., 1946): 31.

10. U.S. Veterans' Administration, *Annual Report of the Administrator of Veterans' Affairs* for Fiscal Year Ending June 30, 1945 (Washington, D.C.: GPO, 1946), p. 2; U.S. Veterans' Administration, Annual Report of the Administrator of Veterans' Affairs for Fiscal Year Ending June 30, 1946 (Washington, D.C.: GPO, 1947), p. 29.

11. U.S. Veterans' Administration, *Annual Report of the Administrator of Veterans' Affairs* for Fiscal Year Ending June 30, 1946 (Washington, D.C.: GPO, 1947), p. 29.

12. U.S. Veterans' Administration, *Annual Report of the Administrator of Veterans' Affairs* for Fiscal Year Ending June 30, 1947 (Washington, D.C.: GPO, 1948), p. 37.

13. Charles Hurd, *The Veterans' Program: A Complete Guide to Its Benefits, Rights, and Options* (New York: McGraw Hill, 1946), pp. 93–94.

14. Nicholas M. McKnight, "They Know What They Want," *School and Society* 63 (June 29, 1946): 449–52.

15. Maj. Harry Ransom, "Educational Plans of AAF Veterans," *Higher Education* (May 15, 1946): 8. These surveys were published by the Army Information and Education Division in May and December, 1945.

16. Spearman and Brown, "When the Veteran Goes to College," p. 35; Lloyd C. Emmons, "College Curricula of World War II Veterans," *School and Society* 64 (Aug. 31, 1946): 152–53.

17. Keith W. Olson, *The GI Bill, the Veterans, and the Colleges* (Lexington: University Press of Kentucky, 1974), p. 35; Olive Remington Goldman, "GI Style: Learning with a Difference," Journal of the American Association of University Women 39 (Summer, 1946): 205–206; Cardozier, Colleges and Universities in World War II, p. 218.

18. Veterans' Administration, Office of Vocational Rehabilitation and Education, Training Facilities Service, "Summary by States of Openings Available

to Veterans in 1,029 Institutions of Higher Education, Present and Fall Term (1946)," Apr. 15, 1946, Old National Archives and Records Administration (hereafter ONARA), RG 15, Veterans' Administration, pamphlets, box 1.

19. Director of War Mobilization and Reconversion, "The Veteran and Higher Education: A Report to the President, 20 May 1946," in *Documentary History of the Truman Presidency: Demobilization and Reconversion, Rebuilding a Peacetime Economy following WWII*, vol. 4, ed. Dennis Merrill (Frederick, Md.: University Publications of America, 1996), pp. 491–94, 542.

20. Edwin Kiester, "The GI Bill May Be the Best Deal Ever Made by Uncle Sam," *Smithsonian* 25 (Nov., 1994): 134.

21. Veterans' Administration, Office of Vocational Rehabilitation and Education, Training Facilities Service, "Supplement to Summary by Field of Education of Openings Available to Veterans in Institutions of Higher Education, Fall Term (1946)," May, 1946, ONARA, RG 15, Veterans' Administration, pamphlets, box 1. An additional 7,176 were listed as "unclassified."

22. Greenberg, *GI Bill*, pp. 54, 56–57.

23. Ibid., p. 36. See also Rufus D. Smith and Ray F. Harvey, "College Population Trends," *School and Society* 66 (July 5, 1947): 1–5.

24. Sgt. Bill Davidson, "Ex-GIs in College," *Yank* (June 29, 1945), p. 6.

25. Nettie Wysor, "Veterans Invade the Varsities," *School and Society* 63 (Mar. 16, 1946): 196; "Brown University's Adjustment to the Veterans' Problem," School and Society 64 (July 13, 1946): 21.

26. Cardozier, *Colleges and Universities in World War II*, p. 211; Peter H. Odegard, "Is This Education?" American Scholar 16 (Autumn, 1947): 477; Sutherland Denlinger, "The Vets' Best Bet," Collier's (Apr. 27, 1946), p. 34; Goldman, "GI Style: Learning with a Difference," p. 205; Norman Frederiksen and W. B. Schrader, Adjustment to College: A Study of 10,000 Veteran and Nonveteran Students in Sixteen American Colleges (Princeton, N.J.: Educational Testing Service, 1951), p. 16.

27. Keith Spalding, "The Contemporary Context," *American Scholar* 16 (Summer, 1947): 345.

28. Spearman and Brown, "When the Veteran Goes to College," p. 36. See also Henry G. Koss, "Education and the Older Veteran," *School and Society* 63 (Feb. 23, 1946): 135, and Donald Hutchins MacMahon, "Vets into Students," School and Society 64 (Sept. 21, 1946): 204–206.

29. Spalding, "Contemporary Context," p. 346.

30. Ibid.

31. Edward C. McDonagh, "Some Hints to Professors," *American Association of University Professors Bulletin* 31 (Winter, 1945): 643–47; Maj. J. L. Rogers, "Additional Hints to Professors," American Association of University Professors Bulletin 32 (June, 1946): 364.

32. S. M. Vincoor, "The Veteran Flunks the Professor: A GI Indictment of Our Institutes of Higher Education!" *School and Society* 66 (Oct. 18, 1947): 290–91.

33. Ibid., p. 290.

34. Olson, *The GI Bill*, pp. 50–51; Frederiksen and Schrader Adjustment to College, pp. 8, 48.

35. U.S. Department of Commerce, *Historical Statistics of the United States: Colonial Times to 1970* (Washington, D.C.: GPO, 1975), p. 140.

36. Daniel A. Clark, "The Two Joes Meet: Joe College, Joe Veteran: The GI Bill, College Education, and Postwar American Culture," *History of Education Quarterly* 38 (Summer, 1998): 165–89.

37. Patterson, *Grand Expectations,* p. 69; Diane Ravitch, Troubled Crusade, p. 183.

38. W. J. Danforth, "J-O-B Spells Rehabilitation," *National News of the American Legion Auxiliary* 19 (Mar./Apr., 1945), p. 13. See also Davis R. B. Ross, Preparing for Ulysses: Politics and Veterans during World War II (New York: Columbia University Press, 1969), pp. 190–92.

39. Robert J. Havighurst et al., *The American Veteran Back Home: A Study of Readjustment* (New York: Longmans, Green, 1951), p. 91.

40. Veterans' Administration, *Occupational Outlook Information Series: California,* VA pamphlet 7-2.3, June, 1947, p. 3; Veterans' Administration, Occupational Outlook Information Series: Illinois: Employment by Industry and Occupation: Background and Industrial Employment Trends: Wartime Expansion: Outlook, VA pamphlet 7-2.4, June, 1947; Veterans' Administration, Occupational Outlook Information Series: Pennsylvania: Employment by Industry and Occupation: Background and Industrial Employment Trends: Wartime Expansion: Outlook, VA pamphlet 7-2.39, June, 1947, pp. 3–4, ONARA, RG 15, Veterans' Administration, pamphlets, box 1.

41. U.S. Office of Education, "Vocational Education in Agriculture for Returning Veterans," n.d., American Legion Archive and Library (hereafter AL), Veterans' Welfare Classification, Vocational Rehabilitation.

42. U.S. Department of Commerce, *Historical Statistics,* p. 166.

43. Hurd, *The Veterans' Program,* p. 97.

44. U.S. Department of Commerce, *Historical Statistics,* pp. 142–44.

45. Benjamin Fine, "Millions in Waste Charged in Schooling for Veterans," *New York Times* (Feb. 6, 1950), p. 1.

46. U.S. Department of Labor, *Thirty-fourth Annual Report of the Secretary of Labor for the Fiscal Year Ended June 30, 1946* (Washington, D.C.: GPO, 1947), pp. 136–37.

47. Nelson Lichtenstein, *The Most Dangerous Man in Detroit: Walter Reuther and the Fate of American Labor* (New York: Basic Books, 1995), pp. 194–95.

48. Pamphlet, *The CIO and the Veteran,* n.d., p. 3, Walter P. Reuther Library, CIO PAC Collection, box 12; John Morton Blum, V Was for Victory: Politics and American Culture during World War Two (New York: Harcourt Brace, 1976), pp. 140–41; U.S. Department of Commerce, Historical Statistics, p. 177. Total union membership grew from 10.5 million in 1941 to 14.75 million by 1945. See also Richard Polenberg, War and Society: The United States, 1941–1945 (New York: Lippincott, 1972), pp. 154–83.

49. Robert H. Zieger, *American Workers, American Unions, 1920–1985* (Baltimore: Johns Hopkins University Press, 1986), pp. 62–99.

50. Ruth Milkman, "Rosie the Riveter Revisited: Management's Postwar

Purge of Women Automobile Workers," in *On the Line: Essays in the History of Auto Work,* ed. Nelson Lichtenstein and Stephen Meyer (Chicago: University of Illinois Press, 1989), pp. 141–43. See also "Veterans Return to Work in the Nation's Factories," Monthly Labor Review 63 (Dec., 1946): 927.

51. Letter, E. J. Lever (War Production Board) to Victor Reuther (War Activities Division of the CIO), Feb. 2, 1944, Walter P. Reuther Library, UAW War Policy Division Collection, Series I, box 23.

52. See, for example, pamphlet, *The CIO and the Veteran,* n.d., p. 1.

53. Letter, Joseph G. Velosky (director, Veterans' Department, War Policy Division) to all regions 2, 2A, and 2B, UAW-CIO local unions, Oct. 31, 1944, Walter P. Reuther Library (hereafter WPRL), UAW War Policy Division Collection, Series I, box 24.

54. Pamphlet, *The CIO and the Veteran,* n.d., p. 3; David M. Kennedy, Freedom from Fear: The American People in Depression and War, 1929–1945 (New York: Oxford University Press, 1999), pp. 626–32.

55. UAW-CIO, *United Auto Worker: Serviceman's Edition* 9, Dec. 1, 1944, WPRL, UAW War Policy Division Collection, Series I, box 23.

56. Pamphlet, *The CIO and the Veteran,* n.d., p. 6.

57. Letter, Emil Mazey (director, UAW Veterans' Department) to Melvin Ryder (editor, *Army Times*), Sept. 23, 1946, WPRL, UAW Veterans' Department Collection, Series II, box 2.

58. Ibid.

59. Veterans of Foreign Wars, press release, July 24, 1944, WPRL, UAW War Policy Division Collection, Series I, box 25; "Recent Decisions of Interest to Labor: Reemployment Rights of Veterans," *Monthly Labor Review* 63 (July, 1946): 98–99.

60. U.S. Department of Commerce, *Historical Statistics,* pp. 176–77. By 1953, it stood at 17.8 million.

61. Robert H. Zieger, *John L. Lewis: Labor Leader* (Boston: Twayne, 1988), pp. 150–53. See also Joshua B. Freeman, Working-Class New York: Life and Labor since World War II (New York: New Press, 2000), pp. 124–40. Many New York organizations such as the International Ladies' Garment Workers' Union eventually had their own health centers. Of the other national unions, only the United Mine Workers pursued a similar type of benefit.

62. Freeman, *Working-Class New York,* pp. 150–80; David McCullough, Truman (New York: Simon and Schuster, 1992), p. 492. For a study of organized labor in the early days of the Cold War, see Steven K. Ashby, "Shattered Dreams: The American Working Class and the Origins of the Cold War, 1945–1949" (Ph.D. diss., University of Chicago, 1993).

63. McKnight, "They Know What They Want," p. 452.

64. Wilbur D. Jones, *Gyrene: The World War II United States Marine* (Shippensburg, Penn.: White Mane Books, 1998), p. 1.

65. Geoffrey Perrett, *Days of Sadness, Years of Triumph: The American People, 1939–1945* (New York: Coward, McCann, and Geoghegan, 1973), p. 408.

66. Goulden, *Best Years,* pp. 70–71.

67. Jennifer E. Brooks, "From Hitler and Tojo to Talmadge and Jim Crow:

World War Two Veterans and the Remaking of Southern Political Tradition"
(Ph.D. diss., University of Tennessee, Knoxville, 1997), pp. 8–10.

68. "Legion's Heart Study Awards," *New York Times* (Sept. 22, 1946), p. 53;
"Dr. Avery Honored for Research Work," New York Times (May 30, 1946), p. 26;
"Hospital Gets $2,000," New York Times (Sept. 17, 1945), p. 31.

69. "Gives $138 to First Lady," *New York Times* (Jan. 31, 1945), p. 38; news-
letter, Helen Fairchild Post 412, Dec., 1947, p. 2, Center for the Study of the
History of Nursing, University of Pennsylvania, records of American Legion
Helen Fairchild Post 412, MC 39, box 1.

70. Ty Cobb, "Batting Out Better Boys," *Rotarian* 71 (July, 1947), p. 11;
"Gets $50 for Oratory," New York Times (Jan. 11, 1947), p. 8; "Legion Baseball
Aug. 27," New York Times (July 6, 1945), p. 15.

71. "Veterans Seek Purchase of Greendale," *American City* 64 (Jan., 1949), p. 73.

72. Vance Packard, *The Status Seekers* (New York: St. Martin's Press, 1959),
pp. 31–42.

73. Adam Rome, *The Bulldozer in the Countryside: Suburban Sprawl and the Rise
of American Environmentalism* (New York: Cambridge University Press, 2001), pp.
119–52; J. John Palen, The Suburbs (New York: McGraw-Hill, 1995), pp. 56–89;
see also Kenneth T. Jackson, Crabgrass Frontier: The Suburbanization of the
United States (New York: Oxford University Press, 1985).

74. George H. Gallup, *The Gallup Poll: Public Opinion, 1935–1971,* vol. 1
(New York: Random House, 1972), pp. 571, 574.

75. U.S. Congress, 92nd Cong., 1st sess., *Biographical Directory of the American
Congress, 1774–1971,* Senate doc. 92-8 (Washington, D.C.: GPO, 1971). For a
roster of lawmakers by state, see pp. 411–16. Short biographical paragraphs follow from p. 489 to p. 1,972.

76. Ibid.

77. Robert A. Caro, *The Lyndon Johnson Years: Means of Ascent* (New York:
Knopf, 1990), p. 19; Robert Dallek, Lone Star Rising: Lyndon Johnson and His
Times, 1908–1960 (New York: Oxford University Press, 1991), pp. 225–41.

78. Richard M. Nixon, *RN: The Memoirs of Richard Nixon* (New York: Grosset
and Dunlap, 1978), p. 35.

79. William Manchester, *The Glory and the Dream: A Narrative History of America, 1932–1972* (New York: Bantam Books, 1975), pp. 394–95.

80. Blum, *V Was for Victory,* p. 340.

81. Caro, *Means of Ascent,* pp. 46–53; Doris Kearns, Lyndon Johnson and
the American Dream (New York: Harper and Row, 1976), pp. 90–96.

82. Allan R. Millett, and Peter Maslowski, *For the Common Defense: A Military
History of the United States of America* (New York: Free Press, 1994), pp. 498–507;
Maurice Matloff, ed., American Military History (Washington, D.C.: GPO,
1973), pp. 538–42. For a scathing indictment of the post-1945 military, see
David H. Hackworth, About Face: The Odyssey of an American Warrior (New
York: Simon and Schuster, 1989).

83. Capt. Francis J. Braceland, *The Retraining and Re-education of Veterans: A
Lecture Delivered for the Nellie Heldt Lecture Fund* (Oberlin, Ohio: Oberlin College,
1945), pp. 4–5.

84. Much has been written of the American replacement system in World War II. See Stephen E. Ambrose, *Citizen Soldiers: The U.S. Army from the Normandy Beaches to the Surrender of Germany, June 7, 1944–May 7, 1945* (New York: Simon and Schuster, 1997), pp. 273–89.

85. Martin Blumenson, *The Patton Papers, 1940–1945* (Boston: Houghton Mifflin, 1974), p. 722.

86. Milton Lehman, "The War's Not Over for Them," *Saturday Evening Post* 220 (Feb. 28, 1948), pp. 41–52.

87. Doris Schwartz, "For These the War Is Not Over," *New York Times Magazine* (Nov. 24, 1946), p. 11.

88. Darrell Berrigan, "New Men Travel the Old Roads," *New Republic* 116 (May 26, 1947): 13. See also Joseph C. Goulden, The Best Years, 1945–1950 (New York: Atheneum, 1976), pp. 49–51.

89. In the epilogue to the well-received 2001 drama *Band of Brothers,* in which interviews of the original members of the 101st Airborne are featured, it is striking to see how reticent they were about their own actions and achievements.

90. James Bradley with Ron Powers, *Flags of Our Fathers* (New York: Bantam Books, 2000), pp. 3–8.

91. Although Ambrose's book by the same title is an excellent study of the wartime experience of American GIs, his later works reflect on the common postwar experience of veterans. See Stephen E. Ambrose, *Comrades: Brothers, Fathers, Heroes, Sons, Pals* (New York: Simon and Schuster, 1999).

92. There are a number of interesting recent studies on this topic. See Karen O. Dunivin, "Military Culture: Change and Continuity," *Armed Forces and Society* 20 (Summer, 1994): 531–47; Barbara Ehrenreich, Blood Rites: Origins and History of the Passions of War (New York: Henry Holt, 1997); Thomas E. Ricks, Making the Corps (New York: Scribner, 1997); Joseph J. Collins, "The Complex Context of American Military Culture: A Practitioner's View," Washington Quarterly 21 (Autumn, 1998): 213–28; Edwin Dorn et al., American Military Culture in the Twenty-first Century (Washington, D.C.: Center for Strategic and International Studies, 2000); Anthony Swofford, Jarhead: A Marine's Chronicle of the Gulf War and Other Battles (New York: Scribner, 2003); Richard D. Hooker Jr., "Soldiers of the State: Reconsidering American Civil-Military Relations," Parameters of the U.S. Army War College 33 (Winter, 2003–2004): 4–18.

93. Stephen E. Ambrose, *Eisenhower: Soldier, General of the Army, President-Elect, 1890–1952,* vol. 1 (New York: Simon and Schuster, 1983), pp. 167–69.

Chapter 4

1. For an interesting contemporary account of this mission, see Therese Benedek, *Insight and Personality Adjustment: A Study of the Psychological Effects of War* (New York: Ronald Press, 1946), pp. 270–71.

2. Leisa D. Meyer, *Creating GI Jane: Sexuality and Power in the Women's Army Corps during World War II* (New York: Columbia University Press, 1996), p. 21; Dorothy Schneider and Carl J. Schneider, Sound Off! American Military

Women Speak Out (New York: Paragon House, 1992), pp. 6–16; Maureen Honey, Creating Rosie the Riveter: Class, Gender, and Propaganda during World War II (Amherst: University of Massachusetts Press, 1984), pp. 97–105; John Costello, Virtue under Fire: How World War II Changed Our Social and Sexual Attitudes (Boston: Little, Brown, 1985), pp. 19–25.

3. Benedek, *Insight and Personality Adjustment*, p. 270.

4. Robin M. Beringer, "Looking Over vs. Overlooking Historic Contributions: Women Veterans' Experiences of WWII" (Ph.D. diss., California School of Professional Psychology at Alameda, 1996), p. 70; Stephen E. Ambrose, *Citizen Soldiers* (New York: Simon and Schuster, 1997), pp. 322–23.

5. Mattie E. Treadwell, *The Women's Army Corps* (Washington, D.C.: GPO, 1954), pp. 191–218.

6. June A. Willenz, *Women Veterans: America's Forgotten Heroines* (New York: Continuum, 1983), p. 20.

7. This theme appears frequently in memoirs written at the time and afterward. See Theresa Archard, *GI Nightingale: The Story of an American Army Nurse* (New York: Norton, 1945); Judy Barrett Litoff and David C. Smith, eds., We're in This War, Too: World War II Letters from American Women in Uniform (New York: Oxford University Press, 1994); Anne Bosanko Green, ed., One Woman's War: Letters Home from the Women's Army Corps, 1944–1946 (St. Paul: Minnesota Historical Society Press, 1989). See also Kathi Jackson, They Called Them Angels: American Military Nurses of World War II (Westport, Conn.: Praeger, 2000), and Brenda McBryde, Quiet Heroines: Nurses of the Second World War (London: Hogarth Press, 1985).

8. Janann Sherman, " 'They Either Need These Women or They Do Not': Margaret Chase Smith and the Fight for Regular Status for Women in the Military," *Journal of Military History* 54 (Jan., 1990): 58–59; D'Ann Campbell, Women at War with America: Private Lives in a Patriotic Era (Cambridge: Harvard University Press, 1984), pp. 22–26.

9. D'Ann Campbell, "Women in Combat: The World War II Experience in the United States, Great Britain, Germany, and the Soviet Union," *Journal of Military History* 57 (Apr., 1993): 301–305.

10. D'Ann Campbell, "Servicewomen of World War II," *Armed Forces and Society* (Winter, 1990): 253–60.

11. Campbell, *Women at War with America*, p. 36. See also Frances Zauhar, Richard D. Wissolik, and Jennifer Campion, eds., Out of the Kitchen: Women in the Armed Services and on the Homefront: The Oral Histories of Pennsylvania Veterans of World War II (Latrobe, Penn.: Saint Vincent College, 1995), pp. 185, 264–65.

12. Litoff and Smith, *We're in This War, Too*, p. 31.

13. Campbell, *Women at War with America*, p. 36.

14. Beringer, "Looking Over vs. Overlooking Historic Contribution," p. 71.

15. Charity Adams Early, *One Woman's Army* (College Station: Texas A&M University Press, 1989), p. 11; Weatherford, American Women and World War II, pp. 220–36.

16. Benedek, *Insight and Personality Adjustment*, p. 272.

17. Archard, *GI Nightingale,* pp. 10, 18.

18. Kathi Jackson, *They Called Them Angels: American Military Nurses of World War II* (Westport, Conn.: Praeger, 2000), p. xvii.

19. LaVonne Telshaw Camp, *Lingering Fever: A World War II Nurse's Memoir* (Jefferson, N.C.: McFarland, 1997), p. 25.

20. Telshaw Camp, *Lingering Fever,* p. 29. For an interesting narrative on volunteerism during the war, see David Brinkley, Washington Goes to War (New York: Ballantine Books, 1988).

21. Benedek, *Insight and Personality Adjustment,* p. 278.

22. James Jones, *WWII* (New York: Ballantine Books, 1975), p. 16.

23. Elizabeth R. Pollock, *Yes, Ma'am! The Personal Papers of a WAAC Private* (New York: Lippincott, 1943), p. 88 (emphasis mine).

24. Green, *One Woman's War,* p. 188.

25. Jeanne Holm, *Women in the Military: An Unfinished Revolution* (San Francisco: Presidio Press, 1992), pp. 98–99.

26. Jackson, *They Called Them Angels,* p. xviii.

27. Joanne Meyerowitz, "Beyond the Feminine Mystique," in *Not June Cleaver: Women and Gender in Postwar America, 1945–1960,* ed. Joanne Meyerowitz (Philadelphia: Temple University Press, 1994), p. 232. Meyerowitz's premise is that postwar mass culture did not automatically consign women to predominantly domestic roles. The representations of women in the mass media were, upon close examination, varied in content and presentation.

28. Doris Kearns Goodwin, *No Ordinary Time: Franklin and Eleanor Roosevelt, the Home Front in World War II* (New York: Simon and Schuster, 1994), p. 623.

29. See James T. Patterson, *Grand Expectations: The United States, 1945–1974* (New York: Oxford University Press, 1996), pp. 32–38. This paradigm shift has become part of the contemporary conventional wisdom in America.

30. Campbell, "Servicewomen of World War II," pp. 257–58; the poll is also cited in Nancy McInerny, "The Woman Vet Has Her Problems Too," *New York Times Magazine* (June 30, 1946), p. 18.

31. "Problems of Women Veterans," *Carry On* 25 (Nov., 1946), pp. 12–13. See also Treadwell, Women's Army Corps, pp. 738–39, and Carol Owen Bell, "The Long-Term Impact of Military Experience on World War II Women's Army Corps Veterans" (M.A. thesis, University of Tennessee, Knoxville, 1996), p. 31.

32. Stilwell, "Pertinent Statistics on Women Veterans," p. 8.

33. Helen G. Brown, "Adjustment Problems of College and Non-College WAC Veterans, 1945–1947" (M.A. thesis, Leland Stanford Junior University, Stanford, Calif., 1947). p. 39.

34. McInerny, "The Woman Vet Has Her Problems Too," p. 18. See also Veterans' Administration, Office of Information Management and Statistics, Statistical Policy and Research Service, "Survey of Female Veterans: A Study of Needs, Attitudes, and Experiences of Women Veterans," Information Management and Statistics (IM&S), report no. 70-85-7 (Washington, D.C.: Veterans' Administration, Sept., 1985), pp. 4–5; Willenz, *Women Veterans,* p. 193.

35. Willenz, *Women Veterans,* pp. 156–57.

36. "Veterans' Benefits as They Pertain to Women in the Army," n.d.,

USMHI, Manuscripts Division. See also *Going Back to Civilian Life,* War Department pamphlet 21-4, Feb., 1946.

37. McInerny, "The Woman Vet Has Her Problems Too," p. 18.

38. "Edith Nourse Rogers to Introduce Legislation for War Women," *Carry On* 26 (Feb., 1947), p. 5.

39. Bettie J. Morden, *The Women's Army Corps, 1945–1978* (Washington, D.C.: GPO, 1992), p. 26.

40. For an example, see UAW Women's Auxiliary, report of the secretary-treasurer, Nov., 1946–Feb., 1947, n.d., Walter P. Reuther Library, Catherine Gelles Collection, Series III, general files, box 2.

41. "Legion Admits All-Woman Post," *New York Times* (Aug. 19, 1945), p. 37.

42. "WAC-Vets Philadelphia Chapter," *WAC Journal* 3 (Dec., 1948): 7.

43. Willenz, *Women Veterans,* p. 203.

44. Newsletter, Helen Fairchild Post 412, Dec., 1947, p. 2, Center for the Study of the History of Nursing, University of Pennsylvania, records of American Legion Helen Fairchild Post 412, MC 39, box 1.

45. Susan M. Hartmann, "Prescriptions for Penelope: Literature on Women's Obligations to Returning World War II Veterans," *Women's Studies* 5 (1978): 223–29; William Graebner, The Age of Doubt: American Thought and Culture in the 1940s (Boston: Twayne, 1991), p. 14; William H. Chafe, The Paradox of Change: American Women in the Twentieth Century (New York: Oxford University Press, 1991), pp. 156–77; Stephanie Coontz, The Way We Never Were: American Families and the Nostalgia Trap (New York: Basic Books, 1992), pp. 23–41; Elizabeth Fox-Genovese, "Mixed Messages: Women and the Impact of World War II," Southern Humanities Review 27 (Summer, 1993): 235–45; Costello, Virtue under Fire, pp. 192–93; Tyler May, Homeward Bound, pp. 63–66; Honey, Creating Rosie the Riveter, p. 97.

46. Tyler May, *Homeward Bound,* pp. 58–59, 103; Leila J. Rupp and Verta Taylor, Survival in the Doldrums: The American Women's Rights Movement, 1945 to the 1960s (Columbus: Ohio State University Press, 1990), pp. 15–20. The Labor Department noted an increase in live births from 1.4 million in 1940 to 1.9 million in 1944. See U.S. Department of Labor, Women's Bureau, Trends and Their Effect on the Demand for Women Workers, bulletin 203-12 (Washington, D.C.: GPO, 1946), p. 20.

47. Al Newman, "Separation for GI Jane Practically Painless," *Newsweek* (Oct. 29, 1945), p. 58.

48. Ibid., pp. 55–58; Mary P. Lord, "The WACs Sight New Objectives," *New York Times Magazine* (Sept. 2, 1945), p. 12. See also Tyler May, Homeward Bound, pp. 62–65.

49. George H. Gallup, *The Gallup Poll: Public Opinion, 1935–1971,* vol. 1 (New York: Random House, 1972), p. 490.

50. Beatrice Berg, "When GI Girls Return," *New York Times Magazine* (Apr. 22, 1945), p. 40.

51. Eleanor Lake, "A Smarter GI Jane Comes Home," *Reader's Digest* 49 (Sept., 1946), p. 34.

52. "Drama for the Brain," *Newsweek* (July 8, 1946), pp. 52, 54.

53. Benedek, *Insight and Personality Adjustment,* pp. 280–82.

54. Evelyn Field, "A Woman Veteran Is Mad . . . Here Are Her Gripes," *Daily World* (June 19, 1946), p. 5.

55. Brown, "Adjustment Problems," p. 50.

56. Historian Doris Weatherford has offered the opinion that what women sought in the postwar period was not so much a new role as a better role in American society. See Weatherford, *American Women and World War II,* pp. 103–11.

57. U.S. Department of Labor, Women's Bureau, *Handbook of Facts on Women Workers,* bulletin no. 225 (Washington, D.C.: GPO, 1946), p. 12.

58. "Post-War Job Role for Women Urged," *New York Times* (May 6, 1944), p. 14. See also "Hines Hails Women in Aid of Disabled," New York Times (Apr. 8, 1944), p. 18.

59. U.S. Department of Labor, *Thirty-fourth Annual Report of the Secretary of Labor for the Fiscal Year Ended June 30, 1946* (Washington, D.C.: GPO, 1947), p. 211; U.S. Department of Labor, Thirty-fifth Annual Report of the Secretary of Labor for the Fiscal Year Ended June 30, 1947 (Washington, D.C.: GPO, 1948), p. 104; Sherna Berger Gluck, Rosie the Riveter Revisited: Women, the War, and Social Change (Boston: Twayne, 1987), p. 16.

60. Berger Gluck, *Rosie the Riveter,* p. 16.

61. U.S. Department of Labor, *Thirty-fifth Annual Report,* p. 104; Chafe, Paradox of Change, p. 161; U.S. Department of Labor, Women's Bureau, Employment of Women in the Early Postwar Period: With Background of Prewar and War Data, bulletin no. 211 (Washington, D.C.: GPO, 1946), p. 13.

62. "Women's Activity in Unions Grows Rapidly in New York Area," *Christian Science Monitor* (Feb. 5, 1943), LOC, records of the National Women's Trade Union League (hereafter NWTUL), subject file, reel 18.

63. U.S. Department of Labor, *Thirty-sixth Annual Report of the Secretary of Labor for the Fiscal Year Ended June 30, 1948* (Washington, D.C.: GPO, 1949), p. 93; letter, Elizabeth Christman (secretary-treasurer, NWTUL) to Dorothy F. Markle (women's personnel advisor, Goodyear Aircraft Corp.), Oct. 13, 1944; memo, Elizabeth Christman (secretary-treasurer, NWTUL) to Elizabeth Pidgeon (Women's Bureau, Department of Labor), "Approximate Numbers of Women in Some Trade Unions," Apr. 25, 1947, Library of Congress, Papers of the National Women's Trade Union League, subject file, reel 18.

64. See, for example, Ruth Milkman, "Rosie the Riveter Revisited: Management's Postwar Purge of Women Automobile Workers," in *On the Line: Essays in the History of Auto Work,* ed. Nelson Lichtenstein and Stephen Meyer (Chicago: University of Illinois Press, 1989), pp. 129–41.

65. U.S. Department of Labor, Women's Bureau, *The Outlook for Women in Chemistry,* bulletin no. 223-2 (Washington, D.C.: GPO, 1948), pp. 2–11; U.S. Department of Labor, Women's Bureau, The Outlook for Women in Science, bulletin no. 223-1 (Washington, D.C.: GPO, 1949), pp. 1–27.

66. Nona Brown, "The Armed Services Find Woman Has a Place," *New York Times Magazine* (Dec. 26, 1946), pp. 14–15, 26; Doris Weatherford, American Women and World War II (New York: Facts on File, 1990), pp. 62–79; Zauhar, Wissolik, and Campion, eds., Out of the Kitchen, pp. 222–23.

67. Weatherford, *American Women in World War II,* p. 64.

68. Samuel Eliot Morison, Henry Steel Commager, and William E. Leuchtenburg, *The Growth of the American Republic,* vol. 2 (New York: Oxford University Press, 1969), pp. 722–27.

69. U.S. Department of Labor, Women's Bureau, "*The Outlook for Women in Occupations in the Medical Services: Professional Nursing,*" bulletin 203-3 (Washington, D.C.: GPO, 1945), 24–26; Susan Rimby Leighow, "A Obligation to Participate: Married Nurses' Labor Force Participation in the 1950s," in *Not June Cleaver,* pp. 42–43.

70. U.S. Department of Labor, Women's Bureau, *Women Workers after VJ Day in One Community: Bridgeport, Connecticut,* bulletin 216 (Washington, D.C.: GPO, 1946), pp. 27–28; McInerny, "The Woman Vet Has Her Headaches Too," p. 18.

71. Weatherford, *American Women and World War II,* p. 100.

72. Ibid., p. 106.

73. McInerny, "The Woman Vet Has Her Headaches Too," p. 18; Anderson, *Wartime Women,* p. 170; Weatherford, American Women and World War II, pp. 103–105. Anderson's examination of employment patterns in the Detroit area points out an interesting paradox. The Detroit USES office commonly denied manufacturing jobs to women who sought them, while also attempting to discourage men from clerical and service work, something counselors considered to be traditionally "women's" work.

74. Anderson, *Wartime Women,* pp. 158–59, 165–71. See also Ruth Milkman, "American Women and Industrial Unionism during World War II," in Behind the Lines: Gender and the Two World Wars, ed. Margaret Randolph Higonnet et al. (New Haven, Conn.: Yale University Press, 1987), pp. 169–80.

75. U.S. Department of Labor, Women's Bureau, *Handbook of Facts on Women Workers,* bulletin no. 237 (Washington, D.C.: GPO, 1950), p. 15.

76. For samplings of these expectations, see U.S. Department of Labor, Women's Bureau, *Women Workers in Ten Production Areas and Their Postwar Plans,* bulletin no. 209 (Washington, D.C.: GPO, 1946), p. 5.

77. Stilwell, "Pertinent Statistics on Women Veterans," p. 8.

78. "For GI Jane," *Reader's Digest* (Jan. 15, 1945), p. 72; Eugenia Kaledin, Mothers and More: American Women in the 1950s (Boston: Twayne, 1984), pp. 43–59.

79. Weatherford, *American Women and World War II,* pp. 104–105; R. W. Babcock, "Youth Wins Out," Survey 32 (July, 1946), pp. 185–86 (emphasis mine).

80. Alice C. Lloyd, "Women in the Postwar College," *Journal of the American Association of University Women* 39 (Spring, 1946): 131–34.

81. Anderson, *Wartime Women,* p. 175. Karen Anderson observes that the GI Bill subsidized "male mobility" while concurrent consideration for women was most often lacking.

82. Campbell, "Servicewomen of World War II," pp. 257–58; a similar poll is also cited in U.S. Department of Labor, Women's Bureau, *Women Workers after VJ Day in One Community: Bridgeport, Connecticut,* bulletin 216 (Washington, D.C.: GPO, 1946), pp. 27–28.

Chapter 5

1. Gunnar Myrdal, *An American Dilemma: The Negro Problem and Modern Democracy* (New York: Harper and Row, 1944), p. 1004; See also Neil A. Wynn, The Afro-American and the Second World War (New York: Holmes and Meier, 1975), pp. 99–106; Robert J. Morrell, "One Thing We Did Right: Reflections of the Movement," in New Directions in Civil Rights Studies, ed. Armstead L. Robinson and Patricia Sullivan (Charlottesville: University Press of Virginia, 1991), pp. 66–69.

2. Neil R. McMillen, "Fighting for What We Didn't Have: How Mississippi Veterans Remember World War II," in *Remaking Dixie: The Impact of World War II on the American South,* ed. Neil R. McMillen (Jackson: University Press of Mississippi, 1997), pp. 96–97.

3. Maggi M. Morehouse, Fighting in the Jim Crow Army: Black Men and Women Remember World War II (New York: Rowman and Littlefield, 2000), p. 202.

4. Ibid.

5. James T. Patterson, *Grand Expectations: The United States, 1945–1974* (New York: Oxford University Press, 1996), p. 22. War Department circular 124, "Utilization of Negro Manpower in the Postwar Army Policy, Apr. 27, 1946," in Blacks in the Military: Essential Documents, ed. Bernard C. Nalty and Morris J. MacGregor (Wilmington, Del.: Scholarly Resources, 1981), p. 192. See also Charles G. Bolté and Louis Harris, "Our Negro Veterans," public affairs pamphlet no. 128 (New York: Public Affairs Committee, 1947), p. 4; Harvard Sitkoff, "African-American Militancy in the World War II South: Another Perspective," in Remaking Dixie, p. 73.

6. Charity Adams Early, *One Woman's Army* (College Station: Texas A&M University Press, 1989), p. 24.

7. For a list of military occupational specialties (MOS) that had civilian applications, see War Manpower Commission, Bureau of Manpower Utilization, *Special Aids for Placing Military Personnel in Civilian Jobs (Enlisted Army Personnel)* (Washington, D.C.: GPO, 1944).

8. Stephen E. Ambrose, *Citizen Soldiers: The U.S. Army from the Normandy Beaches to the Surrender of Germany, June 7, 1944–May 7, 1945* (New York: Simon and Schuster, 1997), pp. 331–50; Steven A. Holmes, "Some Notable Old Soldiers Fight to Avoid Fading Away," New York Times (Sept. 2, 2002), p. A1; Lawrence P. Scott and William M. Womack Sr., Double V: The Civil Rights Struggle of the Tuskegee Airmen (East Lansing: Michigan State University Press, 1994), pp. 185–262.

9. Allan R. Millett and Peter Maslowski, *For the Common Defense: A Military History of the United States of America* (New York: Free Press, 1994), pp. 472–73. For a sample army directive discussing the treatment of African American soldiers, see "Army Service Forces Manual M5: Leadership and the Negro Soldier, October, 1944," in Blacks in the Military, pp. 128–30.

10. James C. Cobb, "World War II and the Mind of the Modern South," in *Remaking Dixie,* pp. 5, 9–10.

11. Allen Cronenberg, *Forth to the Mighty Conflict: Alabama and World War II* (Tuscaloosa: University of Alabama Press, 1995), p. 84.

12. McMillen, "Fighting for What We Didn't Have," p. 106. See also Jessie Parkhurst Guzman, *1952 Negro Yearbook: A Review of Events Affecting Negro Life* (New York: Wm. H. Wise, 1952), p. 11.

13. Bolté and Harris, *Our Negro Veterans,* pp. 4–5, 9–10.

14. Joseph H. Ball, "The Case of the Negro," *Jewish Veteran* 14 (Mar., 1945), p. 5.

15. John Egerton, *Speak Now against the Day: The Generation before the Civil Rights Movement in the South* (New York: Knopf, 1994), p. 245.

16. Michael D. Gambone, ed., *Documents of American Diplomacy: From the Revolution to the Present* (Westport, Conn.: Praeger, 2002), pp. 250–54, 296–97.

17. "Hines Pledges Aid to Negro Veteran," *New York Times* (Mar. 14, 1945), p. 1.

18. Letter, Charles Lett to Jesse O. Dedmon (secretary, Veterans' Affairs, NAACP), May 10, 1945, in *Papers of the NAACP: Part 9: Discrimination in the U.S. Armed Forces, 1918–1955, Series C: Veterans' Affairs Committee, 1940–1950,* ed. Richard M. Dalfiume (Bethesda, Md.: University Publications of America, 1989), reel 7, frame 244.

19. Letter, Frank T. Hines (administrator, VA) to Jesse O. Dedmon (secretary, Veterans' Affairs, NAACP), Apr. 9, 1945, in *Papers of the NAACP: Part 9,* reel 7, frames 180–81.

20. Mark V. Tushnet, *Making Civil Rights Law: Thurgood Marshall and the Supreme Court, 1936–1961* (New York: Oxford University Press, 1994), pp. 67–70; Thurgood Marshall, "The Legal Attack to Secure Civil Rights," in Thurgood Marshall: His Speeches, Writings, Arguments, Opinions, and Reminiscences, ed. Mark V. Tushnet (Chicago: Lawrence Hill Books, 2001), pp. 90–91.

21. Good accounts of this culture shock are given in Kathryn Browne Pfeifer, *The 761st Tank Battalion* (New York: Twenty-First Century Books, 1994).

22. Walter White, "Behind the Harlem Riot," *New Republic* 109 (Aug. 16, 1943): 221.

23. Patricia Sullivan, "Southern Reformers, the New Deal, and the Movement's Foundation," in *New Directions in Civil Rights Studies,* pp. 82–85; David McCullough, Truman (New York: Simon and Schuster, 1992), pp. 247, 528, 587–88. See also Jacqueline Jones, "Federal Power, Southern Power: A Long View, 1860–1940," Journal of American History 87 (Mar., 2001): 1392–96.

24. McCullough, *Truman,* p. 588.

25. For documentation produced by this committee, see U.S. President's Committee on Civil Rights, *To Secure These Rights: The Report of the President's Committee on Civil Rights* (Washington, D.C.: GPO, 1947). See also Tushnet, ed., Thurgood Marshall, p. 93.

26. NAACP memo, "Hospital Status," Nov. 8, 1945, Library of Congress (hereafter LOC), records of the NAACP, Veterans' Affairs, 1940–1955, box G-18.

27. Press service of the NAACP, "Full Integration of Negro Veterans Urged on General Omar Bradley by NAACP," Sept. 20, 1945, LOC, records of the NAACP, branch files, 1940–1955, box A657; letter, Robert D. Beer (manager, VA Regional Office, Chicago) to Henry W. McGee (president, NAACP, Chicago branch), Mar. 18, 1947; letter, Addison V. Pinkney (executive secretary, NAACP, Baltimore branch) to Jessie O. Dedmon (secretary, Veterans' Affairs, NAACP), Apr. 3, 1947, LOC, records of the NAACP, Veterans' Affairs files, 1940–1955, box G-9.

28. For an example of these exchanges, see letter, Jesse O. Dedmon (secretary, Veterans' Affairs, NAACP) to Walter White (secretary, NAACP), Nov. 15, 1946; letter, A. D. Hiller (executive assistant to the administrator) to Walter White (secretary, NAACP), July 4, 1945, LOC, records of the NAACP, branch files, 1940–1955, box A657.

29. "The GI Assault Bill," *New Republic* 112 (Feb. 5, 1945): 166.

30. NAACP, *Veterans' Handbook,* n.d., LOC, records of the NAACP, branch files, 1940–1955, box A658; Morehouse, Fighting in the Jim Crow Army, p. 202.

31. Doug McAdam, *Political Process and the Development of Black Insurgency, 1930–1970* (Chicago: University of Chicago Press, 1982), p. 109; Morehouse, Fighting in the Jim Crow Army, p. 202.

32. Daniel Kryder, *Divided Arsenal: Race and the American State during World War II* (New York: Cambridge University Press, 2000), p. 252; Myrdal, An American Dilemma, p. 1009.

33. George N. Redd, "Present Status of Negro Higher Education and Professional Education: A Critical Summary," *Journal of Negro Education* 17 (Summer, 1948): 402; McAdam, Political Process and the Development of Black Insurgency, p. 102.

34. James A. Atkins, "Negro Educational Institutions and the Veterans' Educational Facilities Program," *Journal of Negro Education* 17 (Spring, 1948): 141–53.

35. Editorial comment, "The Critical Situation in Negro Higher and Professional Education," *Journal of Negro Education* 15 (Fall, 1946): 579–84; editorial comment, "The Improvement of the Negro College Faculty," Journal of Negro Education 16 (Winter, 1947): 1–9.

36. Atkins, "Negro Educational Institutions," pp. 144–45.

37. Guzman, *1952 Negro Yearbook,* p. 218. For a more recent study of the issue, see Sarah Turner and John Bound, "Closing the Gap or Widening the Divide: The Effects of the GI Bill and World War II on the Educational Outcomes of Black Americans," Journal of Labor History 63 (Mar., 2003): 145–77.

38. James T. Patterson, *Brown v. Board of Education: A Civil Rights Milestone and Its Troubled Legacy* (New York: Oxford University Press, 2001), p. 14; Howard Ball, A Defiant Life: Thurgood Marshall and the Persistence of Racism in America (New York: Crown, 1998), pp. 92–95; Tushnet, Making Civil Rights Law, pp. 49, 68.

39. Wynn, *The Afro-American and the Second World War,* p. 129.

40. Patterson, *Brown v. Board of Education,* p. 4; Guzman, 1952 Negro Yearbook, pp. 116–17.

41. "Lag in Jobs Found by Negro Veterans," *New York Times* (Apr. 2, 1946), p. 15.

42. Letter, Paul W. McNutt (War Manpower Commission) to Leslie S. Perry (administrative assistant, Washington Bureau, NAACP), Sept. 2, 1944; memo, "Segregation: United States Employment Service," Sept. 8, 1944, LOC, records of the NAACP, branch files, 1940–1955, box A653.

43. David H. Onkst, " 'First a Negro, Incidentally a Veteran': Black World War Two Veterans and the GI Bill of Rights in the Deep South, 1944–1948," *Journal of Social History* 31 (Spring/Summer, 1998): 517–44; Bolté and Harris, Our Negro Veterans, pp. 11, 20.

44. Bolté and Harris, *Our Negro Veterans,* p. 12. See also "Asks Skilled Jobs for More Negroes," New York Times (June 12, 1946), p. 2.

45. "Jim Crow Hospitals Add to 'Comfort' of Negro Vets, says Bradley," *Chicago Defender* (Feb. 23, 1946): 1, 8 (emphasis mine); memo of conference with General Bradley at Veterans' Administration by Coordinating National Negro Organizations, "Techniques and Procedures for the Complete Integration of Negroes on a Non Segregated [sic] Basis in All Phases of the Veterans' Administration Program," Dec. 20, 1945, in Papers of the NAACP: Part 9, reel 7, frames 612–13. See also Robert F. Jefferson, "Organization Is the Key: Wounded African American World War II Ex-GIs and the Civil Rights Struggles of the Late 1940s" (paper presented at the Veteran and Society Conference, Knoxville, Tenn., Nov., 2000).

46. Patterson, *Brown v. Board of Education,* p. 2; McAdam, Political Process and the Development of Black Insurgency, pp. 102–107.

47. Howard Ball reflects on the general impatience of this new, younger generation of civil rights leaders for action. See Ball, *A Defiant Life,* pp. 92–93.

48. Charles M. Payne, *I've Got the Light of Freedom: The Organizing Tradition and the Mississippi Freedom Struggle* (Berkeley: University of California Press, 1995), pp. 30, 47, 56; Robert J. Norrell, "One Thing We Did Right: Reflections on the Movement," in New Directions in Civil Rights Studies, p. 70.

49. Payne, *I've Got the Light of Freedom,* p. 57.

50. Jesse O. Dedmon (secretary, Veterans' Affairs, NAACP), "When GI Joe Comes Home," May 19, 1945, LOC, records of the NAACP, Veterans' Affairs, 1940–1955, box G-17.

51. Letter, Walter White to Gov. Thomas Dewey, Dec. 18, 1945, LOC, records of the NAACP, branch files, 1940–1955, box A657.

52. Sullivan, "Southern Reformers, the New Deal, and the Movement's Foundation," p. 92.

53. "Birmingham War Vets March through Streets for Vote Rights," *Chicago Defender* (Feb. 2, 1946): 7; Patricia Sullivan, Days of Hope: Race and Democracy in the New Deal Era (Chapel Hill: University of North Carolina Press, 1996), pp. 197–98. For an excellent account of the difficulties faced by African Americans in 1946, see Robert J. Norrell, Reaping the Whirlwind: The Civil Rights Movement in Tuskegee (New York: Knopf, 1985), pp. 59–78.

54. Jennifer E. Brooks, "From Hitler and Tojo to Talmadge and Jim Crow: World War Two Veterans and the Remaking of Southern Political Tradition" (Ph.D. diss., University of Tennessee, Knoxville, 1997), pp. 13, 29, 55–60, 151–60. For an example of a specific organization, see National Council of Negro Veterans, "A Report to Veterans," Oct., 1946, LOC, records of the NAACP, branch files, 1940–1955, box A657.

55. Egerton, *Speak Now against the Day,* pp. 361–69; Sullivan, "Southern Reformers, the New Deal, and the Movement's Foundation," p. 96; Herbert Shapiro, White Violence and Black Response: From Reconstruction to Montgomery (Amherst, Mass.: University of Amherst Press, 1988), pp. 349–55; Donald L. Grant, The Way It Was in the South: The Black Experience in Georgia (New York: Carol Publishing Group, 1993), pp. 366.

Notes to Pages 124–26

56. "Negroes Ask Vote Guard," *New York Times* (May 19, 1946), p. 18.

57. Brooks, "From Hitler and Tojo to Talmadge and Jim Crow," p. 125.

58. Payne, *I've Got the Light of Freedom*, pp. 24–25; Patterson, Brown v. Board of Education, p. 4; "Ouster of Rankin Urged by Veterans," New York Times (Feb. 25, 1946), p. 8.

59. Morehouse, *Fighting in the Jim Crow Army*, p. 205.

60. Patterson, *Brown v. Board of Education*, p. 13.

61. Genna Rae McNeil, *Groundwork: Charles Hamilton Houston and the Struggle for Civil Rights* (Philadelphia: University of Pennsylvania Press, 1983), pp. 134, 183. Harry Briggs, a navy veteran with five children, was one of twenty plaintiffs in an NAACP suit protesting segregation in the South Carolina public schools in 1948. See Patterson, Brown v. Board of Education, p. 4.

62. Mead Calls for Action," *New York Times* (Mar. 17, 1946), V, p. 2.

63. Patterson, *Grand Expectations*, pp. 10–38. A major theme of Patterson's work is the catalyst World War II provided for disenfranchised groups in American society.

64. Census data on the "foreign-born" population of the United States is limited as it applies to Latin America. The 1950 census included only Mexico as a point of origin under the category of "foreign born." The total population for 1940 was 377,433, or 3.3 percent of the total U.S. population. See U.S. Department of Commerce, Bureau of the Census, *Census of Population: 1950*, vol. 2, Characteristics of the Population, Part 1: United States Summary (Washington, D.C.: GPO, 1953), pp. 1–98.

65. Carl Allsup, *The American GI Forum: Origins and Evolution* (Austin: Center for Mexican American Studies, 1982), pp. 21, 32.

66. U.S. Department of Defense, office of the deputy assistant secretary of defense, *Hispanics in America's Defense* (Washington, D.C.: GPO, 1989), p. 27.

67. Lawrence A. Clayton and Michael L. Conniff, *A History of Modern Latin America* (New York: Harcourt Brace College, 1999), p. 374.

68. Henry A. J. Ramos, *The American GI Forum: In Pursuit of the Dream, 1948–1983* (Houston: Arte Publico Press, 1998), p. 2.

69. Clayton and Conniff, *A History of Modern Latin America*, pp. 368–69, 373.

70. Erasmo Gamboa, *Mexican Labor and World War II: Braceros in the Pacific Northwest, 1942–1947* (Austin: University of Texas Press, 1990), pp. 22–73; Juan Gomez-Quiñones, Mexican American Labor, 1790–1990 (Albuquerque: University of New Mexico Press, 1994), pp. 167–68; Alexander Monto, The Roots of Mexican Labor Migration (Westport, Conn.: Praeger, 1994), pp. 55–57.

71. Benjamin Márquez, *LULAC: Evolution of a Mexican American Political Organization* (Austin: University of Texas Press, 1993), pp. 40–41.

72. Ramos, *American GI Forum*, pp. 3–4; Allsup, American GI Forum, p. 32.

73. Allsup, *American GI Forum*, pp. 29, 31.

74. Ramos, *American GI Forum*, pp. 4–6.

75. Ibid., p. 7; Ralph C. Guzmán, *The Political Socialization of the Mexican People* (New York: Arno Press, 1976), pp. 147–49.

76. Allsup, *American GI Forum*, pp. 34–35.

77. Ibid., pp. 8–9, 33–39; Robert A. Caro, *Master of the Senate* (New York: Knopf, 2002), pp. 740–55; Robert Dallek, Lone Star Rising: Lyndon Johnson and His Times, 1908–1960 (New York: Oxford University Press, 1991), p. 369; F. Chris Garcia, ed., Latinos and the Political System (Notre Dame, Ind.: University of Notre Dame Press, 1988), p. 51.

78. Ramos, *American GI Forum*, pp. 22, 52, 77.

79. Ibid., p. 30; Richard Anthony Santillán, "Latino Political Development in the Southwest and Midwest Regions: A Comparative Overview, 1915–1989," in *Latinos and Political Coalitions: Political Empowerment for the 1990s*, ed. Roberto E. Villarreal and Norma G. Hernandez (Westport, Conn.: Praeger, 1991), p. 117. See also George Ochoa, Atlas of Hispanic-American History (New York: Facts on File, 2001), pp. 142–44.

80. Santillán, "Latino Political Development in the Southwest and Midwest Regions," pp. 117–18.

81. Dallek, *Lone Star Rising*, p. 369; Rodolfo Rosales, "Personality and Style in San Antonio Politics: Henry Cisneros and Bernardo Eureste, 1975–1985," in Chicano Politics and Society in the Late Twentieth Century, ed. David Montejano (Austin: University of Texas Press, 1999), p. 3.

82. Mario T. García, *Mexican Americans: Leadership, Ideology, and Identity, 1930–1960* (New Haven, Conn.: Yale University Press, 1989), pp. 13–22; Alejandro Portés and Dag McLeod, "What Shall I Call Myself? Hispanic Identity Formation in the Second Generation," Ethnic and Racial Studies 19 (July, 1996): 523–47; José O. Díaz, "Gender, Ethnicity, and Power: Recent Studies on Puerto Rican History," Latin American Research Review 37 (2002): 215–30.

83. William Hohri, "Redress as a Movement toward Enfranchisement," in *Japanese Americans: From Relocation to Redress*, ed. Roger Daniels, Sandra C. Taylor, and Harry H. L. Kitano (Seattle: University of Washington Press, 1991), pp. 196–97.

84. Tomi Kaizawa Knaefler, *Our House Divided: Seven Japanese American Families in World War II* (Honolulu: University of Hawaii Press, 1991), p. 6.

85. Daniel K. Inouye with Lawrence Elliott, *Journey to Washington* (Englewood Cliffs, N.J.: Prentice-Hall, 1967), pp. 53–55.

86. Tamotsu Shibutani, *The Derelicts of K Company: A Sociological Study of Demoralization* (Berkeley: University of California Press, 1978), pp. 33, 38.

87. Lyn Crost, *Honor by Fire: Japanese Americans at War in Europe and the Pacific* (Novato, Calif.: Presidio Press, 1994), p. 14.

88. Orville C. Shirey, *Americans: The Story of the 442nd Combat Team* (Washington, D.C.: Infantry Journal Press, 1946), p. 19.

89. Inouye, *Journey to Washington*, p. 75.

90. Shirey, *Americans*, p. 101; Hawaii Nikkei History Editorial Board, Japanese Eyes, American Hearts: Personal Reflections of Hawaii's World War II Nisei Soldiers (Honolulu: Tendai Educational Foundation, 1998), p. 6; U.S. Commission on Wartime Relocation and Internment of Civilians, Personal Justice Denied (Washington, D.C.: GPO, 1982), p. 258.

91. Hawaii Nikkei History Editorial Board, *Japanese Eyes, American Hearts*, p. 20; Kaizawa Knaefler, Our House Divided, p. 15.

92. Gary Y. Okihiro, *Storied Lives: Japanese American Students and World War II* (Seattle: University of Washington Press, 1999), pp. 118–39.

93. U.S. Department of the Interior, War Agency Liquidation Unit, *The Postwar Adjustment of the Evacuated Japanese Americans* (Washington, D.C.: GPO, 1947), pp. 7, 17–25; Crost, *Honor by Fire*, pp. 300–305. See also James M. Skinner, "December 7: Filmic Myth as Historical Fact," Journal of Military History 55 (Oct., 1991): 511.

94. Charlotte Brooks, "In the Twilight Zone between Black and White: Japanese American Resettlement and Community in Chicago, 1942–1945," *Journal of American History* 86 (Mar., 2000): 1655–87.

95. Kaizawa Knaefler, *Our House Divided*, p. 41.

96. Shibutani, *Derelicts of K Company*, p. 39.

97. Crost, *Honor by Fire*, pp. 295–301; U.S. Commission on Wartime Relocation and Internment of Civilians, Personal Justice Denied, pp. 117–21.

98. U.S. Department of the Interior, War Relocation Authority (WRA), *Legal and Constitutional Phases of the WRA Program* (Washington, D.C.: GPO, 1946), pp. 56–59; U.S. Department of the Interior, War Relocation Authority, The Wartime Handling of Evacuee Property (Washington, D.C.: GPO, 1946), p. 84.

99. WRA, *Legal and Constitutional Phases of the WRA Program*, pp. 56–59.

100. Crost, *Honor by Fire*, pp. 295–301; U.S. Commission on Wartime Relocation and Internment of Civilians, Personal Justice Denied, pp. 117–21; U.S. Department of Commerce, Bureau of the Census, Sixteenth Census of the United States: 1940: Population, vol. 2, Characteristics of the Population (Washington, D.C.: GPO, 1943), p. 52; U.S. Department of Commerce, Bureau of the Census, Census of Population: 1950, vol. 2, Characteristics of the Population: Part 1: U.S. Summary (Washington, D.C.: GPO, 1953), pp. 1–106.

101. American Council on Race Relations, "Report of Action," Jan. 18, 1945, Walter P. Reuther Library, UAW Office of the President, R. J. Thomas Collection, part II, box 17.

102. Shibutani, *Derelicts of K Company*, p. 24.

103. For a good discussion of these difficulties, see Jack K. Wakamatsu, S*ilent Warriors: A Memoir of America's 442nd Regimental Combat Team* (Los Angeles: JKW Press, 1992), p. 197.

104. U.S. Department of Commerce, Bureau of the Census, *Census of Population: 1950*, vol. 2, Characteristics of the Population: Parts 51–54: Territories and Possessions (Washington, D.C.: GPO, 1953), pp. 52–115; Jere Takahashi, Nisei/Sansei: Shifting Japanese American Identities and Politics (Philadelphia, Penn.: Temple University Press, 1997), pp. 113–31; Harry H. L. Kitano, Japanese Americans: The Evolution of a Subculture (Englewood Cliffs, N.J.: Prentice Hall, 1976), pp. 89–97.

105. Albert Deutsch, "U.S. Agencies Charged with Bias against Vets," *PM* (Apr. 8, 1946), p. 13.

106. War Agency Liquidation Unit, *People in Motion*, p. 24.

107. Deutsch, "U.S. Agencies Charged with Bias against Vets," p. 13.

108. U.S. Commission on Wartime Relocation and Internment of Civilians, *Personal Justice Denied*, pp. 259–60. See also David K. Yoo, Growing Up Nisei:

Notes to Pages 136–40

Race, Generation, and Culture among Japanese Americans of California, 1924–1949 (Urbana: University of Illinois Press, 2000), pp. 135–37.

109. "Aloha to the 442nd Combat Team on Their 10th Anniversary Reunion, Hawaii, 1953," *Honolulu Advertiser* (July 24, 1953), pp. 2, 13; 442nd Reunion Committee, Go for Broke: 442nd Regimental Combat Team, the 442nd Decade, 10th Anniversary Reunion, July 20–31, 1953; Lawrence H. Sakamoto, Hawaii's Own, 1946, p. 93, USMHI, Manuscript Collection.

110. Takahashi, *Nisei/Sansei*, p. 127.

111. Ibid., pp. 126–27.

112. For an excellent study of the propaganda methodologies utilized by both the United States and Japan, see John W. Dower, *War without Mercy: Race and Power in the Pacific War* (New York: Pantheon Books, 1986), pp. 77–202.

113. Inouye, *Journey to Washington*, pp. 243–45.

114. Andrew Michael Manis, *Southern Civil Religions in Conflict: Black and White Baptists and Civil Rights, 1947–1957* (Athens: University of Georgia Press, 1987), pp. 27, 39; David M. Kennedy, Freedom from Fear: The American People in Depression and War, 1929–1945 (New York: Oxford University Press, 1999), pp. 746–97; Patterson, Grand Expectations, pp. 10–60.

115. Manis, *Southern Civil Religions in Conflict*, p. 31; Cronenberg, Forth to the Mighty Conflict, p. 163.

116. NAACP memo, "Negro Accumulated Inductions and Enlistments by State," Aug. 1, 1946, LOC, records of the NAACP, Veterans' Affairs file, 1940–1950, box G-1.

117. George N. Craig, "Something to Remember," excerpt from *American Legion Magazine*, May, 1950, USMHI, Daniel B. Strickler Papers, 28th Infantry Division, 1947–1951, Germany, Occupation.

118. See K. A. Cuordileone, " 'Politics in an Age of Anxiety': Cold War Political Culture and Crisis in American Masculinity, 1949–1960," *Journal of American History* 87 (Sept., 2000): 515–45; Manis, Southern Civil Religions in Conflict, p. 54; Allsup, American GI Forum, pp. 60–62.

119. Ramos, *American GI Forum*, p. 21.

120. See, for example, "Veteran Barred by Law School in Louisiana," *Chicago Defender* (Mar. 2, 1946): 1, 8; "Chicago Vets Endure D.C., Jim Crow to Fight Taxicab Monopoly," Chicago Defender (Mar. 2, 1946): 8.

121. Allsup, *American GI Forum*, pp. 20–31.

122. Márquez, *LULAC*, pp. 39–60.

Chapter 6

1. Marita Sturken, "Reenactment, Fantasy, and the Paranoia of History: Oliver Stone's Docudramas," *History and Theory* 36 (Dec., 1997): 64–79. The April, 1992, edition of the American Historical Review is largely devoted to a discussion of Stone's controversial movie, JFK. See Robert A. Rosenstone, "JFK: Historical Fact/ Historical Film," American Historical Review 97 (Apr., 1992): 506–11.

2. Richard Maltby, ed., *Passing Parade: A History of Popular Culture in the Twentieth Century* (New York: Oxford University Press, 1989), pp. 147–57. See

also Erik Barnouw, Tube of Plenty: The Evolution of American Television (New York: Oxford University Press, 1982).

3. Harlan Jacobson, "Bad Day at Black Rock," *Film Comment* 38 (Jan./Feb., 2002): 28–31.

4. For a thoughtful examination of this topic, see William J. Prior, "*Saving Private Ryan* and the Morality of War," Parameters: U.S. Army War College 30 (Autumn, 2000): 138–46.

5. Michael Valdéz Moses, "Virtual Warriors," *Reason* 33 (Jan., 2002): 54–61.

6. Richard T. Jameson, "*Saving Private Ryan*," Film Comment 34 (Sept./Oct., 1998): 21–23.

7. Jason Katzman, "From Outcast to Cliché: How Film Shaped, Warped, and Developed the Image of the Vietnam Veteran, 1967–1990," *Journal of American Culture* 16 (Spring, 1993): 7–24; J. Hoberman, "America Dearest," American Film 13 (May, 1988): 39–45.

8. Jameson, "*Saving Private Ryan*," pp. 21–23.

9. Jacobson, "Bad Day at Black Rock," p. 28. Many critics of the film have commented on its open glorification of the World War Two generation. See Albert Auster, "*Saving Private Ryan* and American Triumphalism," Journal of Popular Film and Television 30 (Summer, 2002): 98–105. See also Bernard Beck, "The War's Desolation: Saving Private Ryan, the Thin Red Line, and the Baggage of History," Multicultural Perspectives 1 (1999): 19–22.

10. Norman Kagan, *The War Film* (New York: Pyramid, 1974), pp. 56–62. See also Geoffrey B. Pingree, "Visual Evidence Reconsidered: Reflections on Film and History," Public Historian 21 (Spring, 1999): 99–107; Susan Jeffords, "Telling the War Story," in It's Our Military, Too! Women and the U.S. Military, ed. Judith Hick Stiehm (Philadelphia: Temple University Press, 1996), pp. 220–34; James M. Skinner, "December 7: Filmic Myth as Historical Fact," Journal of Military History 55 (Oct., 1991): 507–16.

11. Jonathan Munby, *Public Enemies, Public Heroes: Screening the Gangster from Little Caesar to Touch of Evil* (Chicago: University of Chicago Press, 1999), pp. 144–86; Pierre Sorlin, "The Cinema: American Weapon," Film History 10 (1998): 375–81; Jonathan Buchsbaum, "Tame Wolves and Phony Claims: Paranoia and Film Noir," in The Book of Film Noir, ed. Ian Cameron (New York: Continuum, 1993), pp. 88–89; Richard Maltby, "Film Noir: The Politics of Maladjusted Text," Journal of American Studies 18 (Apr., 1984): 49–70; Barbara Deming, Running Away from Myself: A Dream Portrait of America Drawn from the Films of the Forties (New York: Grossman, 1969), pp. 3–38.

12. Nicholas Christopher, *Somewhere in the Night: Film Noir and the American City* (New York: Free Press, 1997), p. 38.

13. Paul S. Boyer, *By the Bombs' Early Light: American Thought and Culture at the Dawn of the Atomic Age* (New York: Pantheon Books, 1985), p. 15.

14. Richard Severo, *The Wages of War: When America's Soldiers Came Home—from Valley Forge to Vietnam* (New York: Simon and Schuster, 1989), p. 293.

15. Susan M. Hartman, *The Home Front and Beyond: American Women in the 1940s* (Boston: Twayne, 1982), p. 17; Elaine Tyler May, Homeward Bound: American Families in the Cold War Era (New York: Basic Books, 1988), p. 59.

16. William L. O'Neill, *A Democracy at War: America's Fight at Home and Abroad in World War II* (Cambridge: Harvard University Press, 1993), pp. 247–66. David Kennedy underplays the impact of the war on child care, noting that federal day-care centers were consistently undersubscribed during the war. See Kennedy, Freedom from Fear, p. 780.

17. Andrew J. Cherlin, *Marriage, Divorce, Remarriage* (Cambridge: Harvard University Press, 1992), pp. 68–90.

18. Lou Berg, "Veteran-Conscious Hollywood," *American Legion Magazine* 40 (Jan., 1946), p. 32.

19. Martin F. Norden " 'Coward, Take My Hand': Race, Ableism, and the Veteran Problem in *Home of the Brave* and Bright Victory," in Classic Hollywood, Classic Whiteness, ed. Daniel Bernardi (Minneapolis: University of Minnesota Press, 2001), pp. 339–56.

20. Charles Higham and Joel Greenberg, *Hollywood in the Forties* (New York: A. S. Barnes, 1968), p. 15.

21. James I. Deutsch, "Coming Home from 'The Good War': World War II Veterans as Depicted in American Film and Fiction" (Ph.D. diss., George Washington University, 1991), p. 109.

22. Ibid., pp. 58–59, 68–69.

23. William Graebner, *The Age of Doubt: American Thought and Culture in the 1940s* (Boston: Twayne, 1991), p. 41.

24. Bernard Frizell, "Handless Veteran," *Life* 21 (Dec. 16, 1946), pp. 74–75.

25. David A. Gerber, "Heroes and Misfits: The Troubled Social Reintegration of Disabled Veterans in *The Best Years of Our Lives*," in Disabled Veterans in History, ed. David A. Gerber (Ann Arbor: University of Michigan Press, 2000), pp. 80–90.

26. "Gen. Bradley Lauds Film: Praises *Best Years of Our Lives* in Letter to Samuel Goldwyn," New York Times (Dec. 11, 1946), p. 42.

27. "Harold Russell's 'Oscars,' " *New York Times* (Mar. 15, 1947), p. 12.

28. "Redeeming Oscar: Independence Shown in the 1946 Awards," *New York Times* (May 23, 1947), II, p. 1.

29. Deborah Thomas, "How Hollywood Deals with the Deviant Male," in *The Book of Film Noir*, ed. Ian Cameron (New York: Continuum, 1993), pp. 62–64; Bruce Crowther, Film Noir: Reflections in a Dark Mirror (New York: Continuum, 1989), pp. 69–113.

30. Dan Levin, *From the Battlefield: Dispatches of a World War II Marine* (Annapolis, Md.: Naval Institute Press, 1995), p. 123.

31. Steven Mintz and Randy Roberts, eds., *Hollywood's America: United States History through Its Films* (St. James, N.Y.: Brandywine Press, 1993), p. 193.

32. Robert Sklar, *Movie-Made America: A Cultural History of American Movies* (New York: Vintage Books, 1994), p. 255.

33. Colin Shindler, *Hollywood Goes to War: Films and American Society, 1939–1952* (Boston: Routledge and Kegan Paul, 1979), pp. 101, 115; Graebner, The Age of Doubt, p. 25. See also Timothy Shuker-Haines, "Home Is the Hunter: Representations of Returning World War II Veterans and the Reconstruction of Masculinity" (Ph.D. diss., University of Michigan, 1994), pp. 1–52.

34. Christopher, *Somewhere in the Night,* p. 38; Foster Hirsch, Film Noir: The Dark Side of the Screen (New York: A. S. Barnes, 1985), pp. 167–97.

35. O'Neill, *A Democracy at War,* p. 250.

36. Ibid., p. 263.

37. Michael J. Bennett, *When Dreams Come True: The GI Bill and the Making of Modern America* (London: Brassey's, 1996), p. 223; Geoffrey Perrett, Days of Sadness, Years of Triumph: The American People, 1939–1945 (New York: Coward, McCann, and Geoghegan, 1973), pp. 401–402.

38. U.S. President's Commission on Law Enforcement and Administration of Justice, *The Challenge of Crime in a Free Society* (New York: E. P. Dutton, 1968), pp. 101–10.

39. Willard Waller, *The Veteran Comes Back* (New York: Dryden Press, 1944), pp. 124–25.

40. For a contemporary study of the problem of perception, see Roberta Rose, "I'm a Veteran Judge," *American Legion Magazine* 40 (Mar., 1946), pp. 22–23.

41. Paul Arthur, *"Act of Violence,"* Film Comment 35 (July/Aug., 1999): 56–58.

42. Alain Silver and Elizabeth Ward, *An Encyclopedic Reference to the American Style: Film Noir* (New York: Overlook Press, 1992), p. 242.

43. Harry Lever, "They're Out to Get You," *American Legion Magazine* 40 (Mar., 1946), pp. 16, 70; George Kellman, "Some Who Wait for the New Vet," Jewish Veteran 14 (May, 1945), p. 10.

44. Christopher, *Somewhere in the Night,* p. 173.

45. Crowther, *Reflections in a Dark Mirror,* p. 1.

46. See William F. McDermott, "Police Jobs for Veterans," *American Legion Magazine* 41 (Aug., 1946), pp. 24–25; "996 Veterans Join Ranks of Finest," New York Times (Sept. 22, 1946), p. 54.

47. Bowsley Crowther, "The Movies," in *While You Were Gone: A Report on Wartime Life in the United States,* ed. Jack Goodman (New York: Simon and Schuster, 1946), pp. 521–32.

48. Edwin P. Hoyt, *The GIs' War: The Story of American Soldiers in Europe in World War II* (New York: McGraw-Hill, 1988), p. 272; Gerald F. Linderman, The World within War: America's Combat Experience in World War II (New York: Free Press, 1997), pp. 316–17. See also Maurice Zolotow, Shooting Star: A Biography of John Wayne (New York: Simon and Schuster, 1974).

49. Allan R. Millett and Peter Maslowski, *For the Common Defense: A Military History of the United States of America* (New York: Free Press, 1994), p. 653.

50. Richard Severo, *The Wages of War: When America's Soldiers Came Home—from Valley Forge to Vietnam* (New York: Simon and Schuster, 1989).

51. Frank Ninkovich, *Germany and the United States: The Transformation of the German Question since 1945* (Boston: Twayne, 1988).

52. Melvyn P. Leffler, *A Preponderance of Power: National Security, the Truman Administration, and the Cold War* (Stanford: Stanford University Press, 1992); David McCullough, Truman (New York: Simon and Schuster, 1992), pp. 382–84, 390–91; John Lewis Gaddis, Strategies of Containment: A Critical Appraisal of Postwar American National Security Policy (New York: Oxford University Press, 1982), pp. 3–88.

53. Bill Mauldin, *Up Front* (New York: Henry Holt, 1945), p. 60.

54. Tom Englehardt, *The End of the Victory Culture: Cold War America and the Disillusioning of a Generation* (Amherst: University of Massachusetts Press, 1995), pp. 69–89.

55. Patrick Brogan, *The Fighting Never Stopped: A Comprehensive Guide to World Conflict since 1945* (New York: Vintage Books, 1990), pp. 567–84.

56. Dean Acheson, *Present at the Creation: My Years in the State Department* (New York: Norton, 1969), pp. 354–61. Acheson refers to his ongoing battles with Congress in a chapter titled "The Attack of the Primitives Begins."

57. Englehardt, *The End of the Victory Culture,* pp. 58–65. What were veterans' roles in defining the Communist enemy? There was hardly a consensus among the VFW, American Legion, AmVets, and AVC regarding the topic of Communism. See Rodney G. Minott, Peerless Patriots: Organized Veterans and the Spirit of Americanism (Washington, D.C.: Public Affairs Press, 1962), pp. 90–111.

58. The officer as adversary is a familiar theme in many of the popular postwar novels of the forties, including Norman Mailer's *Naked and the Dead* (1948), James Jones's From Here to Eternity (1951), and Herman Wouk's Caine Mutiny (1951). See Lawrence H. Suid, Guts and Glory: Great American War Movies (Reading, Mass.: Addison-Wesley, 1978), pp. 115–17.

59. Lawrence Alloway, *Violent America: The Movies, 1946–1964* (New York: Museum of Modern Art, 1971), p. 10.

60. Jeanine Basinger, *The World War II Combat Film: Anatomy of a Genre* (New York: Columbia University Press, 1986), p. 142.

61. Shindler, *Hollywood Goes to War,* p. 79.

62. Bosley Crowther, "*Battleground,* Metro Film on Heroic Soldiers at Bastogne, Opens at Astor," New York Times (Nov. 12, 1949), p. 8.

63. R. Wilson Brown, "Movie Headliners for November," *American Legion Magazine* 47 (Nov., 1949), p. 44.

64. Beirne Lay and Sy Bartlett, *Twelve O'clock High!* (New York: Ballantine Books, 1948), pp. 70–74, 79–81, 214–22.

65. Bosley Crowther, "*Twelve O'clock High!* Realistic Saga of the Eighth Air Force, Arrives at Roxy Theatre," New York Times (Jan. 28, 1950), p. 10.

66. Basinger, *World War II Combat Film,* pp. 156–57.

67. Gladwin Hill, "Veterans of Bastogne Fight in *Battleground,*" New York Times (May 29, 1949), II, p. 3.

68. Mauldin, *Up Front,* pp. 30–31.

69. Prior, "*Saving Private Ryan* and the Morality of War," pp. 138–46.

Chapter 7

1. George H. Gallup, *The Gallup Poll: Public Opinion, 1935–1971,* vol. 2 (New York: Random House, 1972), p. 951.

2. Maurice Matloff, ed., *American Military History* (Washington, D.C.: GPO, 1969), p. 540.

3. Allan R. Millett and Peter Maslowski, *For the Common Defense: A Military History of the United States of America* (New York: Free Press, 1994), pp. 502–505.

4. Harry S. Truman, *Special Message to the Congress on Reorganization of the National Military Establishment,* Mar. 5, 1949, in Public Papers of the Presidents of the United States, Harry S. Truman, 1949 (Washington, D.C.: GPO, 1964), pp. 163–66.

5. Harry S. Truman, *Annual Budget Message to Congress: Fiscal Year 1950,* Jan. 10, 1949, in Public Papers of the Presidents of the United States, Harry S. Truman, 1949 (Washington, D.C.: GPO, 1964), pp. 44–51; David T. Fautua, "The 'Long Pull' Army: NSC 68, the Korean War, and the Creation of the Cold War U.S. Army," Journal of Military History 61 (Jan., 1997): 94–97.

6. James F. Schnabel, *United States Army in Korea: Policy and Direction: The First Year* (Washington, D.C.: GPO, 1972), pp. 45–46; Fautua, "The 'Long Pull' Army," pp. 99–105.

7. Stephen Howarth, *To Shining Sea: A History of the United States Navy, 1775–1998* (Norman: University of Oklahoma Press, 1999), p. 476.

8. Clay Blair, *The Forgotten War: America in Korea, 1950–1953* (New York: Times Books, 1987), p. 213.

9. Knox, *The Korean War,* pp. 8–9.

10. William D. Dannenmaier, *We Were Innocents: An Infantryman in Korea* (Chicago: University of Illinois Press, 1999), p. 33; Schnabel, United States Army in Korea, pp. 54–59.

11. Schnabel, *United States Army in Korea,* pp. 54–59. See also Robert J. Dvorchak, Battle for Korea: A History of the Korean Conflict (New York: Associated Press, 1993).

12. Michael Schaller, *Douglas MacArthur: The Far Eastern General* (New York: Oxford University Press, 1989), pp. 120–57. See also Stanley Weintraub, "How to Remember the Forgotten War," American Heritage 51 (May/June, 2000): 100–106.

13. Blair, *Forgotten War,* pp. 49–50; Schnabel, United States Army in Korea, p. 59.

14. Blair, *Forgotten War,* pp. 49–50.

15. Knox, *Korean War,* p. 6.

16. John Toland, *In Mortal Combat: Korea, 1950–1953* (New York: William Morrow, 1991), pp. 77–78, 80–82.

17. "Call on Reserves," *Business Week* (Aug. 11, 1951), p. 22; "Turnover Time," Business Week (Oct. 4, 1952), p. 31. The need for trained medical personnel was particularly acute. The army reported a shortage of 3,000 nurses in January, 1951. The air force's figure was 1,000, and the navy's shortfall was 500. See "3,000 Army Nurses Needed," All Women's Services Journal 6 (Jan., 1951): 15.

18. Ed Cray, *General of the Army: George C. Marshall, Soldier and Statesman* (New York: Simon and Schuster, 1990), pp. 679–95; Burton I. Kaufman, The Korean War: Challenges in Crisis, Credibility, and Command (Philadelphia: Temple University Press, 1986), pp. 82–83.

19. Fautua, "The 'Long Pull' Army," pp. 113–14; " '52: Year of Uncertainty for Reserve Officers," *U.S. News and World Report* (Dec. 14, 1951), pp. 39–39; "Reserve, Guard, Draft Status," New York Times (Aug. 13, 1950), p. 54.

20. "The Home Front Becomes Aware of Korea," *Life* 29 (July 17, 1950), pp. 45–47; "Silver City Goes to War Again," Life 27 (Aug. 7, 1950), pp. 25–26.

21. Schnabel, *United States Army in Korea*, pp. 120–25.

22. Ibid., p. 122. Involuntary recalls also extended to service members within the medical fields. See "Involuntary Recall of Women Medical Specialists," *All Women's Services Journal* 5 (Nov., 1950): 3. In testimony before the Senate Committee on Armed Services on Aug. 22, 1950, Gen. Omar Bradley argued that recalled National Guard and Reserve forces would comprise only veterans who volunteered for duty. Others who did not volunteer would be "largely exempt." See Omar Bradley, "Statement before the Senate Committee on Armed Services," Aug. 22, 1950, Library of Congress, Omar N. Bradley Papers.

23. "Reservists Charge Bias," *New York Times* (Sept. 3, 1950), p. 42.

24. "War Held Not Ended for Reserve Officer," *New York Times* (Oct. 9, 1951), p. 14; "Army Captain Loses Plea," New York Times (Oct. 20, 1951), p. 6.

25. "Sergeant Gets 2 Years," *New York Times* (Aug. 5, 1952), p. 10.

26. "New Deal for Reserves," *Time* (Oct. 30, 1950), p. 27; Sam A. Jaffe, "Uncle Sam's Bitter Nephews," Nation (Dec. 29, 1951): 567–68; "Run for the Hills, Boys," Time (Nov. 13, 1950), p. 23; "Marine 'Deadwood' Seen," New York Times (Dec. 4, 1950), p. 3.

27. "Guard Not Ready for Early Combat," *New York Times* (Feb. 11, 1951), p. 10; Hanson W. Baldwin, "Condition of the Army," New York Times (June 22, 1950), p. 5; "Aid to Reserves Derided," New York Times (Aug. 7,1951), p. 16.

28. Lt. Leslie E. This, "Remember Me? I'm Your Dad," *Parents' Magazine* 27 (Mar., 1952), pp. 32–34.

29. "Bleats from the Guard," *Time* (Nov. 5, 1951), p. 22; "Antiquated National Guard," Time (Aug. 27, 1951), p. 22.

30. "Reservists Freed from Forced Duty," *New York Times* (Oct. 24, 1950), p. 20.

31. Gallup, *Gallup Poll*, pp. 938, 943, 956–58.

32. Ibid., pp. 938, 943, 956–58, 969, 972, 993, 1183.

33. Ibid., p. 1019.

34. Stephen E. Ambrose, *Eisenhower: The President*, vol. 2 (New York: Simon and Schuster, 1983), pp. 14–15, 30–32. See also Max Hastings, The Korean War (New York: Simon and Schuster, 1987), pp. 314–17.

35. Michael D. Gambone, *Eisenhower, Somoza, and the Cold War in Nicaragua* (Westport, Conn.: Praeger, 1997), pp. 15–44.

36. Scholarship on this topic is enormous. However, one of the most outstanding studies of this particular process as it applies to Vietnam is Ronald H. Spector, *Advice and Support: The Early Years, 1941–1960* (Washington, D.C.: Center of Military History, 1983).

37. Richard E. Mack, *Memoir of a Cold War Soldier* (Kent, Ohio: Kent State University Press, 2001), p. 15. Mack's account is typical of the situation in 1950 and 1951.

38. J. Lawton Collins, *War in Peacetime: The History and Lessons of Korea* (Boston: Houghton Mifflin, 1969), pp. 294–326. For details on the nature of the fighting at this stage of the war, see David H. Hackworth, About Face: The Odyssey of an American Warrior (New York: Simon and Schuster, 1989), pp. 224–85.

39. "Trouble in the Air," *Time* (Apr. 28, 1952), p. 24; "Air Force 'Mutiny': Veterans Tired of War," U.S. News and World Report (Apr. 25, 1952), pp. 37–40; "The Reservist Revolt," Newsweek (Apr. 28, 1952), p. 25.

40. While the writing on the causes and nature of the Cold War is enormous, one of the better geopolitical discussions of it may be found in Gordon Craig and Alexander George, *Force and Statecraft: Diplomatic Problems of Our Time* (New York: Oxford University Press, 1990).

41. Matloff, ed., *American Military*, pp. 8–9. For an interesting history of the 28th Division from its creation to World War I, see H. G. Proctor, The Iron Division: National Guard of Pennsylvania in the World War (Philadelphia: John C. Winston, 1919).

42. Capt. Thomas R. Nevitt, "A Guard Division Trains for M-Day," *Army Information Digest* 3 (Oct., 1948): 35–45.

43. Army National Guard Training Inspection Report, Company A, 110th Infantry Battalion, July 29, 1950–Aug. 12, 1950; Army National Guard Training Inspection Report, Battery C, 108th Field Artillery Battalion, July 29, 1950–Aug. 12, 1950, Penn. State Archives, record group 19, Correspondence and Reports of the Office of Adjutant General, 1934–1989, Army National Guard Training Inspection Reports, carton 1, folder 1-1.

44. "Report Covering the 28th Infantry Division's Induction in Federal Service," n.d., USMHI, Strickler Papers, Germany, Occupation.

45. See "28th Division of Penna. to Enter U.S. Service Today," *Reading Times* (Sept. 5, 1950), p. 14; "Famed 28th Enters Federal Service," Reading Eagle (Sept. 5, 1950), pp. 1, 15.

46. "Reserve Tank Battalion Here Alerted by Army for Active Duty," *Reading Eagle* (Sept. 7, 1950), p. 1; "Berks Soldier Killed in Korea," Reading Eagle (Feb. 27, 1951), p. 1.

47. "Report Covering the 28th Infantry Division's Induction in Federal Service," n.d.

48. Letter, Lt. Gen. S. J. Chamberlain (commanding general, U.S. Army) to Maj. Gen. Daniel B. Strickler (commanding general, 28th Infantry Division), Oct. 12, 1950, USMHI, Strickler Papers, Germany, Occupation.

49. Blair, *Forgotten War*, pp. 193–94. Blair pays specific attention to the 1st Provisional Marine Brigade.

50. Headquarters, 28th Infantry Division, "Training Program, 28-Week Cycle," Oct. 14, 1950, USMHI, Strickler Papers, Germany, Occupation.

51. Memo, headquarters, 28th Infantry Division, "Battle Indoctrination Courses," Jan. 27, 1951, Annex 1, enclosure #1, p. 5, USMHI, Strickler Papers, Germany, Occupation.

52. Public Information Section, headquarters, 28th Infantry Division, Camp Atterbury, Indiana, press release, May, 1951, USMHI, Strickler Papers, Germany, Occupation; 28th Infantry Division Yearbook, *Roll-On, 1951–1952* (published in 1953), p. 10, USMHI, Manuscript Division Collection.

53. This process is well covered in many military histories and particularly so in Stephen E. Ambrose, *Band of Brothers: E Company, 506th Regiment, 101st Airborne, from Normandy to Hitler's Eagle's Nest* (New York: Simon and Schuster, 1992).

54. Public information section, headquarters, 28th Infantry Division, Camp Atterbury, Indiana, press release, Apr. 23, 1951, USMHI, Strickler Papers, Germany, Occupation.

55. Memo, Capt. Arba G. Williamson (assistant division signal officer) to the assistant division chief of staff, G-4, May 2, 1951; memo, Lt. Col. Chester N. Rees (division ordinance officer) to Division G-4, May 2, 1951, USMHI, Strickler Papers, Germany, Occupation.

56. U.S. Army, 28th Infantry Division Yearbook, *Roll-On, 1951–1952,* p. 10.

57. U.S. Army, 28th Infantry Division, Orientation Booklet, *Know Your Job, Know Your Division,* 1951, p. 12, USMHI, Strickler Papers, Germany, Occupation.

58. Portions of the 28th Mechanized Infantry Division deployed to Bosnia in October, 2002.

59. John Cogley, "Guys Like Yourself," *Commonweal* 57 (Jan. 2, 1953): 322.

60. Benjamin Fine, "Millions in Waste Charged in Schooling for Veterans," *New York Times* (Feb. 6, 1950), p. 1. See also Anthony Leviero, "Truman Asks Congress Curbs on Fly-by-Night GI Schools," New York Times (Feb. 14, 1950), p. 1.

61. "American Colleges and Universities Show a Loss in Fall Enrollment," *New York Times* (Nov. 27, 1950), p. 21.

62. "V.A. to Lay Off 7,800," *New York Times* (Mar. 4, 1950), p. 19; "Defeat of Rehabilitation Program Feared in Retrenchment Move," New York Times (Mar. 20, 1950), p. 20.

63. "Americans Fighting in Korea are Entitled to Full Wartime Benefits, VA Announces," *New York Times* (July 7, 1950), p. 3.

64. "Help for Disabled from Korea Asked," *New York Times* (Dec. 5, 1950), p. 15. Both the American Legion and the Veterans of Foreign Wars engaged in a heavy lobbying effort for the benefits extension. See "Korea Benefits Asked," New York Times (Apr. 26, 1951), p. 3.

65. "Congress Enacts Veterans' Pension over Truman Veto," *New York Times* (Sept. 19, 1951), p. 1.

66. "Benefits for Korea Veterans Voted after Hospital Bars an Ex-Marine," *New York Times* (May 11, 1951), p. 1.

67. "Hospital Cut Assailed," *New York Times* (Apr. 10, 1951), p. 29; "2,250 to Be Dropped by Veterans' Agency," New York Times (Oct. 2, 1952), p. 18.

68. "Hospital Cut Assailed," p. 29.

69. "Cut in Funds Seen Curbing VA Work," *New York Times* (October 17, 1952), p. 16.

Chapter 8

1. James T. Patterson, *Grand Expectations: The United States, 1945–1974* (New York: Oxford University Press, 1996), pp. 3–10.

2. Andy Rooney, *My War* (New York: Public Affairs, 2000), p. 310.

3. James Jones, *WWII* (New York: Ballantine Books, 1975), p. 256.

4. Mark R. Grandstaff, "Making the American Military: Advertising, Reform, and the Demise of an Antistanding Military Tradition, 1945–1955," *Journal of Military History* 60 (Apr., 1996): 299–323. The remnants of this contro-

versy appear even today. See William J. Clinton, "Letter to Colonel Holmes," Dec. 3, 1969, in Letters of a Nation: A Collection of Extraordinary American Letters, ed. Andrew Carroll (New York: Kodansha International, 1997), pp. 169–73.

5. James Webb, *Fields of Fire* (New York: Bantam Books, 1978), pp. 23–25.

6. See, for example, Philip Caputo, *A Rumor of War* (New York: Holt, Rinehart, and Winston, 1977), p. 6. See also Ron Kovic, Born on the Fourth of July (New York: Pocket Books, 1976).

7. Webb, *Fields of Fire*, p. 34.

8. Robert Timberg, *The Nightingale's Song* (New York: Simon and Schuster, 1995), pp. 89–90.

9. Letter, Ralph H. Lavers (American Legion National Economic Commission) to Charles M. Wilson (American Legion Membership and Post Activities), May 10, 1951, American Legion Archive and Library, Veterans' Welfare Classification, GI Bill, folder 10.

10. Ibid.

11. Patterson, *Grand Expectations,* pp. 446–49. The scholarship on this topic is significant. See, for example, Diane Ravitch, The Troubled Crusade: American Education, 1945–1980 (New York: Basic Books, 1983), p. 183, and Kenneth H. Ashworth, American Education in Decline (College Station: Texas A&M University Press, 1979), pp. 30–32.

12. William Graebner, *The Age of Doubt: American Thought and Culture in the 1940s* (Boston: Twayne, 1991), p. 1.

13. Norman L. Rosenberg and Emily S. Rosenberg, *In Our Times: America since World War II* (Englewood Cliffs, N.J.: Prentice Hall, 1995), pp. 167–70.

14. Omar N. Bradley, *Collected Writings: Articles, Broadcasts, and Statements, 1945–1967,* vol. 3 (Washington, D.C.: GPO, 1967), p. 152.

15. Harold M. Hyman, *American Singularity: The 1787 Northwest Ordinance, the 1862 Homestead and Morrill Acts, and the 1944 GI Bill* (Athens: University of Georgia Press, 1986). 71. Hyman talks in particular about the "augmented mobility" produced by the GI Bill.

16. Patterson, *Grand Expectations,* pp. 786–90.

BIBLIOGRAPHIC ESSAY

This bibliographic essay lists the numerous sources I consulted during the preparation of this book.

Archival Sources

One of the core sources for this project was the American Legion Archive and Library located in Indianapolis, Indiana. One of the primary records groups for this project was the Veteran Welfare Classification, a collection of federal and state documents pertaining to employment, housing, loans, pensions, and legislation. A second important source of records was the Great War Classification. Despite its name, this group contains data on World War II topics such as selective service, casualties, and veterans' benefits programs. The archives also contain a wealth of bound periodicals ranging from the *American Legion Magazine* to more esoteric publications such as *Carry On*.

Records of the Veterans' Administration are held in the old National Archives and Records Administration in Washington, D.C. Specifically, this information is housed in Records Group 15, Records of the Veterans' Administration. While this collection contains a staggering amount of minutiae, useful sources such as the *Occupational Outlook Information Series,* annual reports, and some of department circulars issued by Omar Bradley were very helpful in establishing the tactical decisions made by VA officials as well as postwar policy strategy.

The National Archives and Records Administration in University Park, Maryland, also holds a significant body of primary documents related both directly and indirectly to veterans. Of particular use were Records Group 12, Records of the Office of Education; Records Group 112, Records of the Army Surgeon General; Records Group 147, Records of the Selective Service System; Records Group 165, Records of the War Department General Staff; and Records Group 211, Records of the War Manpower Commission. The host of civilian and military agencies represented in these collections provided additional depth for the policy-making context of the postwar period.

In the Manuscript Division of the Library of Congress, I was able to find fairly extensive references to African American veterans in the Records of the NAACP. Particularly useful was the correspondence of NAACP Veterans' Affairs Secretary Jesse O. Dedmon. The Omar N. Bradley Papers, albeit few in number, holds a number of speeches that I was unable to find in other archives.

The Walter P. Reuther Library, Archives of Labor and Urban Affairs, housed at Wayne State University, is a virtual treasure trove of material relevant to the veterans' transition into the peacetime workforce. The Congress of Industrial Organizations (CIO) Political Action Committee (PAC) Collection, the United Auto Workers (UAW) Veterans' Department, and the UAW War Policy Division Collection holds, for example, the union's plans to incorporate the veterans into the ranks of organized labor after the war. The Emil Mazey Papers contain specific references to the soldiers' strikes conducted in early 1946. Also of particular use were the Catherine Gelles Papers; the Olga Hrabar Papers; the UAW Office of the President: R. J. Thomas Collection; the UAW War Policy Division, Women's Bureau Collection; and the United Community Services Central Files Collection.

For the chapter on the Korean War, I visited the Pennsylvania State Archives in Harrisburg, Pennsylvania, in search of information regarding the mobilization of the 28th National Guard Infantry Division. The papers of past state governors, specifically the James H. Duff Papers and those of John S. Fine were of very limited use. Neither collection has more than passing references to the Korean mobilization. Somewhat more useful was Records Group 19, Records of the Department of Military and Veterans' Affairs. This archive contains National Guard training and readiness records that predate the outbreak of hostilities in 1950.

A far better source for Korean War information is the U.S. Military History Institute located at Carlisle, Pennsylvania. There I gained access to the papers of division commander Daniel B. Strickler, a resource that contains training programs, readiness reports, and a substantial body of correspondence relating to the 28th Division's readiness for war.

World War II oral-history collections are prolific and growing. One of the best that I have come across is the Rutgers University Oral History Archives of WWII. Hundreds of interviews conducted by Kurt Piehler are available online for any interested student. Both the World War Two Veterans' Survey Project and the Korean War Veterans' Survey Project, available at the U.S. Military History Institute contain thousands of standardized written questionnaires organized by unit. Responses to questionnaires distributed by the author were uneven at best. Particularly helpful were the wartime experiences of Olive D. Malm of Worcester, Massachusetts.

The Women in Military Service for America Archives located in Arlington, Virginia, is a relatively new but interesting source of primary documents. Specifically useful were the postwar academic works of many female veterans who went to college on the GI Bill in the forties.

Primary Sources

Private organizations have created numerous documents that proved very helpful in this project. Specifically useful were the American National Red Cross, *Helping Disabled Veterans* (Washington, D.C.: American National Red Cross, 1945); Richard M. Dalfiume, ed., *Papers of the NAACP: Part 9: Discrimination in the U.S. Armed Forces, 1918–1955, Series C: Veterans' Affairs Committee, 1940–1950* (Bethesda: University Publications of America, 1989); National Education Association, Educational Policies Commission, *A Program for the Education of Returning Veterans* (Washington, D.C.: National Education Association, 1944).

A multitude of federal agencies provided statistical and reference data for this project. Census data for both 1940 and 1950 created a baseline for vocation, income, residency, and a host of other information fundamental to life in the forties. The Interior Department War Agency Liquidation Unit and War Relocation Authority were instrumental in quantifying the war's impact on Japanese Americans. Justice Department crime statistics fleshed out the historical backdrop to the chapter on film noir. The Labor Department offered extensive primary-source data on employment trends after 1945 as well as efforts to retrain veterans. The Women's Bureau of the Labor Department was equally prolific in its publications addressing female workers and veterans in the postwar era. Finally, the Veterans' Administration annual reports allowed me to trace trends throughout the decade with an important degree of specificity, both in terms of budget numbers and programs.

A few state agencies have essentially mirrored the functions of federal veterans' organizations. See, for example, the Michigan Office of Veterans' Affairs, *Progress Report* (Lansing: Office of Veterans' Affairs, Feb., 1945).

Unit histories and unit yearbooks provided some insights into the process of mobilization and the military experience in general. See 442nd Reunion Committee, *Go for Broke: 442nd Regimental Combat Team, the 442nd Decade, 10th Anniversary Reunion*, 20–31, July, 1953, and United States Army, 28th Infantry Division, Orientation Booklet, *Know Your Job, Know Your Division*, 1951.

Secondary Sources

A number of classic works came to mind during the early research for this project. These general sources include John Keegan, *The Face of Battle: A Study of Agincourt, Waterloo, and the Somme* (New York: Penguin, 1976), and Walter Millis, *Arms and Men: A Study in American Military History* (New Brunswick, N.J.: Rutgers University Press, 1984). A excellent primer of general U.S. military history is Allan R. Millett and Peter Maslowski, *For the Common Defense: A Military History of the United States of America* (New York: Free Press, 1994).

Introduction

A number of excellent secondary sources pertain to eighteenth- and nineteenth-century veterans' policy. William H. Glasson, *History of Military Pension Legislation in the United States* (New York: Columbia University Press, 1900), and his subsequent *Federal Military Pensions in the United States* (New York: Oxford University Press, 1918) are both outstanding references. For more recent scholarship, see Patrick J. Kelly, *Creating a National Home: Building the Veterans' Welfare State, 1860–1900* (Cambridge: Harvard University Press, 1997).

For a usable interpretation of veterans and nineteenth-century American culture, see Eleanor L. Hannah, "Manhood, Citizenship, and the Formation of the National Guards, Illinois, 1870–1917" (Ph.D. diss., University of Chicago, 1997).

Histories of veterans' organizations at both the state and national level are abundant. See Rodney G. Minott, *Peerless Patriots: Organized Veterans and the Spirit of Americanism* (Washington, D.C.: Public Affairs

Press, 1962); Thomas A. Rumer, *The American Legion: An Official History, 1919–1989* (New York: M. Evans, 1990); Terry Radtke, *The History of the Pennsylvania American Legion* (Mechanicsburg, Penn.: Stackpole Books, 1993).

Examples of presidential wartime experience may be found in any notable historical biography. For this work, I looked specifically at Edmund Morris, *The Rise of Theodore Roosevelt* (New York: Ballantine, 1979); William S. McFeeley, *Grant: A Biography* (New York: W. W. Norton, 1982); and David Donald Herbert, *Lincoln* (London: Jonathan Cape, 1995).

For a superior study of World War I that includes veterans, see Nancy Gentile Ford, *Americans All! Foreign-born Soldiers in World War I* (College Station: Texas A&M University Press, 2001). Also useful is Stephen R. Ward, James M. Diehl, Michael A. Ledeen, Donald J. Lisio, and Robert Soucy, eds., *The War Generation: Veterans of the First World War* (Port Washington, N.Y.: Kennikat Press, 1975); William P. Dillingham, *Federal Aid to Veterans, 1917–1941* (Gainesville: University of Florida Press, 1952).

Numerous books discuss postwar America and the impact of World War II. These include Richard Polenberg, *War and Society: The United States, 1941–1945* (New York: J. P. Lippincott, 1972); Geoffrey Perrett, *Days of Sadness, Years of Triumph: The American People, 1939–1945* (New York: Coward, McCann, and Geoghegan, 1973); Martin J. Sherwin, *A World Destroyed: The Atomic Bomb and the Grand Alliance* (New York: Knopf, 1975); Joseph C. Goulden, *The Best Years, 1945–1950* (New York: Atheneum, 1976); John Morton Blum, *V Was for Victory: Politics and American Culture during World War Two* (New York: Harcourt Brace, 1976); Alan S. Milward, *War, Economy, and Society, 1939–1945* (Berkeley: University of California Press, 1977); William E. Leuchtenburg, *A Troubled Feast: American Society since 1945* (Boston: Little, Brown, 1983); David Brinkley, *Washington Goes to War* (New York: Ballantine Books, 1988); William Graebner, *The Age of Doubt: American Thought and Culture in the 1940s* (Boston: Twayne, 1991); William L. O'Neil, *A Democracy at War: America's Fight at Home and Abroad in World War II* (Cambridge: Harvard University Press, 1993); Doris Kearns Goodwin, *No Ordinary Time: Franklin and Eleanor Roosevelt: The Home Front in World War II* (New York: Simon and Schuster, 1994); Michael C. C. Adams, *The Best War Ever: America in World War II* (Baltimore: Johns Hopkins University Press, 1994); and Gerald F. Linderman, *The World within*

War: America's Combat Experience in World War II (New York: Free Press, 1997).

The general history of the American soldier during World War II is replete with outstanding studies. Foremost among these are John Ellis, *The Sharp End: The Fighting Man in World War II* (New York: Charles Scribner's Sons, 1980); Paul Fussell, *Wartime: Understanding and Behavior in the Second World War* (New York: Oxford University Press, 1989); and Stephen E. Ambrose, *Band of Brothers: E Company, 506th Regiment, 101st Airborne: from Normandy to Hitler's Eagle's Nest* (New York: Simon and Schuster, 1992).

A multitude of works focuses on the creation of the Serviceman's Readjustment Act of 1944. These include Harold M. Hyman, *American Singularity: The 1787 Northwest Ordinance, the 1862 Homestead and Morrill Acts, and the 1944 GI Bill* (Athens, Ga.: University of Georgia Press, 1986), and Milton Greenberg, *The GI Bill: The Law That Changed America* (New York: Lickle, 1997). The latter work offers a somewhat superficial view of the law's impact but is very readable.

The best example of recent scholarship on veterans after World War II may be found in Mark D. Van Ells, *To Hear Only Thunder Again: America's World War II Veterans Come Home* (Lanham, Mass.: Lexington Books, 2001). However, while the books provides some information on the overall scope of veterans' history, its case studies are largely limited to the state of Wisconsin.

Other histories of veterans' experiences include Davis R. B. Ross, *Preparing for Ulysses: Politics and Veterans during World War II* (New York: Columbia University Press, 1969); Sar A. Levitan and Karen A. Cleary, *Old Wars Remain Unfinished: The Veterans' Benefits System* (Baltimore: Johns Hopkins University Press, 1973); Robert Klein, *Wounded Men, Broken Promises* (New York: Macmillan, 1981); Richard Severo and Lewis Milford, *The Wages of War: When America's Soldiers Came Home, from Valley Forge to Vietnam* (New York: Simon and Schuster, 1989); Raymond B. Lech, *Broken Soldiers* (Urbana: University of Illinois Press, 2000). Many of these, however, focus specifically on the veterans' benefits system with an emphasis on medical treatment. For a good recent example of this, see David A. Gerber, ed., *Disabled Veterans in History* (Ann Arbor: University of Michigan Press, 2000).

Chapter 1. Home

The climax of the war has been well addressed by authors, particularly in recent scholarship. See Paul Boyer, *By the Bomb's Early Light: American Thought and Culture at the Dawn of the Atomic Age* (New York: Pantheon Books, 1985); John C. Sparrow, *History of Personnel Demobilization in the United States Army* (Washington, D.C.: Center of Military History, 1994); Stanley Weintraub, *The Last Great Victory: The End of World War II, July/August 1945* (New York: Truman Talley Books/Dutton, 1995); Tom Englehardt, *The End of the Victory Culture: Cold War America and the Disillusioning of a Generation* (Amherst: University of Massachusetts Press, 1995). Although it deals with the postwar period as a whole, the early chapters of James T. Patterson, *Grand Expectations: The United States, 1945–1974* (New York: Oxford University Press, 1996), are useful. See also David M. Kennedy, *Freedom from Fear: The American People in Depression and War, 1929–1945* (New York: Oxford University Press, 1999), for a highly detailed and cogent study. For an excellent Department of War survey of returning GIs, see Samuel A. Stouffer, Arthur A. Lumsdaine, Robin M. Williams, M. Brewster Smith, Irving L. Janis, Shirley A. Star, and Leonard S. Cottrell, *The American Soldier: Combat and Its Aftermath*, vol. 2 (Princeton: Princeton University Press, 1949).

The collection of personal memoirs and accounts of war service is voluminous. Some of the most useful published in the postwar era include William Manchester, *Goodbye, Darkness: A Memoir of the Pacific War* (Boston: Little, Brown, 1979); James Jones, *WWII* (New York: Ballantine, 1975); T. Grady Gallant, *On Valor's Side* (New York: Doubleday, 1963), and *The Friendly Dead* (New York: Popular Library, 1964); Janice Holt Giles, *The GI Journal of Sergeant Giles* (Boston: Houghton Mifflin, 1965); Audie Murphy, *To Hell and Back* (New York: Holt, Rinehart, and Winston, 1949); John Dos Passos, *Tour of Duty* (Boston: Houghton Mifflin, 1946; Thomas R. St. George, *C/o Postmaster* (New York: Thomas Y. Crowell, 1943); and Marion Hargrove, *See Here, Private Hargrove* (New York: Henry Holt, 1942).

One of the most readable set of books addressing the war experience remains Bill Mauldin, *Up Front* (New York: Henry Holt, 1945), and *Back Home* (New York: Bantam Books, 1948). The books by Ernie Pyle relating his observations are classics. See Ernie Pyle, *Last Chapter* (New York: Henry Holt, 1946), *Brave Men* (New York: Grosset and Dunlap, 1944), and *Here Is Your War* (New York: Henry Holt, 1943).

For more recently published personal accounts of the war, see Richard Aquila, *Home Front Soldier: The Story of a GI and His Italian American Family during World War II* (Albany: State University of New York Press, 1999); Lawrence Percival Hall and Lawrence Percival Hall Jr., *My Brother's Letters Home: Blutiger Eimer (28th) Division Field Artillery Officer's Letters Home*, ed. John M. Hall (New York: Vantage Press, 1999); Russell E. McLogan, *Boy Soldier: Coming of Age during World War II* (Reading, Mich.: Terrus Press, 1998); Dan Levin, *From the Battlefield: Dispatches of a World War II Marine* (Annapolis, Md.: Naval Institute Press, 1995); Robert Peters, *For You, Lili Marlene: A Memoir of World War II* (Madison: University of Wisconsin Press, 1995); Leon C. Standifer, *Not in Vain: A Rifleman Remembers World War II* (Baton Rouge: Louisiana State University Press, 1992); Howard S. Hoffman and Alicia M. Hoffman, *Archives of Memory: A Soldier Recalls World War II* (Lexington: University Press of Kentucky, 1990); and Annette Tappert, ed., *Lines of Battle: Letters from American Servicemen, 1941–1945* (New York: Times Books, 1987). A classic in this genre remains Studs Terkel, *The Good War: An Oral History of World War Two* (New York: Pantheon, 1984). See also Henry Berry, *Semper Fi, Mac: Living Memories of the U.S. Marines in World War II* (New York: Quill, 1982). For a thoughtful piece on the nature of oral history, see Edward M. Coffman, "Talking about War: Reflections on Doing Oral History and Military History," *Journal of American History* (Sept., 2000): 582–91.

More specific scholarship has also focused on American society, families, sexuality, and children. One of the earliest is the alarmist account of what might happen to American society upon the return of veterans. See Willard Waller, *The Veteran Comes Back* (New York: Dryden Press, 1944). More recent examples include John Costello, *Virtue under Fire: How World War II Changed Our Social and Sexual Attitudes* (Boston: Little, Brown, 1985); Elaine Tyler May, *Homeward Bound: American Families in the Cold War Era* (New York: Basic Books, 1988); Stephanie Coontz, *The Way We Never Were: American Families and the Nostalgia Trap* (New York: Basic Books, 1992); William M. Tuttle Jr., *"Daddy's Gone to War": The Second World War in the Lives of America's Children* (New York: Oxford University Press, 1993); and John D'Emilio and Estelle B. Friedman, *Intimate Matters: A History of Sexuality in America* (Chicago: University of Chicago Press, 1997).

For an account of the Truman administration's early struggles, see Robert J. Donovan, *Conflict and Crisis: The Presidency of Harry S. Truman, 1945–1948* (New York: W. W. Norton, 1977), and David McCullough, *Truman* (New York: Simon and Schuster, 1992).

A lengthy set of literature pertains to the veterans' benefits system published after the war. See also Dixon Wecter, *When Johnny Comes Marching Home* (Boston: Houghton Mifflin, 1944); E. Jay Howenstine, *The Economics of Demobilization* (Washington, D.C.: Public Affairs Press, 1944); George K. Pratt, *Soldier to Civilian: Problems of Readjustment* (New York: McGraw Hill, 1944); Grace Sloan Overton, *Marriage in War and Peace: A Book for Parents and Counselors of Youth* (New York: Abingdon-Cokesbury Press, 1945); Maxwell Drake, *Good-by to GI: How to Be a Successful Civilian* (New York: Abingdon-Cokesbury Press, 1945); Alexander G. Dumas and Grace Keen, *A Psychiatric Primer for the Veteran's Family and Friends* (Minneapolis: University of Minnesota Press, 1945); Eli H. Mellan, *Your Rights as a Veteran* (New York: Bernard Ackerman, 1945); Ira D. Scott, *Manual of Advisement and Guidance* (Washington, D.C.: Government Publication Office, 1945); Jack Goodman, ed., *While You Were Gone: A Report on Wartime Life in the United States* (New York: Simon and Schuster, 1946); Tracy E. Goodwin, *Veterans' Handbook and Guide* (Cincinnati: Goodwin, 1946); Charles Hurd, *The Veterans' Program: A Complete Guide to Its Benefits, Rights, and Options* (New York: McGraw Hill, 1946); and Dorothy W. Baruch and Lee Edward Travis, *You're Out of the Service Now: A Veteran's Guide to Civilian Life* (New York: D. Appleton-Century, 1946).

Chapter 2. Healing the Wounds

General studies of medical treatment during the war are plentiful. Two of particular use were Clarence McKittrick Smith, *The Medical Department: Hospitalization and Evacuation, Zone of the Interior* (Washington, D.C.: Government Publication Office, 1956), and Gertrude Keough, *History and Heritage of the Veterans' Administration Nursing Service, 1930–1980* (New York: National League for Nursing, 1981).

Contemporary periodical literature on war wounded is extensive. See "Take Up Thy Bed," *Time* 45 (May 21, 1945), p. 90; "They're Telling Us," *Saturday Evening Post* 218 (July 7, 1945), p. 4; "How We're Healing the Scars of Battle," *Popular Science Monthly* 146 (June, 1945), pp. 88–93; William Best, "They Won't All Be Psychoneurotics!" *Saturday Evening Post* 217 (Apr. 14, 1945), p. 112; "The Army and the Deaf," *New York Times Magazine* 28 (Oct. 14, 1946), p. 78; Ralph Knight, "How Veterans Get What's Due Them," *Saturday Evening Post* 218 (Feb. 2, 1946), p. 6; Bernard Frizell, "Handless Veteran," *Life* 21 (Dec. 16, 1946), pp. 74–75; "Army Blind School," *Life* 21 (Nov. 11, 1946), pp. 101–102. Some of the articles are remarkably upbeat: See Walter P. Pitkin, "The Advantage of Handicaps," *Rotarian* 67 (Oct., 1945), pp. 16–18.

Parallel works are also contained in many period professional journals. See Howard P. Rome, "The Neuropsychiatric Problem in Returning Servicemen," *Diseases of the Nervous System* 6 (Nov., 1945): 333–36; Lee Yugend, "Brief Case Work Services in a Military Hospital," *American Association of Medical Social Workers Bulletin* 18 (Sept., 1945): 66–70; Louis J. Schuldt, "Psychiatric Case Work in an Army Air Force Hospital," *Social Science Review* 20 (June, 1946): 212–20; Saul Hofstein, "Differences in Military Psychiatric Work Practices," *Journal of Psychiatric Social Work* 16 (Winter, 1946–1947): 74–82; Winifred Zwemer, "Psychiatric Social Work in a Volunteer Clinic for Veterans," *Journal of Psychiatric Social Work* 17 (Autumn, 1947): 42–43; Philip B. Reichline, "The Role of the Psychiatric Social Worker in a Veterans' Administration Mental Hygiene Clinic," *Journal of Psychiatric Social Work* 17 (Autumn, 1947): 61–65; and Edith Beck, "Coordination of Treatment in Winter Veterans' Administration Hospital," *Journal of Psychiatric Social Work* 19 (Summer, 1949): 3–8.

The body of contemporary monographs addressing both mental and physical injury grew significantly as a result of the war. See the excellent study by Therese Benedek, *Insight and Personality Adjustment: A Study of the Psychological Effects of War* (New York: Ronald Press, 1946). See also Edward A. Strecker and Kenneth E. Appel, *Psychiatry in Modern Warfare* (New York: MacMillan, 1945); Roy R. Grinker and John P. Spiegel, *Men under Stress* (Philadelphia: Blakiston, 1945); Bruno Bettelheim and Morris Janowitz, *Dynamics of Prejudice: A Psychological and Sociological Study of Veterans* (New York: Harper and Brothers, 1950); Gilbert W. Beebe and Michael E. DeBakey, *Battle Casualties: Incidence, Mortality, and Logistical Considerations* (Springfield, Ill.: Charles C. Thomas, 1952); Norman Q. Brill and Gilbert W. Beebe, *A Follow-up Study of War Neuroses* (Washington, D.C.: Veterans' Administration, 1955); Alan G. Gowman, *The War Blind in the American Social Structure* (New York: American Foundation for the Blind, 1957); and Nelson C. Woodfork and Francis K. Hayes, *Social Work Techniques Utilized in the Treatment of Psychotic Patients* (Northampton, Mass.: Veterans' Administration Hospital, 1957).

For more modern examples of this scholarship, see Richard Holmes, *Acts of War: The Behavior of Men in Battle* (New York: Free Press,

Bibliographic Essay

1985); Albert E. Cowdrey, *Fighting for Life: American Military Medicine in World War II* (New York: Free Press, 1994); Galen L. Barbour, Larry Malby, Richard R. Lussier, R. W. Thonale Jr., Judith A. Lerner, *Quality in the Veterans' Health Administration* (San Francisco: Jossey-Bass, 1996); Hans Binneveld, *From Shell Shock to Combat Stress,* trans. John O'Kane (Amsterdam: Amsterdam University Press, 1997); Paul Wanke, "American Military Psychiatry and Its Role among Ground Forces in World War II," *Journal of Military History* 63 (Jan., 1999): 127–46; and Megan Barke, Rebecca Fribush, and Peter N. Stearns, "Nervous Breakdown in Twentieth-Century American Culture," *Journal of Social History* 33 (Spring, 2000): 565–84.

Omar Bradley wrote extensively of his postwar time in the Veterans' Administration. See Omar N. Bradley, *A Soldier's Story* (New York: Henry Holt, 1951) and *The Collected Writings of General Omar N. Bradley,* 4 vols. (Washington, D.C.: Government Publication Office, 1967); also see Omar N. Bradley and Clay Blair, *A General's Life: An Autobiography by General of the Army Omar N. Bradley* (New York: Simon and Schuster, 1983). Bradley also authored many contemporary articles such as "Protecting the Mental Health of the Veteran," *Mental Hygiene* 30 (Jan., 1946): 1–8. Subordinates who served under Bradley in the VA later offered their own reflections on the experience. See Paul B. Magnuson, *Ring the Night Bell: The Autobiography of a Surgeon* (Boston: Little, Brown, 1960).

The controversy regarding medical treatment at the end of the war is contained in numerous 1945 and 1946 publications. See Leo Egan, "Veterans' Hospitals Widely Criticized," *New York Times* (May 16, 1945), p. 36; Albert Q. Maisel, "The Veterans Betrayed," *Reader's Digest* (May, 1945), pp. 22–26; Albert Deutsch, "U.S. Agencies Charged with Bias against Vets," *PM* (Apr. 8, 1946), p. 13; Doris Schwartz, "For These the War Is Not Over," *New York Times Magazine* 28 (Nov. 24, 1946), pp. 11, 51; Sutherland Denlinger, "The Vets' Best Bet," *Collier's* (Apr. 27, 1946), pp. 53–55; and Ralph G. Martin, "They Must Be Awfully Bitter," *New Republic* 114 (Jan. 7, 1946): 12–14. Examples of this journalism reappear throughout much of the late forties. See Perry Brown, "The Growing Attack on Veterans' Benefits," *American Legion Magazine* 47 (July, 1949), pp. 14–15.

An essential early study of veterans' reassimilation is contained in Robert J. Havighurst, Walter H. Eaton, John W. Baughman, and Ernester W. Burgess, *The American Veteran Back Home: A Study of Veteran Readjustment* (New York: Longmans, Green, 1951).

A large body of contemporary writing addresses the veteran in American education: J. Hillis Miller and Dorothy V. N. Brooks, *The Role of Higher Education in War and After* (New York: Harper and Brothers, 1944); Edward C. McDonaugh, "Some Hints to Professors," *American Association of University Professors Bulletin* 31 (Winter, 1945): 643–47; Walter Spearman and Jack R. Brown, "When the Veteran Goes to College," *South Atlantic Quarterly* 45 (Jan., 1946): 31–41; Maj. Harry Ransom, "Educational Plans of AAF Veterans," *Higher Education* (May 15, 1946): 8–9; Maj. J. L. Rogers, "Additional Hints to Professors," *American Association of University Professors Bulletin* 32 (June, 1946): 363–66); Robert M. Hutchins, "A Plan to Meet 'The Crisis in Education,'" *New York Times Magazine* 28 (June 9, 1946), pp. 11, 53–54; Nicholas M. McKnight, "They Know What They Want," *School and Society* 63 (June 29, 1946): 449–52; Donald Hutchins MacMahon, "Vets into Students," *School and Society* 64 (Sept. 21, 1946): 204–206; William H. Martin and Virgil A. Clift, "The Place of Values in Education for Returning Veterans," *Quarterly Review of Higher Education among Negroes* 14 (Jan., 1946): 3–10; S. M. Vincoor, "The Veteran Flunks the Professor: A GI Indictment of Our Institutes of Higher Education!" *School and Society* 66 (Oct. 18, 1947): 289–92; M. T. Cook, "The Need for Direction and Meaning," *American Scholar* 16 (Summer, 1947): 344–45; and Peter H. Odegard, "Is This Education?" *American Scholar* 16 (Autumn, 1947): 477–79. For a superior and extensive survey, see Norman Frederiksen and W. B. Schrader, *Adjustment to College: A Study of 10,000 Veteran and Nonveteran Students in Sixteen American Colleges* (Princeton, N.J.: Educational Testing Service, 1951).

Equally so is a separate cottage industry offering educational advice to the returning veteran. Peter T. Dondlinger, *Manual of What and Where in Up-to-Date GI Education: For Returned Service Men and Women and Others* (New York: Richard R. Smith, 1946).

For more modern studies of the veterans' impact on American education, see Oscar Handlin and Mary F. Handlin, *The American College and American Culture: Socialization as a Function of Higher Education* (New

York: McGraw-Hill, 1970); and Thomas N. Bonner, "The Unintended Revolution in America's Colleges since 1940," *Change* 18 (Sept./Oct., 1986): 44–51. For a very good study of changes already under way during the war, see V. R. Cardozier, *Colleges and Universities in World War II* (Westport, Conn.: Praeger, 1993); Edwin Kiester, "Uncle Sam Wants You . . . to Go to College," *Smithsonian* 25 (Nov., 1994): 128–39; Daniel A. Clark, "The Two Joes Meet: Joe College, Joe Veteran: The GI Bill, College Education, and Postwar American Culture," *History of Education Quarterly* 38 (Summer, 1998): 165–89. For an example of unpublished scholarship, see James E. Schmaedeke, "World War Two Veterans and Their Participation in College Life at the University of Kansas, 1944–1952" (Ph.D. diss., University of Kansas, 1995).

Studies particular to the educational provisions of the GI Bill include Michael J. Bennett, *When Dreams Come True: The GI Bill and the Making of Modern America* (London: Brassey's, 1996). Although dated, Keith W. Olson, *The GI Bill, The Veterans, and the Colleges* (Lexington: University Press of Kentucky, 1974), is a superior piece of scholarship on the topic.

A number of histories are much less sanguine about American education after 1945. See Kenneth H. Ashworth, *American Education in Decline* (College Station: Texas A&M University Press, 1979); and Diane Ravitch, *The Troubled Crusade: American Education, 1945–1980* (New York: Basic Books, 1983).

For studies of the veteran in the postwar work force, see Morse A. Cartwright, *Marching Home: Educational and Social Adjustment after the War* (New York: Institute of Adult Education, 1944); Morse A. Cartwright and Glen Burch, *Adult Adjustment: A Manual on the Coordination of Existing Community Services and the Establishment and Operation of Community Adjustment Centers for Veterans and Others* (New York: Institute of Adult Education, 1945); Capt. Francis J. Braceland, "The Retraining and Re-education of Veterans," a lecture delivered for the Nellie Heldt Lecture Fund, Oberlin College, Oberlin, Ohio, 1945; and W. Leslie Barnette, *Occupational Aptitude Patterns of Selected Groups of Counseled Veterans* (Washington, D.C.: American Psychological Association, 1950).

Modern scholarship in the field of labor history includes Joshua B. Freeman, *Working-Class New York: Life and Labor since World War II* (New York: New Press, 2000). For an older example in the same area, see "Veterans Return to the Nation's Factories," *Monthly Labor Review* 63 (Dec., 1946): 924–34.

Military service is included in many excellent biographies of American politicians. See Robert A. Caro, *The Years of Lyndon Johnson: Means of Ascent* (New York: Knopf, 1990), as well as the same author's excellent *Master of the Senate* (New York: Knopf, 2002). See also Robert Dallek, *Lone Star Rising: Lyndon Johnson and His Times, 1908–1960* (New York: Oxford University Press, 1991). The same is true with respect to autobiographies. See Richard M. Nixon, *RN: The Memoirs of Richard Nixon* (New York: Grosset and Dunlap, 1978).

For stories of community involvement, see Ty Cobb, "Batting Out Better Boys," *Rotarian* 71 (July, 1947): 10–12; Clarice H. L. Pennock, "The GI Volunteer," *Compass* 27 (Apr., 1946): 10–12; and "Veterans Seek Purchase of Greendale," *American City* 64 (Jan., 1949): 73–74.

For useful histories regarding American suburbia, see J. John Palen, *The Suburbs* (New York: McGraw-Hill, 1995); Tom Martinson, *American Dreamscape: The Pursuit of Happiness in Postwar Suburbia* (New York: Carroll and Graf, 2000); and Adam Rome, *The Bulldozer in the Countryside: Suburban Sprawl and the Rise of American Environmentalism* (New York: Cambridge University Press, 2001).

Chapter 4. GI Jane Comes Home

A number of general surveys of women during the war years were valuable to this project. See Susan M. Hartmann, "Prescriptions for Penelope: Literature on Women's Obligations to Returning World War II Veterans," *Women's Studies* 5 (1978): 223–29, and *The Home Front and Beyond: American Women in the 1940s* (Boston: Twayne, 1982) by the same author; Karen Anderson, *Wartime Women: Sex Roles, Family Relations, and the Status of Women during World War II* (Westport, Conn.: Greenwood Press, 1981); Maureen Honey, *Creating Rosie the Riveter: Class, Gender, and Propaganda during World War II* (Amherst: University of Massachusetts Press, 1984); Eugenia Kaledin, *Mothers and More: American Women in the 1950s* (Boston: Twayne, 1984); D'Ann Campbell, *Women at War with America: Private Lives in a Patriotic Era* (Cambridge: Harvard University Press, 1984); Sherna Berger Gluck, *Rosie the Riveter Revisited: Women, the War, and Social Change* (Boston: Twayne, 1987); Margaret Randolph Higonnet, Jane Jenson, Sonya Mitchell, and Margaret Collins Weitz, eds., *Behind the Lines: Gender and the Two World Wars* (New Haven, Conn.: Yale University Press, 1987); Doris Weatherford, *American Women and World War II* (New York: Facts on File, 1990); Judy Barrett

Litoff and David C. Smith, eds., *Since You Went Away: World War II Letters from American Women on the Home Front* (New York: Oxford University Press, 1991); William H. Chafe, *The Paradox of Change: American Women in the Twentieth Century* (New York: Oxford University Press, 1991); Elizabeth Fox-Genovese, "Mixed Messages: Women and the Impact of World War II," *Southern Humanities Review* 27 (Summer, 1993): 235–45; Joanne Meyerowitz, ed., *Not June Cleaver: Women and Gender in Postwar America, 1945–1960* (Philadelphia: Temple University Press, 1994); Frances Zauhar, Richard D. Wissolik, and Jennifer Campion, eds., *Out of the Kitchen: Women in the Armed Services and on the Homefront: The Oral Histories of Pennsylvania Veterans of World War II* (Latrobe, Penn.: Saint Vincent College, 1995); Sarah Armstrong, "Work, Womanpower, and World War II," *Reference Services Review* 26 (Spring, 1998): 31–36, 42; and Eugenia Kaledin, *Daily Life in the United States, 1940–1959: Shifting Worlds* (Westport, Conn.: Greenwood Press, 2000).

The scholarship addressing women in the military has grown in recent years. Of particular note is Jeanne Holm, *Women in the Military: An Unfinished Revolution* (San Francisco: Presidio Press, 1992). This body of work also includes June A. Willenz, *Women Veterans: America's Forgotten Heroines* (New York: Continuum, 1983); Brenda McBryde, *Quiet Heroines: Nurses of the Second World War* (London: Hogarth Press, 1985); Shelley Saywell, *Women in War* (London: Costello, 1987); Janann Sherman, " 'They Either Need These Women or They Do Not': Margaret Chase Smith and the Fight for Regular Status for Women in the Military," *Journal of Military History* 54 (Jan., 1990): 47–78; Dorothy Schneider and Carl J. Schneider, *Sound Off! American Military Women Speak Out* (New York: Paragon House, 1992); Bettie J. Morden, *The Women's Army Corps, 1945–1978* (Washington, D.C.: Government Publication Office, 1992); Judy Barrett Litoff and David C. Smith, eds., *We're in This War, Too: World War II Letters from American Women in Uniform* (New York: Oxford University Press, 1994); R. Claire Snyder, *Citizen-Soldiers and Manly Warriors: Military Service and Gender in the Civic Republican Tradition* (Lanham, Md.: Rowman and Littlefield, 1995); Leisa D. Meyer, *Creating GI Jane: Sexuality and Power in the Women's Army Corps during World War II* (New York Columbia University Press, 1996); Judith Hick Stiehm, *It's Our Military, Too! Women and the U.S. Military* (Philadelphia: Temple University Press, 1996); Paula Nassen Poulous, ed., *A Woman's War, Too: Women in the Military in World War II* (Washington, D.C.: National Archives and Records Administration,

1996); Donna M. Dean, *Warriors without Weapons: The Victimization of Military Women* (Pasadena, Md.: Minerva Center, 1997); Lois Ann Lorentzen and Jennifer Turpin, eds., *The Women and War Reader* (New York: New York University Press, 1998); Mary T. Sarnecky, *A History of the U.S. Army Nurse Corps* (Philadelphia: University of Pennsylvania Press, 1999); Kathi Jackson, *They Called Them Angels: American Military Nurses of World War II* (Westport, Conn.: Praeger, 2000). Some of the best work in this area has been accomplished by D'Ann Campbell. See "Servicewomen of World War II," *Armed Forces and Society* 16 (Winter, 1990): 251–70; "Women in Combat: The World War II Experience in the United States, Great Britain, Germany, and the Soviet Union," *Journal of Military History* 57 (Apr., 1993): 301–23; and "Women in the Military," *Choice* 31 (Sept., 1993): 63–70.

A number of unpublished studies also proved useful in this study. They include Carol Owen Bell, "The Long-Term Impact of Military Experience on World War II Women's Army Corps Veterans" (M.A. thesis, University of Tennessee, Knoxville, 1996); Robin M. Beringer, "Looking Over vs. Overlooking Historic Contributions: Women Veterans' Experiences of WWII" (Ph.D. diss., California School of Professional Psychology at Alameda, 1996).

A considerable number of memoirs were written during the forties and afterward. Examples include Elizabeth R. Pollock, *Yes, Ma'am! The Personal Papers of a WAAC Private* (New York: J. B. Lippincott, 1943); Theresa Archard, *GI Nightingale: The Story of an American Army Nurse* (New York: W. W. Norton, 1945); Charity Adams Early, *One Woman's Army* (College Station: Texas A&M University Press, 1989); Anne Bosanko Green, ed., *One Woman's War: Letters Home from the Women's Army Corps, 1944–1946* (St. Paul: Minnesota Historical Society Press, 1989); and LaVonne Telshaw Camp, *Lingering Fever: A World War II Nurse's Memoir* (Jefferson, N.C.: McFarland, 1997).

Contemporary accounts of returning female veterans populate a great deal of the literature in the early postwar period. See Beatrice Berg, "When GI Girls Return," *New York Times Magazine* (Apr. 22, 1945), p. 40; Eleanor Lake, "A Smarter GI Jane Comes Home," *Reader's Digest* 49 (Sept., 1946), pp. 33–35; Nancy McInerny, "The Woman Vet Has Her Problems, Too," *New York Times Magazine* (June 30, 1946), pp. 18, 39–40; Evelyn Field, "A Woman Veteran Is Mad . . . Here Are Her Gripes," *Daily World* (June 19, 1946), p. 5; Nona Brown, "The Armed Forces Find Woman Has a Place," *New York Times Magazine* (Dec. 26, 1948), p. 14.

The postwar assimilation of women attracted a great deal of attention, particularly in professional education journals. See Olive Remington Goldman, "GI Style: Learning with a Difference," *Journal of the American Association of University Women* 39 (Summer, 1946): 205–207; and Alice C. Lloyd, "Women in the Postwar College," *Journal of the American Association of University Women* (Spring, 1946): 131–34. A number of these studies may be found in the graduate scholarship of the forties. See Helen G. Brown, "Adjustment Problems of College and Non-College WAC Veterans, 1945–1947" (M.A. thesis, Leland Stanford Junior University, Stanford, Calif., 1947).

Chapter 5. Minority Veterans Come Home

Scholarship regarding World War II and the civil rights movement in the forties is plentiful. Perhaps the most famous work is Gunnar Myrdal, *An American Dilemma: The Negro Problem and Modern Democracy* (New York: Harper and Row, 1944). See also Neil A. Wynn, *The Afro-American and the Second World War* (New York: Holmes and Meier, 1975); Doug McAdam, *Political Process and the Development of Black Insurgency, 1930–1970* (Chicago: University of Chicago Press, 1982); Genna Rae McNeil, *Groundwork: Charles Hamilton Houston and the Struggle for Civil Rights* (Philadelphia: University of Pennsylvania Press, 1983); Aldon D. Morris, *The Origins of the Civil Rights Movement: Black Communities Organizing for Change* (New York: Free Press, 1984); Robert J. Norrell, *Reaping the Whirlwind: The Civil Rights Movement in Tuskegee* (New York: Knopf, 1985); Andrew Michael Manis, *Southern Civil Religions in Conflict: Black and White Baptists and Civil Rights, 1947–1957* (Athens: University of Georgia Press, 1987); Herbert Shapiro, *White Violence and Black Response: From Reconstruction to Montgomery* (Amherst, Mass.: University of Amherst Press, 1988); Armstead L. Robinson and Patricia Sullivan, eds., *New Directions in Civil Rights Studies* (Charlottesville: University Press of Virginia, 1991); Donald L. Grant, *The Way It Was in the South: The Black Experience in Georgia* (New York: Carol Publishing Group, 1993); John Egerton, *Speak Now against the Day: The Generation before the Civil Rights Movement in the South* (New York: Knopf, 1994); Charles M. Payne, *I've Got the Light of Freedom: The Organizing Tradition and the Mississippi Freedom Struggle* (Berkeley: University of California Press, 1995); Allen Cronenberg, *Forth to the Mighty Conflict: Alabama and World War II* (Tuscaloosa: University of Alabama Press, 1995); and Patricia Sullivan, *Days of Hope: Race and Democracy in the New Deal Era* (Chapel Hill: University of North Carolina Press, 1996); relevant chapters of Howard Ball, *A Defiant Life: Thurgood Marshall and the Persistence of Racism in America* (New York: Crown, 1998), are also illustrative of specific legal efforts to further civil rights. For more on Marshall and civil rights law, see Mark V. Tushnet, *Making Civil Rights Law: Thurgood Marshall and the Supreme Court, 1936–1961* (New York: Oxford University Press, 1994), and Mark V. Tushnet, ed., *Thurgood Marshall: His Speeches, Writings, Arguments, Opinions, and Reminiscences* (Chicago: Lawrence Hill, 2001). See also Neil R. McMillen, ed., *Remaking Dixie: The Impact of World War II on the American South* (Jackson: University Press of Mississippi, 1997); Daniel Kryder, *Divided Arsenal: Race and the American State during World War II* (New York: Cambridge University Press, 2000); Jacqueline Jones, "Federal Power, Southern Power: A Long View, 1860–1940," *Journal of American History* 87 (Mar., 2001): 1392–96; and James T. Patterson, *Brown v. Board of Education: A Civil Rights Milestone and Its Troubled Legacy* (New York: Oxford University Press, 2001).

Many monographs relate the African American military experience. This body includes Hondon B. Hargrove, *Buffalo Soldiers in Italy: Black Americans in World War II* (Jefferson, N.C.: McFarland, 1985); Martha S. Putney, *When the Nation Was in Need: Blacks in the Women's Army Corps during World War II* (Metuchen, N.J.: Scarecrow Press, 1992); Kathryn Browne Pfeifer, *The 761st Tank Battalion* (New York: Twenty-First Century Books, 1994); Lawrence P. Scott and William M. Womack Sr., *Double V: The Civil Rights Struggle of the Tuskegee Airmen* (East Lansing: Michigan State University Press, 1994); and Maggi M. Morehouse, *Fighting in the Jim Crow Army: Black Men and Women Remember World War II* (New York: Rowman and Littlefield, 2000). For relevant primary-source collections, see Bernard C. Nalty and Morris J. MacGregor, *Blacks in the Military: Essential Documents* (Wilmington, Del.: Scholarly Resources, 1981). An outstanding piece of scholarship directly related to this project is David H. Onkst, "'First a Negro . . . Incidentally a Veteran': Black World War Two Veterans and the GI Bill of Rights in the Deep South, 1944–1948," *Journal of Social History* 31 (Spring/Summer, 1998): 517–44. For a more recent account, see Sarah Turner and John Bound, "Closing the Gap or Widening the Divide: The Effects of the GI Bill and World War II on the Educational Outcomes of Black Americans," *Journal of Labor History* 63 (Mar., 2003): 145–77. Perhaps one of the best unpublished sources on the postwar experience of

African American veterans is Jennifer E. Brooks, "From Hitler and Tojo to Talmadge and Jim Crow: World War Two Veterans and the Remaking of Southern Political Tradition" (Ph.D. diss., University of Tennessee, Knoxville, 1997). See also Robert F. Jefferson, "Organization Is the Key: Wounded African American World War II ex-GIs and the Civil Rights Struggles of the Late 1940s" (paper presented at the Veteran and Society Conference, Knoxville, Tenn., Nov., 2000).

On the postwar educational opportunities available for African American veterans, see Caliver Ambrose, *Postwar Education of Negroes: Educational Implications of Army Data and Experiences of Negro Veterans and War Workers* (Washington, D.C.: Office of Education, 1945); and James A. Atkins, "Negro Educational Institutions and the Veterans' Educational Facilities Program," *Journal of Negro Education* 17 (Spring, 1948): 141–53.

The sizable number of African American veterans spawned a distinct collection of private and public literature. For examples, see Charles G. Bolté, *The New Veteran* (New York: Reynal and Hitchcock, 1945), and "We're on Our Own," *Atlantic Monthly* 179 (May, 1947): 27–33 by the same author. See also Charles G. Bolté and Louis Harris, *Our Negro Veterans* (Public Affairs Pamphlet no. 128 (New York: Public Affairs Committee, 1947). Particularly helpful for statistical data is Jessie Parkhurst Guzman, ed., *Negro Yearbook: A Review of Events Affecting Negro Life, 1941–1946* (Tuskegee: Department of Records and Research, Tuskegee Institute, 1946), and his later *1952 Negro Yearbook: A Review of Events Affecting Negro Life* (New York: Wm. H. Wise, 1952).

This chapter benefited from a number of general works relevant to Latinos in U.S. history. See Ralph C. Guzmán, *The Political Socialization of the Mexican People* (New York: Arno Press, 1976); Griswold del Castillo, *La Familia: Chicano Families in the Urban Southwest, 1848 to the Present* (Notre Dame: University of Notre Dame Press, 1984); Joan Moore and Harry Pachon, *Hispanics in the United States* (Englewood Cliffs, N.J.: Prentice-Hall, 1985); F. Chris Garcia, ed., *Latinos and the Political System* (Notre Dame: University of Notre Dame Press, 1988); Mario T. Garcia, *Mexican Americans: Leadership, Ideology, and Identity, 1930–1960* (New Haven, Conn.: Yale University Press, 1989); Roberto E. Villarreal and Norma G. Hernandez, eds., *Latinos and Political Coalitions: Political Empowerment for the 1990s* (Westport, Conn.: Praeger, 1991); Juan Gomez-Quiñones, *Mexican American Labor, 1790–1990* (Albuquerque: University of New Mexico Press, 1994); Alejandro Portes and Dag

McLeod, "What Shall I Call Myself? Hispanic Identity Formation in the Second Generation," *Ethnic and Racial Studies* 19 (July, 1996): 523–47; David Montejano, ed., *Chicano Politics and Society in the Late Twentieth Century* (Austin: University of Texas Press, 1999); and José O. Diaz, "Gender, Ethnicity, and Power: Recent Studies on Puerto Rican History," *Latin American Research Review* 37 (2002): 215–30.

A significant body of recent scholarship has lent attention to the Latino population's contribution to the war effort. See Otey M. Scruggs, *Braceros, "Wetbacks," and the Farm Labor Problem: Mexican Agricultural Labor in the United States, 1942–1954* (New York: Garland, 1988); Erasmo Gamboa, *Mexican Labor and World War II: Braceros in the Pacific Northwest, 1942–1947* (Austin: University of Texas Press, 1990); Alexander Monto, *The Roots of Mexican Labor Migration* (Westport, Conn.: Praeger, 1994).

A small number of books address Latino veterans' organizations created after the war. Especially valuable is Carl Allsup, *The American GI Forum: Origins and Evolution* (Austin: Center for Mexican American Studies, 1982). A more recent work is Henry A. J. Ramos, *The American GI Forum: In Pursuit of the Dream, 1948–1983* (Houston: Arte Publico Press, 1998). See also Benjamin Márquez, *LULAC: Evolution of a Mexican American Political Organization* (Austin: University of Texas Press, 1993), for a history of counterpart organizations to the American GI Forum.

The experiences of Nisei and Issei Japanese are well recorded in the scholarship. See John A. Rademaker, *These Are Americans: The Japanese Americans in Hawaii in World War II* (Palo Alto: Pacific Books, 1951); Harry H. L. Kitano, *Japanese Americans: The Evolution of a Subculture* (Englewood Cliffs, N.J.: Prentice Hall, 1976); Peter Irons, *Justice at War: The Story of the Japanese American Internment Cases* (New York: Oxford University Press, 1983); Roger Daniels, Sandra C. Taylor, and Harry H. L. Kitano, eds., *Japanese Americans: From Relocation to Redress* (Seattle: University of Washington Press, 1991); Jere Takahashi, *Nisei/Sansei: Shifting Japanese American Identities and Politics* (Philadelphia: Temple University Press, 1997); Gary Y. Okihiro, *Storied Lives: Japanese American Students and World War II* (Seattle: University of Washington Press, 1999); Charlotte Brooks, "In the Twilight Zone between Black and White: Japanese American Resettlement and Community in Chicago, 1942–1945," *Journal of American History* 86 (Mar., 2000): 1655–87. Especially useful is Tomi Kaizawa Knaefler, *Our House Divided: Seven Japanese American Families in World War II* (Honolulu: University of Hawaii Press, 1991).

Similarly, the combat experience of Japanese American service-men has drawn considerable attention from a variety of writers. For one of the oldest examples, see Orville C. Shirey, *Americans: The Story of the 442nd Combat Team* (Washington, D.C.: Infantry Journal Press, 1946). For more recent writing, see Tamotsu Shibutani, *The Derelicts of K Company: A Sociological Study of Demoralization* (Berkeley: University of California Press, 1978); Joseph D. Harrington, *Yankee Samurai: The Secret Role of Nisei in America's Pacific Victory* (Detroit: Harlo Press, 1979); Jack K. Wakamatsu, *Silent Warriors: A Memoir of America's 442nd Regimental Combat Team* (Los Angeles: JKW Press, 1992); Lyn Crost, *Honor by Fire: Japanese Americans at War in Europe and the Pacific* (Novato, Calif.: Presidio Press, 1994); Wayne Kiyosaki, *A Spy in Their Midst: The World War II Struggle of a Japanese-American Hero* (Lanham, Md.: Madison Books, 1995); Tom McGowan, *"Go for Broke": Japanese Americans in World War II* (New York: Franklin Watts, 1995); Hawaii Nikkei History Editorial Board, *Japanese Eyes, American Hearts: Personal Reflections of Hawaii's World War II Nisei Soldiers* (Honolulu: Tendai Educational Foundation, 1998); Carina A. del Rosario, ed., *A Different Battle: Stories of Asian Pacific Veterans* (Seattle: University of Washington Press, 1999); and David K. Yoo, *Growing Up Nisei: Race, Generation, and Culture among Japanese Americans of California, 1924–1949* (Chicago: University of Illinois Press, 2000).

Chapter 6. The Veteran and the Postwar Film

For general studies on film, see Barbara Deming, *Running Away from Myself: A Dream Portrait of America Drawn from the Films of the Forties* (New York: Grossman, 1969); Lawrence Alloway, *Violent America: The Movies, 1946–1964* (New York: Museum of Modern Art, 1971); Richard Maltby, *Passing Parade: A History of Popular Culture* (New York: Oxford University Press, 1989); Steven Mintz and Randy Roberts, eds., *Hollywood's America: United States History through Its Films* (St. James, N.Y.: Brandywine Press, 1993); Robert Sklar, *Movie-Made America: A Cultural History of American Movies* (New York: Vintage Books, 1994); Robert A. Rosenstone, ed., *Revisioning History: Film and the Construction of a New Past* (Princeton: Princeton University Press, 1995); Geoffrey B. Pingree, "Visual Evidence Reconsidered: Reflections on Film and History," *Public Historian* 21 (Spring, 1999): 99–107; and Daniel Bernardi, ed., *Classic Hollywood, Classic Whiteness* (Minneapolis: University of Minnesota Press, 2001).

The combat film has garnered particular attention by scholars and critics. For examples of this work, see Norman Kagan, *The War Film* (New York: Pyramid, 1974); Lawrence H. Suid, *Guts and Glory: Great American War Movies* (Reading, Mass.: Addison-Wesley, 1978); Colin Shindler, *Hollywood Goes to War: Films and American Society, 1939–1952* (Boston: Routledge and Kegan Paul, 1979); Michael T. Isenberg, *War on Film: The American Cinema and World War I, 1914–1941* (Madison, N.J.: Farleigh Dickinson University Press, 1980); Bernard F. Dick, *The Star-Spangled Screen: The American World War II Film* (Lexington: University Press of Kentucky, 1985); Jeanine Basinger, *The World War II Combat Film: Anatomy of a Genre* (New York: Columbia University Press, 1986); Albert Auster and Leonard Quart, *How the War Was Remembered: Hollywood and Vietnam* (New York: Praeger, 1988); James M. Skinner, "Dec. 7: Filmic Myth as Historical Fact," *Journal of Military History* 55 (Oct., 1991): 507–16; Frank J. Wetta and Stephen J. Curley, *Celluloid Wars: A Guide to Film and the American Experience of War* (Westport, Conn.: Greenwood Press, 1992); Robert Fyne, *The Hollywood Propaganda of World War II* (London: Scarecrow Press, 1994); Robert Castle and Stephen Donatelli, "Full Metal Jacket," *Film Comment* 34 (Sept./Oct., 1998): 24–28; James Morrison, "The Thin Red Line," *Film Quarterly* 53 (Fall, 1999): 35–38; and Harlan Jacobson, "Bad Day at Black Rock," *Film Comment* 38 (Jan./Feb., 2002): 28–31.

For works on the film noir genre, see Richard Maltby, "Film Noir: The Politics of the Maladjusted Text," *Journal of American Studies* 18 (Apr., 1984): 49–70; Foster Hirsch, *Film Noir: The Dark Side of the Screen* (New York: Da Capo Press, 1985); Bruce Crowther, *Film Noir: Reflections in a Dark Mirror* (New York: Continuum, 1989); Ian Cameron, ed., *The Book of Film Noir* (New York: Continuum, 1993); Nicholas Christopher, *Somewhere in the Night: Film Noir and the American City* (New York: Free Press, 1997); Paul Arthur, "Act of Violence," *Film Comment* 35 (July/Aug., 1999): 56–58; Jonathan Munby, *Public Enemies, Public Heroes: Screening the Gangster from Little Caesar to Touch of Evil* (Chicago: University of Chicago Press, 1999); and Nicole Rafter, *Shots in the Mirror: Crime Films and Society* (New York: Oxford University Press, 2000).

The impact of *Saving Private Ryan* has generated enormous commentary. See Richard Jameson, "*Saving Private Ryan,*" *Film Comment* 34 (Sept./Oct., 1998): 21–23; Karen Jaehne, "*Saving Private Ryan,*" *Film Quarterly* 53 (Fall, 1999): 39–41; Bernard Beck, "The War's Desolation:

Saving Private Ryan, The Thin Red Line, and the Baggage of History,"
Multicultural Perspectives 1 (1999): 19–22; William J. Prior, "*Saving Private Ryan* and the Morality of War," *Parameters: U.S. Army War College* 30 (Autumn, 2000): 138–46; John Bodnar, "*Saving Private Ryan* and Postwar Memory in America," *American Historical Review* 106 (June, 2001): 805–17; and Albert Auster, "*Saving Private Ryan* and American Triumphalism," *Journal of Popular Film and Television* 30 (Summer, 2002): 98–105.

For examples of movies that address returning veterans, see Philip D. Beidler, "Remembering *The Best Years of Our Lives,*" *Virginia Quarterly Review* 72 (Autumn, 1996): 589–605. See also James I. Deutsch, "Coming Home from 'The Good War': World War II Veterans as Depicted in American Film and Fiction" (Ph.D. diss., George Washington University, Washington, D.C., 1991).

Chapter 7. Retreads

Readers interested in background on the Korean War might consult Francis H. Heller, ed., *The Korean War: A Twenty-Five-Year Perspective* (Lawrence: Regents Press of Kansas, 1977); Joseph C. Goulden, *Korea: The Untold Story of the War* (New York: Times Books, 1982); Burton I. Kaufman, *The Korean War: Challenges in Crisis, Credibility, and Command* (Philadelphia: Temple University Press, 1986); Max Hastings, *The Korean War* (New York: Simon and Schuster, 1987); Roy E. Appleman, *East of Chosin: Entrapment and Breakout in Korea, 1950* (College Station: Texas A&M University Press, 1987); Clay Blair, *The Forgotten War: America in Korea, 1950–1953* (New York: Times Books, 1987); and Michael Schaller, *Douglas MacArthur: The Far Eastern General* (New York: Oxford University Press, 1989). For a forensic tome that addresses both the geopolitical context and cultural background, see Bruce Cumings, *The Origins of the Korean War,* vol. 2, *The Roaring of the Cataract, 1947–1950* (Princeton, N.J.: Princeton University Press, 1990). See also John Toland, *In Mortal Combat: Korea, 1950–1953* (New York: William Morrow, 1991); Robert J. Dvorchak, *Battle for Korea: A History of the Korean Conflict* (New York: Associated Press, 1993); David T. Fautua, "The 'Long Pull' Army: NSC 68, the Korean War, and the Creation of the Cold War U.S. Army," *Journal of Military History* 61 (Jan., 1997): 93–120; and Stanley Weintraub, "How to Remember the Forgotten War," *American Heritage* 51 (May/June, 2000): 100–106.

For personal recollections of the Korean War period, see Bill Mauldin, *Bill Mauldin in Korea* (New York: W. W. Norton, 1952); Donald Knox, *The Korean War: Pusan to Chosin: An Oral History* (New York: Harcourt Brace Jovanovich, 1985); Sandy Strait, ed., *What Was It Like in the Korean War? Honest Answers to Students' Questions from Men and Women Who Served in Korea* (Unionville, N.Y.: Royal Fireworks Press, 1999); William D. Dannenmaier, *We Were Innocents: An Infantryman in Korea* (Chicago: University of Illinois Press, 1999); and Richard E. Mack, *Memoir of a Cold War Soldier* (Kent, Ohio: Kent State University Press, 2001).

The mobilization of the National Guard and Reserves has attracted a degree of scholarly attention. An early example may be found in Capt. Thomas R. Nevitt, "A Guard Division Trains for M-Day," *Army Information Digest* 3 (Oct., 1948): 35–45. For a highly informative nuts-and-bolts history, see James F. Schnabel, *United States Army in Korea: Policy and Direction: The First Year* (Washington, D.C.: Government Printing Office, 1972). One of the best recent examples of this subfield is William M. Donnelly, *Under Army Orders: The Army National Guard during the Korean War* (College Station: Texas A&M University Press, 2001).

Chapter 8. Legacies

Wartime memoirs have become increasingly popular, particularly in the wake of *Saving Private Ryan* (1998) and the more recent cable production of Stephen Ambrose's *Band of Brothers* (2001). See Andy Rooney, *My War* (New York: Essay Productions, 1995), and James Bradley with Ron Powers, *Flags of Our Fathers* (New York: Bantam Books, 2000).

The legacy of World War II is frequently mentioned in the biographies and autobiographies of Vietnam veterans. See Ron Kovic, *Born on the Fourth of July* (New York: Pocket Books, 1976); Philip Caputo, *A Rumor of War* (New York: Holt, Rinehart, and Winston, 1977); David H. Hackworth, *About Face: The Odyssey of an American Warrior* (New York: Simon and Schuster, 1989); and Robert Timberg, *The Nightingale's Song* (New York: Simon and Schuster, 1995). Although a work of fiction, James Webb, *Fields of Fire* (New York: Bantam Books, 1978), remains impressive for its vivid description of the cultural legacies that World War II created.

For writing that addresses the military as a separate subculture, see J. Glenn Gray, *The Warriors: Reflections on Men in Battle* (New York:

Harper and Row, 1970), and Gwynne Dyer, *War* (New York: Crown, 1985). For more recent academic observations, see Anne L. Shewring, "We Didn't Do That, Did We? Representation of the Veteran Experience," *Journal of American and Comparative Cultures* 23 (Winter, 2000): 51–66; Edward W. Wood, "On Judging World War Two: The Greatest Generation?" *War, Literature, and the Arts* 12 (Fall/Winter, 2000): 213–24; and Neils Sorrells, "An Ever-Increasing Divide: Lawmaker-Veterans Becoming a Rare Breed on Capitol Hill," *Armed Forces Journal International* 139 (Oct., 2001): 10–12.

INDEX